The
Throne
of Money

SPIRITUALITY, ECONOMETRICS, GEOPOLITICAL SYSTEMS, AND KINGDOM PRINCIPLES.

OTHNIEL U. IKECHUKWU

This edition published by: Seraph Creative 2025

First Edition: April 28, 2025

Scripture References: Unless otherwise indicated, all Bible verses are taken from the New King James Version (NKJV) and other translations for deeper revelation.

Disclaimer: This book is a prophetic, educational, and spiritual work. While references are made to scientific research, historical sources, and global perspectives, the intent remains to inspire, equip, and align readers with the Kingdom of Christ in all spheres of influence.

Contact: Email: apstothnieliyke@gmail.com

ISBN 978-1-964959-86-3 (Paperback)

ISBN: 978-1-964959-93-1 (Hardcover)

ISBN 978-1-964959-87-0 (eBook)

Dedication

This book is dedicated first and foremost to

Yeshua Hamashiach (Jesus Christ), the King of Kings and Lord of Lords, who sits enthroned above all nations, governments, and dominions.

To the rising generation of Kingdom reformers, entrepreneurs, policymakers, prophets, and innovators may you carry the flame of divine wisdom and establish Christ's throne in every sphere of the earth.

And to every hidden intercessor, Kingdom economist, and marketplace apostle, this is your trumpet call to occupy until He comes.

ACKNOWLEDGMENTS

First and forever, I acknowledge **Abba Father**, the **Ancient of Days**, for the breath of inspiration, wisdom, and understanding poured into this work. Every revelation, every page, and every decree in this book is offered back as a living sacrifice to Your Eternal Throne.

To **Jesus Christ (Yeshua Hamashiach), the Word made flesh**, and the Sovereign King whose Kingdom shall never end, this manuscript stands as a testimony that You reign over all realms: spiritual, scientific, economic, and cosmic.

To the **Holy Spirit**, the Spirit of Wisdom, Revelation, and Counsel, who carried me through every dimension of insight, prophetic utterance, and strategic blueprint, thank You for the rivers of living water that flowed without ceasing.

To the **great cloud of witnesses**, the apostolic fathers, prophets, marketplace reformers, and innovators of ancient and modern times whose hidden legacies breathe through the corridors of history, you are honored here.

Special gratitude to the scholars and researchers whose work laid stones upon which further revelation was built:

Greg Reid, Fritz Springmeier, T. Harv Eker, Darius Foroux, Seamus Bruner, Peter Schweizer, Ernst Wolff, Niall Ferguson, Noam Chomsky, Nicholas Kralev, John Perkins, Milton Friedman, Jason Brennan, Warren Buffet, Scott Walter, Guled Ahmed, Ray Dalio, David E. Hoffokin, Steven D. Strauss, Adam Smith, Herbert Joly, Ian Clayton, Dr. Adonijah Ogbonnaya, and many others whose research inspired deep exploration.

I honor the Kingdom generals, prophetic scribes, apostolic architects, and digital warriors arising across nations, you are the living letters of God's strategies for this hour.

Finally, to my family, friends, spiritual sons and daughters, and covenant partners in destiny who stood in prayer, counsel, and encouragement, your faith and love are embedded in these pages.

To Christ be all the glory.

Apostolic Council

FOREWORD

There are moments in history when the realms of heaven issue a call so urgent, so catalytic, that it demands a response from the sons and daughters of God across every nation. *The Throne of Money: Spirituality, Science, and the Technology of Politics* is born out of such a time, a kairos moment where heaven's economy is shaking the foundations of the earth.

This book is not merely a study; it is a **kingdom summons**. It invites you to see beyond the surface of political economies, banking systems, global markets, and technological innovation, into the **ancient thrones and altars** that have ruled behind the scenes for millennia. You will encounter the spiritual architectures that have shaped empires, the scientific principles encoded into the fabric of creation, and the technologies that have been wielded to govern nations and souls.

This work is deeply prophetic, yet profoundly researched, melding the ancient wisdom of sacred texts, the revelations of modern science, the insights of leading economic scholars, and the enduring truth of the **eternal Kingdom of Christ**. You will navigate the hidden bloodlines of global wealth, the covert priesthoods of political power, the rise of digital empires, and the unseen battles raging in marketplaces and nations.

In this unveiling, Apostle Othniel Uzorma Ikechukwu does more than analyze systems, he charts a path for **reformation, dominion, and kingdom establishment**. He equips the ecclesia to rise as governors, innovators, economists, architects, and prophetic strategists who build according to heaven's blueprints.

As you journey through these pages, prepare to be challenged, provoked, enlightened, and ignited. Prepare for **activation** into the high calling of governing from the heavenly realms into the earthly domains.

The Spirit of the Lord is releasing a new company of **kingdom economists, apostolic entrepreneurs, marketplace reformers**, and **cyber prophets**, voices who will reframe global systems and steward the wealth of nations for the glory of Christ.

May your heart burn with revelation.

May your mind be expanded by wisdom.

May your spirit be enthroned with Christ's authority.

This is your hour to reclaim the thrones.

Welcome to the convergence of heaven's economy and earth's destiny.

Selah.

Ancient Witness

TESTIMONIALS

"The Throne of Money" is a bold, profound, and timely exploration of the spiritual, historical, and socio-economic forces that have shaped the global monetary system.

A revelatory work that pierces through the veil of global finance to expose the spiritual architecture behind money, wealth, power, and influence. With deep prophetic insight and historical clarity, the author traces the evolution of money from a medium of exchange to a seat of dominion, unmasking the throne of Mammon that governs the systems of this world.

This book is a must-read for those who seek to walk in financial wisdom, spiritual authority, and kingdom stewardship in these last days.

Vincent Ameh (Rabbi)

"Throne of Money is a transformative revelation that uncovers the deep spiritual realities governing global economies, politics, and technology. Apostle Othniel masterfully blends timeless biblical truths with cutting-edge insights to expose the throne of Mammon and its modern manifestations. This book is a must-read for kingdom stewards, providing both prophetic clarity and practical strategies to reclaim dominion in the marketplace and reclaim God's rightful rule."

Murphy Unuakhe

"The Throne of Money: Spirituality, Science, and the Technology of Politics" is a thought-provoking book that explores the intersection of spirituality, economics, and politics. Presented from a prophetic perspective, it urges readers to reclaim dominion and establish kingdom principles in the economic and political spheres.

From my observation, the book delves into themes such as the spiritual DNA of money, cyber-intelligence, fintech, and the battle for dominion. It offers practical guidance for navigating the complexities of the global economic system and encourages readers to think critically about the role of spirituality in shaping economic and political systems.

Like in Algorithms, Apostle Othniel uses established data and biblical references, framed through prophetic language, to highlight the importance of spiritual discernment and righteous governance. His call to action for believers to rise as governors, innovators, and kingdom agents—reclaiming dominion and establishing kingdom principles in every sphere of influence—is both appropriate and galvanising.

I particularly appreciate the chapterisation, which covers a divinely inspired range of topics, from the spiritual DNA of money to cyber-intelligence and the battle for dominion. Reading it has given me a deeper understanding of the unseen forces shaping our world, as well as practical, workable strategies for reclaiming dominion and applying kingdom principles.

Overall, *The Throne of Money* is a valuable resource for anyone seeking to understand the intersection of spirituality, economics, and politics. Its prophetic perspective and practical guidance make it a compelling and timely read for those desiring to make a positive impact in today's world.

Elder BabaJide Attah, PhD (Nigeria)

This book is not just a publication—it is a prophetic trumpet. In The Throne of Money, Apostle Othniel Uzorma Ikechukwu pierces the illusion of earthly wealth to unveil the spiritual architecture behind the world's financial systems. This is apostolic intelligence at its finest—where biblical truth, prophetic insight, and economic strategy converge to equip a new breed of kingdom reformers. With every chapter, you are not merely reading—you are being enlisted into a war for altars, thrones, and territories. It is a wake-up call to those who dare to govern with God. I recommend this book to every leader, economist, intercessor, and nation-builder seeking to steward wealth with revelation and rule with righteousness."

— Archbishop-Elect Anthony Osuobeni
Pastor | Author | Legal Historian | Apostolic Reformer

I am deeply honored to have encountered Throne of Money Insights—a revelatory and timely masterpiece that does not just speak to the intellect, but pierces through to the very spirit. Apostle Othniel Uzorma Ikechukwu has written more than a book; he has released a prophetic mandate, a strategic blueprint, and a divine trumpet call for this generation. This work is a profound convergence of spiritual intelligence, historical revelation, economic deconstruction, and kingdom alignment. Every chapter is layered with deep prophetic insight, unveiling the hidden thrones, altars, and principalities that have long governed the world's economic and political systems. It challenges the Church to stop reacting to the economy and to start governing it—from the secret place of the altar to the gates of policymaking, innovation, and enterprise. What moved me most is the way the book marries deep scholarship with unapologetic spirituality. From ancient altars and priesthoods to the digital empires and AI thrones of today, Apostle Othniel fearlessly exposes the systems of Mammon while equipping Kingdom sons to take their rightful place in the marketplace. This is not motivational fluff—it is war strategy for end-time reformers, innovators, and divine nation-builders. Every page echoes a call to rise—into righteous dominion, prophetic discernment, and kingdom stewardship. It carries the same weight as the writings of reformers who shaped eras and shifted nations. If there is one book I would recommend to every believer called to finance, government, technology, entrepreneurship, or ministry in this critical hour, it is Throne of Money Insights. It is both a sword and a scroll. A wake-up call and a map. A throne room perspective for those ready to reign with Christ. This is more than timely—it is eternal.

David C. Othniel Kingdom Strategist | Marketplace Intercessor | Prophetic Builder

In this book, The Throne of Money, Apostle Othniel appears as a messenger who has transcended into the eternal topography and watched the entire matter play from alpha to omega and seen the establishment of the justified one, the Lord in His original purpose and agenda regarding this matter. In this, every matter is encapsulated, what was intended, the interceptions, the redemption plan, and the re-establishment of the divine purpose. The matrix of this has dealt with the integrity details of dethroning the serpent and reestablishing the kingdom economy and governance as per the blueprint. It takes the reader to be transported to this arena, and with the Lord watch through this reading, be clothed and empowered for the purpose of the warfare to reclaim the throne of money. The virtues are relayed. Whoever reads in the spirit of the breath of these letters, shall be clothed and be fully equipped for the work ahead. This book has genuinely been plucked from the eternal realm. It is of one who must have stood with the father, and through the father's eyes, and bosom harvested His desire regarding this matter, embodies the father's groanings and outlet the same through the expressions of this realm, the expression of writing. As you read, be changed as an emissary of your father in heaven for this noble work. Blessings as you embark on this journey of transcension regarding the throne of money and economic governance.

Apostle Dr. Daniel Wesonga Kingdom,
Touch Ministries, Nairobi, Kenya

If you are a leader — or preparing to step into leadership — I strongly recommend The Throne of Money. This book is not just another discourse on finances; it is a revelation and a guide that every visionary needs to encounter.

Leadership is inseparable from vision, and vision, while divine in origin, requires resources for its realization. As leaders, we quickly discover that passion, clarity, and purpose, though vital, cannot by themselves build institutions, sustain projects, or transform societies. At some critical juncture, the question of resources will confront us. It is at this point that the wisdom contained in The Throne of Money becomes indispensable.

Apostle Othniel Ikechukwu offers profound enlightenment and practical education on navigating the often-convoluted dynamics of resources — how to access them, manage them, and channel them for the fulfillment of vision. His treatment of this subject is both spiritual and strategic, empowering leaders to embrace money not as a master, but as a throne: a tool of dominion, stewardship, and advancement of God's purposes.

I deeply salute God's servant for this great assignment. The Throne of Money is a timely gift to the Body of Christ and to leaders from all walks of life who seek to translate vision into tangible impact. I wholeheartedly recommend this book to every leader and aspiring leader who desires to consistently marry vision with provision.

— Adewole Emmanuel
Lead Pastor, Factmission Global Church

Most mainstream discussions about money are superficial and fail to capture its true nature. This book, The Throne of Money, presents a new understanding of money from a multidimensional perspective, moving beyond common clichés.

Money is not simply a world power currency or paper with faces of historical figures. It's not what most people believe it to be. Currency values are merely physical representations of a larger spiritual reality. Money exists within and for humanity, a tool for navigating life and exercising dominion on Earth. This spiritual reality is so powerful that nations and rulers engage in cross-border transactions for human lives and property.

Traditional economic systems like central banks and fiat currencies do not guarantee lasting wealth. Hard work alone doesn't make someone rich, nor do connections guarantee the stability of systems that affect our standard of living.

Governments and their agencies don't truly control the world's money or regulate exchange with human intelligence alone. There is a spiritual throne of money, and on it sits a being—Mammon—that preys on human ego, greed, and insatiable desires. This being has long competed with God for the human heart. Mammon thrives in economic chaos, using it to manipulate people. As daily needs become seemingly uncontrollable, people have less time to find real solutions, instead turning to human-made financial laws driven by greed.

Ancient financial structures and algorithms reveal Mammon's influence, which has spiraled through generations. Inventions and institutions have been created, all in an attempt to promote a system opposing God's kingdom. We have been schooled by this taskmaster, Mammon, and have passed on this knowledge to others, training them to serve systems that work against the kingdom we represent. We admire and chase after these systems because we've been taught they will meet our needs.

Yet, Jesus challenges this belief, stating, "Seek ye first the kingdom of God and its righteousness, and all these things will be added unto you" (Matthew 6:33). This reorients our focus from chasing money to following God. As Jesus also said, "You cannot serve two masters." You must choose between God and Mammon. Those who pursue money systems, believing they are in control, are being manipulated in a larger game. When it comes to money, it is a war of deities. You don't get money by chasing it; you get the throne that controls it, and money will follow you.

This exposé from my father, Apostle Othniel Ikechukwu, serves as a manual for my ministry team, empowering us to expand God's kingdom across all aspects of human life through a ripple cosmic terraformation.

Apostle Emmanuel Adakole Michael,
C-in-C, Ekklēsia Omni Missions, Liberia.

INTRODUCTION

THE HIDDEN ALTAR OF GLOBAL POWER

This introduction explores how the global system is governed by altars, spiritual and technological, that uphold the current financial and political structures. It reveals how ancient priesthoods, prophetic scrolls, spiritual frequencies, and algorithmic dominions still control modern institutions like central banks, intelligence agencies, and trade alliances. It challenges the reader to see the throne of money as a contested space, a battleground of influence, calling forth sons of God to rise in divine alignment and reclaim dominion.

Beneath the dazzling surface of politics, stock markets, economic alliances, and global summits lies an invisible infrastructure, an altar that fuels and governs human affairs. This altar is not just symbolic; it is spiritual, technological, and cosmic in origin. It operates through thrones, dominions, principalities, and power structures that enforce patterns over territories, economies, and civilizations.

Money, while presented as a neutral medium of exchange, is, in reality, a **spiritual weapon** and a **technology of allegiance**. It binds people, cities, and even nations to unseen covenants, whether to the kingdom of darkness or to the Kingdom of God.

The Scriptures declare:

> *"The love of money is the root of all evil."*
> **(1 Timothy 6:10)**

Yet in the Kingdom of God, resources are vital for dominion, stewardship, and the fulfillment of divine mandates (Deuteronomy 8:18). Thus, the battle for the throne of money is not merely about currency, it is about **worship**, **governance**, and **inheritance**.

The ancient world understood this deeply. Civilizations like Egypt, Babylon, Tyre, and Rome constructed complex financial and political systems not merely to sustain economies, but to secure spiritual authority over territories.

These systems were often undergirded by priesthoods, sorcery, cosmic alignments, and metaphysical structures designed to perpetuate control over wealth and power.

In modern times, these ancient structures have been digitized and globalized, through banking systems, intelligence agencies, cyber-finance, and even artificial intelligence. However, the spiritual roots remain unchanged.

This book calls you to pierce beyond the veil, to perceive the unseen, understand the true thrones that govern money and politics, and arise as a kingdom agent in Christ to reclaim dominion in every sphere of influence.

CONTENTS

1. **The Thrones of Mammon: The Ancient spirit Behind Money** - *Exploring biblical and historical spirits behind wealth and commerce; from Tyre to Babylon.*   22

2. **The Currency of Thrones: Understanding the Spiritual DNA of Money**   47

3. **Priesthood and Politics: The Convergence of Altars and Thrones** - *How spiritual priesthoods influence political decisions and territorial rulership.*   66

4. **The Architectonics of Mammon, How Spiritual Thrones Influence Financial Systems**   78

5. **Global Banking Dynasties, The Hidden Bloodlines of Economic Power** - *Examining divine and demonic algorithms in policy and economic systems.*   91

6. **The Spirit of Pharaoh and the Economy of Bondage** - *Exposing the Spirit of Pharaoh behind economic slavery from Egypt to modern systems.*   116

7. **The Mind of the Investor, Building Kingdom Wealth with Righteous Intelligence** - *Unveiling Kingdom principles for wise, prophetic, and righteous financial stewardship.*   123

8. **The Geometry of Wealth, Sacred Systems of Divine Prosperity Cyber Thrones: Finance, Surveillance, and the New World Order** - *Understanding the role of cyber-intelligence, fintech, and control systems.*   131

9. **Thrones of Wealth, Ancient Texts, Modern Masters, and the Christ Alignment** - *Revealing ancient and modern thrones behind wealth, and aligning them under Christ's dominion.*   142

10. **Marketplace Thrones and the Battle for Territory -** *Uncovering the spiritual battle for marketplace thrones and the call to reclaim territory for Christ.*   149

11. **Cyber Thrones: Finance, Intelligence, and the Digital Battle for Souls**   *156*

12. **Stock Market Scrolls: Decoding Spiritual Patterns in Economic Cycles** - *Prophetic insight into financial cycles, trading frequencies, and God's timings.*   168

13. **The Innovation Mandate: Creators, Inventions, and Kingdom Culture** - *Raising kingdom inventors and entrepreneurs to disrupt industries.*   176

14. **Deep Sea Wealth: Mysteries of Marine Trade and Hidden Treasures** - *Biblical and spiritual revelation on maritime power, trade, and ancient wealth systems.*   188

15. **Territorial Thrones and Geopolitical Architectures: The Dominion Mandate** - *Exploring territorial thrones and spiritual forces shaping nations, borders, and global dominion.*   200

16. **Territorial Wealth: Dominion in Infrastructure and Land Systems** - *Understanding how land, cities, and infrastructure are governed by spiritual gates.*   217

17. **The Melchizedek Economic Blueprint: Building Kingdom Economies Beyond Capitalism** - *Unveiling Heaven's economic blueprint through the Melchizedek order beyond capitalism and socialism.*   229

18. **The War of Trade – Global Sanctions and Spiritual Economics** *240*

19. **Wealth Gateways: Spiritual Portals for Resources, Innovation, and Expansion** - *Revealing spiritual gateways that unlock divine resources, innovation, and territorial expansion.* *247*

20. **Dominion Over Digital Economy and the Rise of AI Thrones** - *Unmasking the spiritual architecture of the digital age and reclaiming AI thrones for Kingdom dominion.* *259*

21. **Kingdom Cyber Warfare Training Module & Prophetic Strategic Blueprint for Ecclesia in Digital Economy and AI Systems** - *Equipping the Ecclesia for prophetic governance in cyberspace, waging strategic Kingdom warfare over AI, data, and digital dominions.* *273*

22. **Reclaiming the Thrones: Building Nations in Christ's Name** - *Building Apostolic cities and economic systems to advance Christ's Kingdom.* *282*

23. **The Merchant Thrones: Trade, Navigation, and the Battle for Economic Gateways** - *Exploring trade thrones and spiritual battles for global economic gateways and dominion.* *289*

24. **The Throne Room Economy – Government from Heaven to Earth** *295*

25. **Kingdom Investment Architectures: Building Eternal Value Systems** - *Building eternal wealth through Kingdom-aligned investments and divine stewardship.* *306*

26. **Economic Thrones: Building Apostolic Cities and Financial Ecosystems for Christ** - *Building Apostolic cities and economic ecosystems that honor Christ's Kingdom rule.* *312*

27. **Kingdom Cryptography: Spiritual Codes for Wealth and Innovation in the Age of Digital Currency** - *Unlocking Kingdom codes for wealth and innovation in the digital currency age.* 318

28. **Currency Wars: Discerning Babylon's Digital Trap vs Zion's Kingdom Economy** - *Navigating Currency Wars: Zion's Kingdom economy versus Babylon's digital trap.* 324

29. **The Grand Dominion - Subduing the Banking Systems and Global Economic Thrones** - *Empowering the Ecclesia to subdue and rule global banking under Christ's dominion.* 330

30. **Demystifying Taxes, Credit Systems, and Financial Slavery: A Kingdom Perspective on Global Debt Institutions** - *Unveiling spiritual chains in taxes and debt; pursuing Kingdom financial freedom.* 338

31. **Thrones of Evasion: How Global Elites Escape Taxes and Redefine Financial Systems** - *Exposing global elites' tax evasion and the spiritual fight for financial justice.* 344

32. **Thrones of Greed, Corporate Corruption and the Crime of Political Power** - *Revealing corporate greed and corruption; calling Ecclesia to reclaim justice.* 350

33. **Greed, Capital, and the Corruption of Sacred and Social Institutions** - *Exposing Mammon's corruption in church, medicine, and humanitarian institutions.* 356

34. **Global Structures of Greed – The Economy of Human Trafficking and the Hyper-Mobility of Narcotics** - *Exposing global greed behind human trafficking and narcotics through Kingdom justice.* 362

35. **Cyber-Gates of Prostitution, Sexual Enslavement at the Altars of Mammon** - *Unveiling digital prostitution's rise as spiritual enslavement under Mammon's throne.*   368

36. **The Love of Money and Global Corporate Monetization** - *Exposing the love of money fueling global corporate monetization and spiritual bondage.*   373

37. **Soul Economies, The Trade of Eternity for Earthly Gain** - *Exposing how souls are traded for worldly gain in global systems of power and greed.*   378

38. **The Sacredness and Lawlessness of the Throne of Money** - *The dual power of money: sacred influence and spiritual deception unveiled.*   385

39. **Dominion Over the Spirits of Mammon, the Matrix of Heartless Emperors, the Mind of the Beast, and Vicious Monsters of Money** - *Conquering mammon's spirits and beastly empires through Christ's dominion.*   391

40. **Thrones Reclaimed - The Final Clarion Call to Rescue Nations and Men** - *A prophetic call to reclaim thrones and restore Christ's Kingdom rule.*   397

41. **My Pledge, Oath, Allegiance, and Mystical Vows on the Throne of Money**   403

CHAPTER 1

The Thrones Of Mammon: The Ancient Spirit Behind Money

"No one can serve two masters; for either he will hate the one and love the other, or else he will be loyal to the one and despise the other. You cannot serve God and mammon." – *Matthew 6:24 (NKJV)*

UNDERSTANDING MAMMON: BEYOND A DEMON OF GREED

In Christ's teachings, **Mammon** is not simply "money", it is a **spirit**, a throne, and a master. **The Throne of Money"** refers to the invisible, spiritual seat of power that governs and manipulates the global economic systems. While money appears to be a neutral tool, this concept reveals that behind every financial system, banks, stock markets, corporate power, and even digital currency, **there are spiritual thrones** and unseen authorities that either align with the Kingdom of God or with Mammon (the spirit of greed, fear, and control).

It is not about money as paper or numbers, but about who or what is enthroned behind it.

They work behind the scenes to shape how wealth flows, how people value money, and how economic systems function, often pulling hearts away from God's true provision and leading them to trust in material things instead.

So, while currency, banks, markets, and businesses are the visible, physical side, these thrones are the **spiritual engines or powers behind them** that give those systems their direction, influence, and sometimes bondage.

When you begin to perceive money as a spirit, a throne, and a master, you will truly understand how to engage with it and subdue it as your slave.

> *"No one can serve two masters...You cannot serve God and Mammon."* **(Matthew 6:24)**

You can **have money and serve God**, but you **cannot serve Mammon and still claim God's dominion**.

The Greek word *Mamōnas* derives from an Aramaic root meaning "wealth personified." Jesus presented Mammon as a **rival god**, capable of commanding **loyalty**, **service**, and **worship**.

Thus, Mammon is an **ancient principality** that seeks to enthrone itself in the hearts of men, institutions, and nations, establishing systems where **trust shifts from God to material wealth**.

From the Tower of Babel (Genesis 11) to the financial empires of Tyre (Ezekiel 28), Mammon has hidden behind human structures of commerce, trade, and economy, always demanding allegiance.

HOW MAMMON OPERATES: WHAT IT FEELS LIKE WHEN MAMMON SPEAKS

1. Fear of Lack: The Voice That Whispers at Night

Imagine this.

It's 2 AM. You're lying in bed, staring at the ceiling. Bills are due. Your account balance is shrinking. And a voice quietly asks:

"What if you run out?"

You feel it deep in your chest. The tension. The panic.

The next morning, you take a job you hate, one that drains your soul, just so you don't "fall behind." You skip giving at church, even though your heart nudged you to. And you stop praying with expectation.

You're surviving, but not living.

That's Mammon's first language: fear.

It's not just a feeling, it's a force. And it's trying to replace your trust in God with trust in money.

2. Identity Swap: Status Over Substance

Ever been in a room where everyone seems to "have it together"?

Suddenly, you start comparing:

Her dress.

His car.

Their vacation.

Your shoes.

And without realizing it, something inside you whispers:

"You don't matter unless you have more."

Now, you're chasing image instead of impact. You're buying things not because you need them, but because you're trying to keep up.

Mammon reshapes your identity. It tells you that your worth is measured by what you wear, where you live, or what people think of your success.

But that's a lie. You were never meant to build your value outside of God.

3. Silent Chains: Oppression in Disguise

Look around.

A young man works three jobs. He can't rest. He's always tired. But every month, after rent and food, there's barely enough left to breathe.

A single mother is underpaid by a company that posts record profits. Her manager tells her she should be "grateful."

This is not just bad business. It's Mammon's system.

It thrives in:

- Exploitation
- Hoarding
- Unfair wages
- Work without Sabbath

The goal? Keep people so tired, so desperate, that they don't even have time to hear God's voice. It's economic slavery with a digital smile.

4. False Security: The Trap of Self-Sufficiency

There's something seductive about having "enough."

Savings. Insurance. Investments.

It feels safe. In control.

Until God tells you to take a leap of faith... and suddenly, you freeze.

"What if this ruins everything I've built?"

Mammon offers

- Comfort without peace.
- Control without surrender.
- Power without protection.

It teaches you that faith is a backup plan, not a lifestyle.

But the Kingdom doesn't work that way. God asks you to walk on water, because He is your boat.

5. War Against Generosity: The Tug-of-War Inside You

You're sitting in church. Or maybe scrolling your phone. A cause stirs your heart. You want to give.

Then it hits you:

"What if you need this later?"

"Play it safe. Be wise."

The nudge fades. You scroll past.

That hesitation is not always logic, it's warfare.

Mammon knows that every time you give freely, you declare, "I trust God, not money."

So it whispers fear. It breeds caution.

Because generosity is rebellion against its throne.

6. The Hustle that Never Ends

You wake up tired.

Emails. Messages. Deadlines.

A voice inside says:

"Keep going. You can't afford to rest."

You skip family dinners. Cut corners on prayer. Say, "Just one more month of grinding," but it turns into a year.

Mammon fuels the lie that your value is in your output. That if you slow down, you'll lose.

But God says the opposite:

"In returning and rest you shall be saved; in quietness and trust is your strength." ~ *Isaiah 30:15*

Mammon drives.

God invites.

BOTTOM LINE: MAMMON'S GOAL IS NOT JUST YOUR WALLET, IT WANTS

Your Worship.

It doesn't matter whether you're rich or poor.

Mammon doesn't care about your balance sheet; it wants to sit on the throne of your heart.

SIGNS MAMMON IS AT WORK IN A LIFE:

- Fear and anxiety about money, even when you have it.
- Inability to rest or stop chasing more.
- Holding back generosity using "logic" as an excuse.
- Bitterness or jealousy when others prosper.
- Making life choices based only on money, not on calling, peace, or purpose.

HOW TO RESIST MAMMON

- Submit your finances to God every day.
- Practice regular generosity, this breaks Mammon's hold.
- Rest confidently in God's provision, don't hustle out of fear.
- Declare your trust in God as your Provider, not your salary, job,

or connections.

- Discern the systems around you: Are they built on fear, greed, or trust in God?

HISTORICAL PERSPECTIVES: ANCIENT THRONES OF WEALTH

Back in ancient times, money was way more than just coins or trading goods, it was tied up with gods and cosmic powers. Imagine Egypt, where people depended on the Nile flooding each year to grow crops. The Pharaoh wasn't just a king; he was seen as the "son of Ra," the sun god, basically the ultimate controller of wealth. So, when the Nile flooded, it wasn't just nature doing its thing, it was a cosmic event connected to the Pharaoh's power.

Over in Babylon, trade was protected by gods like Marduk, and laws about business were wrapped in astrology and cosmic cycles. They believed the stars and planets had a say in how wealth should flow.

Tyre was this huge trading city, rich and proud, but it got called out in the Bible for putting money above God, showing how economic power could become a kind of idol.

And Rome? Rome built its fortune on conquering lands, collecting taxes, and using slaves to work the empire, all tied into worshiping the emperor like a god. Wealth wasn't just power, it was sacred power.

So, money back then wasn't just about the dollars or coins, it **was the currency of spiritual thrones**, wrapped up with gods, cosmic order, and power.

In all these cases, **money was never secular**, it was the **currency** of spiritual thrones.

SCIENTIFIC AND COSMIC KNOWLEDGE: WEALTH IN THE QUANTUM FIELD

Modern science shows that money functions as **energy**, not in a mystical sense, but as **organized information** that carries **human trust, emotion, and collective agreement**. A currency note has no value by itself; its power comes from what people *agree* it represents. Central banks confirm this: money works because people believe in it.

In **behavioral economics**, it's proven that our beliefs and emotions, like **fear, trust, and expectation**, influence how we give, spend, and attract wealth. Fear leads to hoarding and panic. Trust opens up generosity and investment. These emotional "fields" can shape entire markets, which is why economists often track *confidence indexes*.

Even **quantum physics** supports this: value isn't fixed or intrinsic. Reality shifts based on observation and interaction. Jesus echoed this same principle when He said,

> **"Where your treasure is, there your heart will be also"** (Matthew 6:21).

In essence, your focus, trust, and desire shape what you attract or lose.

At a **cosmic level**, gravitational forces that pull stars and galaxies together mirror how wealth and resources flow: **powerful centers** (like major cities or influential people) pull in opportunities, while **weaker or scattered systems** fade, merge, or collapse. In both the cosmos and economics, **attraction follows focus and mass**, what you consistently *honor, trust, and dwell on* begins to flow toward you.

This is the spiritual battlefield where **Mammon** operates. Mammon isn't just greed, it's a spiritual influence that **manipulates emotional fields** like fear, pride, scarcity, and control to direct how wealth moves. It tempts people to **trust in money instead of God**, to hustle in anxiety instead of walk in peace.

In the language of both **science and spirit**, wealth behaves gravitationally. Your internal world, what you trust, love, and honor, pulls resources toward you or repels them. What you *behold*, you eventually *become a magnet for.*

KABBALISTIC TEACHINGS: THE TREE OF LIFE AND WEALTH DIMENSIONS

In the Kabbalistic tradition, particularly in interpretations of the **Sephiroth** (Tree of Life), **wealth** is linked to **Malkuth** (Kingdom), the final emanation where spiritual energy materializes into the physical world.

- **Keter** (Crown) represents divine will.

- **Malkuth** represents manifestation, where divine abundance should flow into earthly reality.

However, when this flow is corrupted, either by pride, fear, or manipulation, the spiritual circuit is broken, and **klipot** (husks, shells of impurity) form.

Mammon operates as a corrupted force at the level of Malkuth, **trapping divine flow** into distorted systems of debt, slavery, and oppression.

In Christ, however, believers are reconnected directly to the Father through the **true Tree of Life**, Jesus Himself (John 15:5), restoring the pure flow of abundance.

> **"I am the vine; you are the branches. If you remain in me and I in you, you will bear much fruit."**

Thus, true wealth in Christ bypasses the corruption of Mammon and flows from the Father's heart.

SPIRITUAL STRUCTURES OF MAMMON IN TODAY'S WORLD

In today's world, **Mammon no longer hides**, it operates through powerful systems that shape how money flows, how people live, and what nations pursue. These systems are not neutral; they carry **spiritual signatures** that can either align with God's order or entrap people in cycles of fear, greed, and control.

Here are some of Mammon's modern strongholds:

- **Banking and Credit Systems**: Many global economies are built on debt. What looks like opportunity often becomes invisible slavery, trapping individuals, families, and entire nations in cycles of repayment and dependency.

- **Stock Markets**: Originally built for investment, many markets now thrive on speculation, panic, and manipulation. Emotional waves of fear and greed often drive decisions, not truth, value, or purpose.

- **Cyber Finance**: While technologies like cryptocurrency and AI offer new potential, they also carry unseen patterns, often shaped by the values of their creators. Without spiritual awareness, believers can unknowingly interact with systems rooted in rebellion or pride.

- **Government Treasury and Trade Systems**: Global agreements, economic policies, and resource flows are often influenced by secret alliances, unrighteous covenants, or power-driven agendas that oppose the kingdom of God.

These systems form an invisible **matrix of Mammon**, subtle yet powerful. Without spiritual discernment, even well-meaning people can get pulled into its web, chasing wealth but losing rest, joy, and purpose.

> *"For what will it profit a man if he gains the whole world and forfeits his soul?"* ~**Mark 8:36**

CHRIST'S DOMINION OVER MAMMON

Christ does not reject wealth; **He reclaims it from the grip of Mammon**.

In the wilderness temptation (Matthew 4:8–10), Satan showed Jesus "all the kingdoms of the world and their glory", offering Him the global economic and political systems in exchange for worship.

> *"All these things I will give you, if you will fall down and worship me."*

But Jesus refused. He didn't deny the legitimacy of influence; **He rejected the means**. He restored the divine order: *Worship belongs to God alone.*

> *"You shall worship the Lord your God, and Him only shall you serve."*

This moment was not just about personal temptation; it was a **spiritual confrontation between two economic thrones**:

- One built on **fear, compromise, and control** (Mammon),
- The other on **righteousness, alignment, and sonship** (Kingdom).

THE GOAL IS NOT POVERTY, BUT HOLY DOMINION

Jesus never preached poverty as a virtue. Instead, He redefined **how wealth is handled** and **who should hold it**.

True kingdom wealth is not for flaunting or enslaving others, it's for **building, freeing, and stewarding**:

- **Abraham** was exceedingly rich in silver, gold, and livestock, yet he was God's friend and intercessor (Genesis 13:2, James 2:23).
- **Joseph** administered Egypt's entire economy under Pharaoh, yet preserved the nations and honored God.
- **Daniel** held authority over multiple empires, yet bowed only to God.

These were men of influence who walked in intimacy. Their wealth and power were platforms for divine purpose.

THE CHURCH'S CALL: NOT TO FLEE, BUT TO ASCEND

We are not called to **withdraw from marketplaces, boardrooms, and policy rooms.**

We are called to **occupy them with light.**

> *"Arise, shine, for your light has come, and the glory of the Lord rises upon you."* , **Isaiah 60:1**

Isaiah 60 goes on to speak of **nations, wealth, and rulers coming to the brightness of our rising.** This is not just poetic, it's prophetic. The wealth of the nations is meant to be drawn into the hands of the righteous, not through force or manipulation, but through **wisdom, excellence, and covenant alignment.**

PRACTICAL PRINCIPLES FOR RULING IN THE MARKETPLACE WITHOUT COMPROMISE

1. **Maintain the Altar First**

   Never let your success outrun your intimacy. The altar must be stronger than the throne you sit on. Like Daniel, pray consistently even if you're in the king's court.

2. **Discern Spiritual Gateways in Business**

   Every business system has spiritual covenants behind it. Seek God's wisdom to know where not to partner, what deals to reject, and when to walk away, even from seemingly "profitable" ventures.

3. **Value People Above Profits**

   Kingdom wealth is people-centered. Mammon sacrifices people for profit; the Kingdom serves people and receives wealth as a consequence.

4. **Be Governed by Integrity, Not Pressure**

In financial stress or high-stakes moments, remember: desperation opens doors to compromise. Train your heart to say *no* when necessary, even if the opportunity looks glittering.

5. **Build with Eternity in Mind**

The legacy of your work should extend beyond you. Ask: Does this honor God? Will it bless generations? Is it aligned with Kingdom values?

6. **Honor God Publicly**

Never be ashamed to attribute your success to divine wisdom and favor. When Joseph interpreted Pharaoh's dream, he gave glory to God, and that posture promoted him (Genesis 41:16).

IN SUMMARY:

Christ came not to strip us of dominion, but to **retrain and re-seat us** on thrones that serve the Kingdom, not Mammon. Wealth in the hands of the righteous becomes a weapon against injustice, a channel for compassion, and a tool for transformation.

"You will be called priests of the Lord... You will feed on the wealth of nations, and in their riches you will boast." ~**Isaiah 61:6**

CAPITALISM: A MODERN MASK FOR AN ANCIENT ALTAR

Capitalism is a system where people and businesses try to make money by owning things, selling goods or services, and competing with others. The main goal is to make a profit, even if some people are left behind. In this system, people are often seen as valuable if they make a lot of money, even if they lie, cheat, or hurt others. But those who are kind, honest, and helpful but poor are often ignored.

But behind this system, underneath the bank accounts, shopping malls, and business meetings, is something deeper. Capitalism is not just about money. It has become a **spiritual system**, a **modern altar** where people **sacrifice** their time, peace, morals, families, and even faith, all in the name of "success."

EVERYDAY EXAMPLES TO MAKE IT CLEAR:

1. **The Sacrifice of Time**

   A father works **14 hours a day** chasing promotion after promotion. He buys his family expensive gifts but **rarely spends time with them**. His kids grow distant.

   He didn't kill a goat on an altar, but he sacrificed his family at the altar of career and success.

2. **The Sacrifice of Morals**

   A young woman is offered a big contract, but only if she **compromises her integrity** or body. She agrees, chasing fame and wealth.

   She didn't kneel at a stone idol, but she bowed to the spirit of greed and recognition.

3. **The Sacrifice of Rest and Health**

   A man hustles non-stop, working 7 days a week, skipping sleep, burning out his health.

   He never went to a temple, but his body became the sacrifice on the altar of financial gain.

4. **Churches and Capitalism**

   Some churches **water down the gospel** to please wealthy donors, or they **market themselves like businesses** to grow numbers, not souls.

   The pulpit becomes a stage, and the cross becomes a brand, faith is offered up to the idol of popularity and profit.

ANCIENT PATTERN, NEW PACKAGING

In ancient times, people gave offerings to gods like **Baal**, **Mammon**, or **Molech**, hoping to get rain, success, or protection.

Today, people do the same, but instead of altars made of stone, we have:

Ancient Altars	Modern Altars
Baal (prosperity god)	Banks, markets, brand obsession
Molech (sacrificing kids)	Parents sacrificing time/family
Mammon (spirit of money)	Obsession with wealth and status

ANCIENT ECHOES: THE TEMPLE ECONOMY REIMAGINED

In ancient temple systems:

- **Farmers, traders, and rulers** brought **offerings** to **gods and goddesses** for **rain**, harvest, war victory, or fertility.

- These temples were not just religious centers, they were **economic hubs**, collecting, storing, and redistributing wealth through **spiritual protocol**.

Fast forward to today:

- **Consumers are the worshippers**, returning again and again to the altar of consumption.

- **Corporations function as temples**, amassing offerings (money, attention, data) and dispensing 'blessings' (products, services, status).

- **Brands and logos are the idols**, capturing loyalty and emotional allegiance, Apple, Nike, Tesla, Amazon, they are more than companies; they're icons of meaning.

- **Central banks and global markets are the modern altars**, redistributing the sacrifices of nations, printing value into existence, and commanding obedience through inflation, interest rates, and policy decisions.

CASE EXAMPLES THAT REVEAL THE PATTERN

1. **Black Friday & Global Sales Rituals**

    Every year, millions trample over one another in stores and online platforms, not out of necessity, but because of a ritualized belief that **scarcity and speed unlock blessing**. This is not just consumerism; it's a scripted ritual of allegiance.

2. **Cryptocurrency Hype & Digital Altars**

    Many buy, sell, and hold tokens not just for profit but for identity, belonging, and faith in a decentralized "salvation" from government control, **a digital religion without a god but full of evangelists, doctrines, and rewards.**

3. **National Economies Aligned to Spiritual Covens**

    Some nations' economic deals, especially involving global loans, natural resource contracts, or elite societies, are made through **unseen spiritual agreements**, creating systemic oppression and cycles of dependency. These are not merely political; they are spiritual structures cloaked as economic policy.

THE SPIRITUAL INFRASTRUCTURE: CLOAKED BUT REAL

Behind spreadsheets and banknotes is a spiritual system that:

- Demands **daily allegiance** through schedules, debts, and consumption.

- Requires **sacrifice** of personal values, family time, and even moral integrity.

- Promises survival or success, but **at the price of surrendering identity and divine purpose.**

This is not just capitalism, it is **Mammon globalized, digitized, and disguised as economic freedom.**

"You cannot serve both God and Mammon.", **Matthew 6:24**

Mammon doesn't just want your money; it seeks **your loyalty, time, and spiritual posture**.

DISCERNING THE DIFFERENCE: CAPITAL VS. MAMMON

We must understand: **capital itself is not evil**. Resources, business, and trade can be **righteous tools** when governed by the Spirit of God.

The problem is when **systems become spiritual strongholds**, requiring **unholy sacrifices** and offering counterfeit blessings.

- **Kingdom economy** is founded on honor, stewardship, rest, and covenant.

- **Mammon economy** is fueled by fear, pressure, competition, and loss.

IN SUMMARY:

Today's economic systems are more than neutral; they are deeply spiritual. They resemble ancient temples more than we realize, demanding sacrifices and offering false security. The true believer must **see beyond the visible**, recognizing which system they're feeding, and which kingdom they're aligning with.

"Do not conform to the pattern of this world, but be transformed by the renewing of your mind." ~Romans 12:2

HISTORICAL CONSTRUCTION OF THE CAPITALIST ALTAR

The altar of Mammon, now fully global, digitized, and enthroned in the modern economy, was not built overnight. It evolved through a series of historical epochs, each embedding **spiritual architecture** into economic development. Behind the rise of global capitalism lies a **carefully layered structure** of economic power, mysticism, empire, and idolatry.

EPOCHS THAT BUILT THE ALTAR

1. **Medieval Banking Families (Venice, Genoa, Florence)**

   - The roots of modern finance can be traced to elite families such as the **Medici** and **Fugger**, who created early banking systems and currency exchange methods.

   - Many of these families were not merely financial strategists, they were connected to **esoteric orders, secret societies, and mystical worldviews** that merged **economic control with spiritual influence**.

   - Banking houses began to function as **shadow temples**, shaping destinies of nations behind closed doors.

   These early systems shifted trust from the **church and feudal lords** to private **financial intermediaries**; a change not just political, but spiritual.

2. **The East India Companies (British, Dutch, French)**

   - These were not just trade companies; they were **military-economic empires** given authority to colonize, wage war, and govern lands.

   - Under the guise of commerce, they **enslaved entire populations**, seized resources, and **baptized economies into submission**, often under flags bearing Christian imagery, yet aligned with Mammon.

- Spiritual domination accompanied economic conquest. Indigenous gods were displaced not only by European weapons but by **European banks and trade laws.**

These companies effectively **married Babylonian commerce to imperial rule**, institutionalizing economic exploitation as "civilization."

3. The Rise of Rothschilds & Central Banks

- The 18th–19th centuries marked a critical turn: the creation of **central banking systems** that replaced national sovereignty with **institutional debt.**

- The **Rothschild dynasty** and similar banking houses financed kings, wars, and revolutions, **shifting the spiritual headship of nations from monarchs to financiers.**

- Debt became the new chain, and compound interest the new whip.

National currencies were no longer backed by gold or silver, but by **trust in invisible systems**, locking entire nations into spiritual bondage.

4. The Industrial Revolution: The Rise of the Profit Priesthood

- As machines replaced manual labor, **moguls and tycoons** like Rockefeller, Carnegie, and Morgan emerged, not just as business leaders but as **priests of a new economic religion.**

- Factories became temples of labor; workers sacrificed health, time, and family to feed systems that placed **productivity over purpose.**

- The Sabbath was abandoned; human dignity traded for efficiency.

This age built the **"machine altar"**, offering prosperity to the few and exhaustion to the many.

5. The Digital Revolution: Data as Devotion

- With the rise of the internet, smartphones, and artificial intelligence, **tech giants** now operate as **high priests of modern culture.**

- Algorithms dictate attention. Social networks shape desire. Data is extracted like offerings to invisible gods, every click, view, and scroll feeds a vast, unseen altar.
- The line between commerce, culture, and control is blurred. Humans become both the product and the offering.

This is the **altar of illusion**, where **virtual realities substitute eternal truths**, and digital values displace divine principles.

SPIRITUAL MECHANICS OF THE CAPITALIST ALTAR

Beneath the machinery of global capitalism lies a **hidden altar**, upheld not by visible economic laws but by **three spiritual pillars** that manipulate the heart, reshape identity, and demand continual sacrifice. These pillars form the inner architecture of Mammon's dominion, a counterfeit spiritual system masquerading as economic progress.

THREE INVISIBLE PILLARS OF MAMMON'S THRONE

1. Fear – The Engine of Servitude

At the root of most economic activity today is not vision, joy, or purpose, but **fear**.

- Fear of poverty.
- Fear of obscurity.
- Fear of irrelevance.
- Fear of not having "enough."

This fear drives **endless consumerism**, compulsive labor, and **debt-based cycles**, entrapping both nations and individuals in a psychological Egypt.

"You were slaves in Egypt, and the Lord brought you out with a mighty hand..." ~**Deuteronomy 5:15**

Just as Pharaoh manipulated the Israelites with bricks and quotas, modern economies enslave through **targets, metrics, and credit scores**.

Fear becomes loyalty to Mammon, a twisted covenant of anxiety in exchange for momentary provision.

2. Identity Worship – The Hijacking of the Soul

In the modern marketplace, **brands have replaced totems**. Lifestyles, labels, and logos now serve as extensions of self, false altars where identity is shaped not by the **image of God**, but by curated aesthetics and possessions.

- "I buy, therefore I am."
- "I wear this, so I belong."
- "I achieve; therefore, I matter."

Advertising has evolved into a **spiritual disciple**, teaching people to place **value in image** rather than essence.

"You are not your own; you were bought with a price."
~ **1 Corinthians 6:19–20**

This is more than consumerism, it is **identity colonization**. The altar of Mammon demands that individuals trade their **divine sonship** for cultural labels and status symbols.

3. Sacrificial Exchange – The Offering of Destiny

Mammon doesn't simply ask for money, it demands **sacrifices**: time, health, marriages, children, calling, and legacy.

It redefines worship: not as **adoration of God**, but as relentless **labor for temporal success**.

People offer their lives, day after day, on the altar of:

- Promotions.
- Paychecks.
- Public approval.
- Personal ambition.

"Offer your bodies as a living sacrifice, holy and pleasing to God, this is your true worship." ~**Romans 12:1**

Yet instead of presenting themselves to the Lord, many present themselves to systems that **burn destiny for visibility**, and **exchange eternal purpose for applause.**

THE COUNTERFEIT RELIGIOUS SYSTEM

Global capitalism, when **divorced from the Spirit of Christ**, becomes more than an economy.

It becomes a **counter-religion:**

Kingdom of God	Capitalist Altar (Under Mammon)
Faith	Fear
Identity in Christ	Identity through brands/status
Sacrificial love	Sacrificial labor
Divine stewardship	Ownership obsession
Rest in God	Perpetual hustle

It has temples (corporations), priests (influencers and CEOs), sacraments (purchases), and congregations (consumers).

It replaces communion with **consumption.**

THE CALL TO DISCERNMENT

The danger is not wealth itself, but **misaligned worship**.

Mammon doesn't simply want to fund you, it wants to **father you**. And if believers are not discerning, they can unconsciously **submit to a foreign spiritual yoke**, thinking they're just "working hard.

The Church must wake up to this counterfeit system, not with fear, but with **clarity, authority, and kingdom alignment.**

"No one can serve two masters... You cannot serve both God and Mammon." ~**Matthew 6:24**

THE SCIENCE OF MASS MANIPULATION

As global capitalism evolves, it no longer depends solely on raw labor or tangible assets, it now **hijacks human consciousness**. In this new terrain, the marketplace has become a **battlefield of the mind**, where souls are subtly programmed through science-backed systems that echo ancient spiritual manipulation.

What began as mere marketing has now matured into a **techno-priesthood**, drawing from the disciplines of behavioral economics, neuroscience, and data analytics, not to serve humanity, but to **reshape desire**, control attention, and deepen allegiance to Mammon's altar.

PRAYER POINTS

Dethroning Mammon and Restoring Kingdom Alignment

1. **I Reject the Spirit of Fear Masquerading as Financial Wisdom**

    Spirit of fear disguised as logic, I expose you and cast you down.

    I declare that I will no longer make decisions based on survival, but by divine trust.

    I reject anxiety as a financial compass and receive the peace of Jehovah Jireh.

2. **I Break Every Mental Idol Formed Around Money and Image**

    Every thought exalting status over substance, performance over presence, I pull you down.

    I cast out every false identity rooted in possessions and public approval.

    I reclaim my identity as a son/daughter of the Most High, not a slave of image or industry."

3. **I Renounce the Chains of Economic Slavery in My Lineage**

"By the blood of Jesus, I renounce generational systems of toil, hustle, and oppression.

I break every ancestral agreement that glorifies bondage in the name of success.

I declare rest, multiplication, and stewardship as my new inheritance."

4. **I Restore the Altar of Worship Above the Altar of Wealth**

"Let my heart be Your throne, O God.

I tear down every high place that has stolen my time, attention, or affection.

Rebuild the altar of devotion within me, where Your presence governs my financial life."

5. **I Declare a New Economy Governed by the Spirit, Not by Mammon**

"I invite the Holy Spirit to be the financial strategist of my life.

Let Your wisdom, not the pressure of the world, guide my investments, work, and generosity.

Let my income be the fruit of covenant, not compromise."

6. **I Sever from the Hustle Culture and Enter Divine Flow**

"I release the addiction to overwork, the fear of falling behind, and the lie that my worth is in my output.

I receive the rhythm of grace, creativity, and supernatural rest.

I declare: I work from identity, not for identity."

PROPHETIC DIRECTIONS & ACTIVATIONS

1. Altar Reset Activation

   Action: Take time today to physically clean, reset, or symbolically rebuild your devotional altar.

Prayer:

"Lord, as I reset this altar, I dethrone every idol that has stolen my affection. Let this place be governed by intimacy, not ambition."

2.   **Identity Warfare Decree**

Action: Stand in front of a mirror and declare:

"I am not my possessions. I am not my productivity. I am not my performance."

"I am a child of the King. I am royal. I am righteous. I am resourceful in Christ."

3.   **Restoration of Rest Act**

Action: Schedule a personal Sabbath or rest day and honor it as a prophetic protest against Mammon.

Prayer:

"I refuse to serve a system that never lets me breathe. As I rest, I prophesy: God is my Source, and my soul is not for sale."

4.   **Mammon Dethronement Decree**

Declare aloud with authority:

Mammon, your throne is overthrown.

I renounce every agreement with greed, fear, and false security.

The throne of my heart belongs to Christ alone.

My money serves His Kingdom. My life is not for sale.

CHAPTER 2

The Currency of Thrones: Understanding the Spiritual DNA of Money

"The silver is Mine, and the gold is Mine, says the Lord of hosts." ~*Haggai 2:8 (NKJV)*

UNVEILING THE SPIRITUAL DNA AND DOMINION CODES OF MONEY

Money is more than paper, metal, or digital code.

At its core, **money is a covenantal symbol,** an invisible agreement of trust, value, and dominion between peoples, territories, and thrones.

Every currency, whether gold, fiat, cryptocurrency, or commodities, carries **spiritual DNA**: a story, an altar, a throne.

Until the Ecclesia understands the **spiritual engineering** of money, we will only react to financial systems rather than **govern them.**

This chapter unlocks the **ancient, scientific, and spiritual revelations** about money,

how it is created, who governs it, and how Christ's Kingdom must reclaim it.

ANCIENT PERSPECTIVES: THE ORIGIN OF MONEY

In Ancient Civilizations:

- In Sumer (Babylonia), money (silver bars) was consecrated through temple altars.

- In Egypt, grain and gold were currencies linked to the Pharaoh's divine authority.

- In Rome, the denarius bore the image of Caesar as "son of the gods."

Money was not just commerce; it was priesthood and worship.

This is why Jesus said:

> **"Show Me the coin used for the tax." And they brought Him a denarius. And He said to them, 'Whose image and inscription is this?'"** - *(Matthew 22:19-20, NASB)*

Money bore **spiritual allegiance**.

It was a **token of governance**.

Whoever controlled the currency controlled the allegiance of the people.

Thus, economies were actually **spiritual ecosystems**.

SCIENTIFIC AND ECONOMIC RESEARCH: THE EVOLUTION OF CURRENCY

Modern research into the evolution of money shows key patterns:

- **Trust is the Foundation:** Whether gold, paper, or digital currency, money depends on collective belief.

- **Energy Transfer:** Scientists like Nassim Taleb describe money as a system for transferring energy (labor, resources) efficiently across time and space.

- **Network Dynamics:** Bitcoin and blockchain technologies demonstrate that decentralized trust networks (without a central bank) are possible, but also vulnerable to new spiritual dynamics.

Key Scientific Insight:

Money systems behave like **living organisms**, growing, mutating, and adapting based on trust, fear, greed, and faith.

Thus, every **economic crash** (like 1929, 2008) is not just market failure, it is **a spiritual shaking of thrones**.

MYSTICAL UNDERSTANDING: THE SPIRITUAL DNA OF MONEY

In the mystical realm, **money is a carrier of agreements**.

It can either carry the **DNA of mammon** (greed, fear, exploitation) or the **DNA of Kingdom stewardship** (trust, generosity, creation, righteousness).

Jesus taught:

> **"You cannot serve God and Mammon."** - *(Matthew 6:24, NKJV)*

He revealed that Mammon is **a spirit**, a counterfeit throne trying to hijack the currency of trust and transfer.

Spiritual laws of currency:

- **Honor:** Money flows toward honor (Proverbs 3:9–10).
- **Trustworthiness:** Kingdom economics are built on faithful stewardship (Luke 16:10–11).
- **Seed Principle:** Money is a seed that reproduces after its spiritual kind (2 Corinthians 9:6–11).

Thus, wealth in the Kingdom is not accumulation, it is **transformation and multiplication under divine governance.**

SCRIPTURAL FOUNDATIONS FOR KINGDOM CURRENCY:

In the Bible, Kingdom economics are visible:

- **Gold of Havilah:** (Genesis 2:11–12) God mentions gold early, implying it is meant for righteous stewardship.
- **Storehouses of Joseph:** (Genesis 41) Joseph built economic infrastructure to sustain generations during famine.
- **The Treasury of the Temple:** (2 Kings 12) Offerings and wealth were guarded and governed under prophetic and priestly oversight.
- **Revelation 21:** In the New Jerusalem, streets are paved with gold, meaning wealth serves as infrastructure, not as idol.

Money must bow to the throne of Christ, not dominate His people.

PROPHETIC INSIGHTS: THE FUTURE OF KINGDOM MONEY

The Spirit is raising **kingdom financiers, innovators, technologists, and marketplace apostles** who:

- See money as a **weapon of righteousness.**
- Build **alternative economic systems** that serve human dignity, innovation, and justice.
- Sanctify wealth through prophetic blueprints and financial ecosystems aligned with Heaven.

Cryptocurrencies, new fintech systems, decentralized economies, all are **transition points** for divine repositioning of wealth.

The prophecy of Haggai is accelerating:

> **"The silver is Mine, and the gold is Mine, declares the Lord of hosts."** - *(Haggai 2:8, ESV)*

THE EVOLUTION OF MONEY: FROM TANGIBLE TO ILLUSORY

In the modern world, money has become less of a substance and more of a shared belief, a digital phantom that governs our lives with startling authority. We rarely hold it, yet we trust it. A few taps on a screen can transfer "wealth" across continents, settle debts, or make fortunes disappear. But what exactly are we moving? Not coins. Not paper. Just digits. Records. Promises.

This illusion of money is maintained by complex systems we cannot see and rarely question. We get paid without touching cash. Our purchases vanish with a beep. We check our balances, not our wallets. But what if the network went down? If your banking app crashed for a day, or your country experienced a cyberattack, what would your money be? Just a number you can no longer reach. For instance, in 2023, several major banks in Europe temporarily froze digital transfers due to security updates, leaving millions unable to access their funds for hours or days (Reuters, 2023). No vaults were empty, just screens.

Even cash, which once symbolized physical wealth, is now largely ignored. In many countries, entire cities run cashless, Sweden is often cited as a leading example, where over 80% of transactions are cashless (Riksbank Report, 2022). A coffee, a ride, or a doctor's visit, all paid without anything you can hold. And the moment your card is declined or your app fails, you realize: the value wasn't ever really in your possession. It was a permission, not a possession.

Governments can also create money out of thin air. In response to economic crises, trillions of dollars were "printed", not by running printing presses, but by typing numbers into systems. No gold was mined. No work was done. For example, during the COVID-19 pandemic, the U.S. Federal Reserve increased its balance sheet by over $3 trillion within months through quantitative easing, effectively creating money digitally to support the economy (Federal Reserve, 2020). Yet this invisible influx devalued savings and inflated prices. Real people paid the cost of imaginary money.

And then there are cryptocurrencies, where the illusion is even more naked. Many of them are created from nothing but code and hype, no physical form, no state backing, no collateral. Dogecoin, created as a joke, rose to a market cap of over $30 billion at its peak simply because enough people believed in it and traded it (CoinMarketCap, 2021). Fortunes made and lost on collective sentiment, not substance.

Even your bank account works on this illusion. When you deposit money, it doesn't just sit there. Banks lend most of it out and keep only a fraction. In fact, they create new money through fractional reserve lending. For every $1 deposited, banks may lend out $9 or more, effectively creating money that didn't exist before (Bank of England, 2014). The system only works as long as you don't ask for it all back at once. That's why when too many people do, like in a bank run, the system collapses.

We are trading real time, talent, and life for something that can vanish with policy, code, or power outage. And yet, the system holds, because belief holds. Perhaps the greatest trick money ever played was convincing the world it still exists, even as it slipped further into abstraction. But behind the screen, the illusion is paper-thin.

Here's the critical insight: since money can be created, it means you don't always have to work traditionally to earn it, if you know how to create or leverage it, **especially in the digital realm**. The very fact that governments and banks can create trillions by typing numbers, or that cryptocurrencies can rise from code and collective trust, means money is, at its core, a system of belief and creation.

Take the U.S. Federal Reserve's response to recent crises, for example. Over $3 trillion was "printed" by simply adding digits to accounts, not by producing anything tangible (Federal Reserve, 2020). This new money flooded markets, inflated asset prices, and altered the economy, **all without direct labor to back it**. People lost jobs, yet this invisible money made some billionaires.

Then there's crypto, which shows the illusion nakedly. Dogecoin began as a joke but gained real buying power because enough people believed in it. Today, people buy cars, pay rent, and shop with coins that exist only as code on a blockchain (Tesla Purchase Announcement, 2021).

Even more, decentralized finance allows people to earn interest or yields on crypto holdings without traditional work, just by moving assets through smart contracts. Money is literally making money, often beyond the reach of those who labor daily for wages that depreciate (DeFi Pulse Report, 2023).

This flip side of the illusion means that those who understand how to create, harness, or manipulate money in its intangible forms can bypass the old rules and the grind many accept as unavoidable. Meanwhile, most people continue working hard for currency that is losing value or slipping further into abstraction.

In the end, the power of money lies not in what it is, but in what we collectively believe it to be, and in who controls its creation.

Era	Currency Type	Spiritual Shift
Ancient	Gold/Silver	Value was **tied to creation**, tangible, God-given resources.
Medieval	Promissory Notes	Value based on **trust in men**, not divine provision.
Industrial	Paper Money	Mass printing created value **detached from substance.**
Modern	Digital Currency	Value is now **invisible**, based on data, speed, and speculation.

This progression mirrors the nature of Satan, who in **Luke 4:5–7** offered Jesus "all the kingdoms of the world" without the process of righteousness or covenant. He traffics in illusions, **promising power with no foundation**, glory without the cross, and prosperity without purpose.

In Summary:

Each stage of economic history did more than reshape trade, it **reconfigured the spiritual landscape** of the world. Behind the banks, companies, empires, and tech platforms are ancient altars redressed in modern robes. The altar of Mammon has been **intentionally constructed across centuries**, not just to capture wealth, but to **enslave worship**.

> "The love of money is the root of all kinds of evil." ~**1 Timothy 6:10**

It is not money itself, but the **systemic devotion to it** that builds the altar.

KEY TECHNIQUES OF THE NEW PRIESTHOOD

1. Neuro-Marketing: Tapping the Brain's Worship Center

Corporations now scan brain activity to identify what triggers **pleasure, loyalty, and impulse**. Ads are no longer designed, they are engineered.

- Emotional storytelling is calibrated to bypass rationality.
- Music, color, and timing are calculated to **imprint desire**.
- Dopamine spikes are strategically triggered, reinforcing consumption with spiritual undertones of **false satisfaction**.

   "Their god is their stomach..." ~**Philippians 3:19**

In essence, this is **modern sorcery**, hacking the soul's attention to keep it orbiting around materialism.

2. Algorithmic Targeting: The Digital Oracle

Through search histories, voice recognition, GPS data, and online behavior, algorithms now **predict and influence** future choices, often before a person becomes consciously aware of them.

- Ads "follow" users, like spirits whispering unseen prompts.
- Personalized feeds reinforce worldviews, values, and insecurities.
- AI learns to feed the flesh while numbing the spirit.

   "They prophesy from their own imaginations..."
   ~**Ezekiel 13:2**

These systems now act like **digital prophets**, shaping destinies without prayer, fasting, or discernment.

3. Scarcity Engineering: The Cult of Urgency

"Only 3 left."

"Sale ends in 2 hours."

"Exclusive offer, just for you."

These are not harmless marketing tactics, they are tools of **artificial urgency**, designed to provoke **fear of lack** and bypass the soul's stillness.

- They mirror ancient oracles that stirred panic to provoke offerings.
- The modern equivalent? Flash sales, viral trends, and planned obsolescence.

"You shall not covet..." ~**Exodus 20:17**

The system is built to prevent **contentment**, ensuring that the soul remains in **perpetual agitation**, always chasing the next product, the next fix, the next false fulfillment.

AN ECHO FROM EDEN

At the core of this manipulation lies the **serpent's ancient whisper**:

"You shall be as gods..." ~**Genesis 3:5**

Just as Eve was seduced by the **promise of enlightenment and empowerment** outside of God's will, today's consumers are drawn to products that promise identity, transformation, and transcendence, without submission to the Creator.

The **technological sophistication** only masks the **spiritual reality**: every click, every purchase, every algorithm-driven indulgence can form an **invisible agreement**, tightening the soul's entanglement with the **unredeemed structures of Mammon**.

THE WARFARE IS SUBTLE, BUT REAL

This is not mere marketing, its **spiritual warfare disguised as convenience**. When manipulation is baptized in data science and offered through sleek devices, discernment becomes the believer's most urgent weapon.

"Do not conform to the pattern of this world, but be transformed by the renewing of your mind..."
~**Romans 12:2**

The question is no longer, "What do I want to buy?"

But rather, **"Who is shaping what I desire?"**

SCRIPTURAL PATTERNS: BABYLON'S ECONOMIC SYSTEM

To understand the climax of unredeemed capitalism, one must look beyond the natural into the prophetic blueprint of **Mystery Babylon**, a spiritual and commercial empire portrayed in **Revelation 17–18**. Babylon is not merely a city, it is a **spiritual-economic system** that spans empires and ages, culminating in a final expression that touches every sphere of trade, culture, and power.

Revelation 18 speaks with chilling clarity of her fall. This collapse is not just financial; it is **spiritual judgment**. And the indictment is not only about currency or commodities but about what lies **beneath** the transactions:

> *"...cargoes of gold, silver, precious stones... fine linen... cattle and sheep... and **bodies and souls of men**."*,
> **Revelation 18:12–13**

BABYLON'S MARKETPLACE: A SPIRITUAL TRADE ZONE

Babylon is not just buying and selling, it is **sacrificing**.

In this economy:

- **Gold and silver** represent **material wealth**.

- **Precious stones and fine linen** symbolize **vanity, luxury, and status**.

- **Cattle and livestock** stand for **food, agriculture, and production systems**.

- And tragically, **"bodies and souls of men"** reflect **human exploitation, identity trade, and spiritual enslavement**.

This shows that **commerce and worship are inseparable**. In Babylon's system, every transaction is a spiritual act, an offering on her hidden altar.

MODERN ECHOES OF BABYLON

Just as Babylon's traders wept at her fall (Rev. 18:11), today's systems are structured to **resist collapse**, not because of righteousness, but because of **entanglement**. The global capitalist structure, when removed from the throne of Christ, is simply Babylon with new clothing:

- **Sorcery**, Manipulation of perception through media, tech, and false prophecy.

- **Lust**, Advertising driven by covetousness and sensuality.

- **Exploitation**, Labor systems that commodify human beings for profit.

- **Idolatry**, Worship of brands, celebrities, and luxury.

- **Soul Trade**, Exchange of identity, values, and integrity for influence and survival.

> *"For all the nations were deceived by your sorcery..."*
> ~**Revelation 18:23**

This verse uncovers the **spiritual technologies** behind Babylon's strength, systems of **mass deception**, **emotional control**, and **unrighteous covenants** that pull entire nations into her grasp.

INEVITABLE JUDGMENT

Babylon's fall is swift. Her riches, her splendor, her illusion of security, all vanish in **one hour** (Rev. 18:10). This prophetic picture is a warning: **no economic system, no empire, no market can escape the justice of God** when it stands on the **blood of souls and the pride of rebellion**.

For the believer, this judgment is not cause for fear but for **discernment**. It is a trumpet call to **come out from her midst** (Rev. 18:4), not physically, but **spiritually and ideologically**:

> *"Come out of her, My people, so that you will not share in her sins or receive any of her plagues."* ~**Revelation 18:4**

DISCERNING THE HIDDEN ALTAR

To walk in purity and dominion, believers must **discern the altars beneath economies**:

Is this transaction a matter of **necessity or identity?**

Is my labor aligned with **Kingdom purpose or Babylon's matrix?**

Am I giving my time, mind, or integrity to a system that traffics in **souls?**

This is not a call to poverty, but to **righteous wealth**: wealth not stained with compromise, manipulation, or spiritual debt.

CHRIST'S CALL: SONS OF GOD IN THE MARKETPLACE

Christ does not call His people to **abandon economies**; He calls them to **govern them**. The wilderness temptation (Matthew 4:8–10) wasn't just a battle over worship; it was a **power struggle over systems**, thrones, and glory. Satan offered the kingdoms of this world because he understood their **spiritual infrastructure**, and Christ refused the offer not to discard those kingdoms, but to **redeem and reclaim them** through the **cross, resurrection, and the enthronement of His sons.**

Now, in this era, **Jesus is raising a remnant**, a new breed of **entrepreneurial priests and kings**, whose allegiance is not to Mammon, but to the **Kingdom of Heaven.**

WHO ARE THESE SONS?

They are not just businessmen, tech founders, or economists. They are **prophetic architects of new economies**, governing by the Spirit, functioning as priests on the altar and kings in the gates.

These sons of God:

- **Build businesses on righteousness**, not greed or exploitation.
- **Innovate technologies** that serve humanity, not enslave or extract identity.
- **Create wealth streams** that fund kingdom purposes: missions, education, healing, restoration.
- **Restore economic systems** to reflect the **justice, creativity, stewardship, and compassion** of the Father.

Their work becomes worship. Their companies become altars. Their strategies become prophecy.

> *"The kingdoms of this world have become the kingdoms of our Lord and of His Christ, and He shall reign forever and ever."* ~**Revelation 11:15**

This is not passive waiting for Christ's return, it is **active enthronement** of the King in every realm **through His body**.

FROM HIDDEN ALTARS TO HOLY THRONES

The hidden altar of global capitalism, powered by fear, identity worship, and sacrificial exploitation, will not be defeated through mere activism or escape. It will be dismantled when **sons of light arise**, not just in churches but in:

- **Markets** (to overturn corrupt pricing, unjust profit, and false value),
- **Nations** (to rebuild policy and governance on truth),
- **Industries** (to restore the balance between innovation and integrity).

Wherever the enemy has built **false thrones**, God is sending His **sons to plant true altars** of worship, wisdom, and supernatural provision.

These are not altars of ritual, but of **reality**, where decisions, creativity, leadership, and capital **bow to the Lordship of Christ**.

MODERN EXAMPLES OF MARKETPLACE SONS

David Green (Hobby Lobby), Built a multi-billion-dollar company while honoring biblical principles and funding Christian missions.

Strive Masiyiwa (Econet, Africa), A telecom magnate who leveraged business to serve millions, while advancing kingdom values.

Daniel in Babylon, governed an empire without compromise, carrying the spirit of excellence and prophecy within a hostile economic and political system.

Joseph in Egypt, architected an entire economic system to preserve nations, stewarding resources under Pharaoh without losing his identity in God.

PROPHETIC CALL TO RISE

"Arise, shine, for your light has come, and the glory of the Lord rises upon you." ~**Isaiah 60:1**

This is a prophetic call, not just to church leadership, but to **every believer called to the marketplace**: arise. Shine. Let the **glory of divine wisdom** manifest in economic creativity, in governance, in innovation.

The marketplace is a mountain of worship, and God is calling His sons to **ascend it**, not just to survive, but to **govern in righteousness**.

CLOSING REFLECTION

The throne of Mammon **will fall**, but the **sons of the Kingdom** will rise.

We are not called to run from the world's systems, but to **redeem and reform them**. Like Joseph, we are called to manage the **storehouses of nations**. Like Daniel, to **counsel kings** and dismantle empires of deceit. Like Solomon, to **establish a wisdom economy** grounded in covenant, not covetousness.

The **throne of money** must be reclaimed:

- Not by **greed**, but by **glory**.
- Not by **manipulation**, but by **manifestation** in Christ.
- Not by **worldly systems**, but by **heavenly order**.

Welcome to the **unveiling** of the **true throne of wealth**.

PRAYER POINTS

1. I Dethrone Mammon from the Inner Sanctuary of My Soul

"Ancient spirit of Mammon, I confront you now in the secret places of my heart and mind. By the fire of the Living God, I uproot your throne and cast down your invisible scepter. I rend the veil that has hidden your dominion and declare:

The King of Glory reigns in me.

No idol, no altar, no spirit of wealth shall hold dominion over my soul."

2. I Sever Every Soul-Tie and Covenant with the Thrones of Mammon

"Blood of Jesus, flow through every spiritual contract and soul-tie that binds me to the altars of Mammon.

I break the chains forged by fear, pride, and deception.

I nullify every unholy covenant made in darkness, whether by my ancestors or myself.

I declare freedom by the power of the Lamb's blood, and I seal this release with the breath of the Spirit."

3. I Reclaim the Divine Flow of Abundance from the Tree of Life

"O Root of Jesse, I reach through the cosmic veil and connect to the pure stream of **Malkuth**, the Kingdom where heaven's abundance manifests.

I reject the **klipot**, the husks of impurity, that choke the flow of Your provision.

Let the sap of Your eternal life course through my veins, transforming every seed of fear into fruitfulness and divine wealth."

(Visualize roots growing from your spirit into a radiant Tree of Life, drawing pure light and abundance.)

4. I Transmute the Quantum Field of My Finances from Fear to Faith

"Spirit of the Living God, I command the energetic field around my finances to shift from scarcity to supernatural abundance.

I declare that value is assigned by the heart of God, not by the illusions of Mammon.

I release all gravitational pulls of fear, manipulation, and control.

I magnetize divine favor, creative ideas, and open doors aligned with Your Kingdom."

5. I Anoint My Mind with the Mind of Christ to See Through Mammon's Illusions

"Holy Spirit, anoint my intellect and imagination to discern the hidden altars and idols that masquerade as 'economic freedom.'

Remove every veil of deception and spiritual blindness.

Let the eyes of my heart be enlightened to see the true nature of wealth as **Your servant**, not my master."

6. I Proclaim the Fall of Babylon's Economic Throne Over My Life and Nation

"By the voice of the Spirit, I declare the collapse of Mystery Babylon's throne over my finances, my family, and my nation.

Let the sorcery of greed, lust, and exploitation be exposed and dismantled.

I call forth the sons and daughters of light to arise as priests and kings, rebuilding altars of justice, mercy, and divine economy."

7. I Activate My Divine Dominion as a Son/Daughter of the Kingdom

"Lord Jesus, You have reclaimed all kingdoms for Your glory.

I step into my priestly and kingly authority in the marketplace.

I anoint my hands, my mind, and my spirit to govern with righteousness, innovation, and compassion.

Let every venture I touch become a living altar of worship and blessing."

8. I Release the Spirit of Generosity and Kingdom Creativity

"Spirit of God, breathe upon me the breath of generosity, creativity, and kingdom stewardship.

Let my resources flow like rivers of living water, breaking every dam of selfishness or fear.

I declare that my wealth is a conduit for Your justice, healing, and restoration in this earth."

PROPHETIC DIRECTIONS & ACTIVATIONS

1. Prophetic Act: Renouncing Mammon's Throne

Stand and declare aloud:

> "I dethrone Mammon from my life. I break every allegiance and enthrone Christ as King over my finances, my work, and my desires."

(You may physically remove a symbolic object from a chair or altar to represent this dethronement.)

2. Marketplace Anointing Activation

Anoint your hands with oil and pray:

> "These hands are set apart for righteous work, innovation, and stewardship.
>
> Let everything I touch in the marketplace reflect the glory and justice of God."

3. Prophetic Decree Over Financial Systems

Lay your hand on your wallet, bank card, or business ledger and decree:

"You are not my master. You are a tool for the Kingdom.

I command every resource under my stewardship to align with God's purposes and overflow with blessing for others."

4. High Praise and Warfare

Engage in **high praise** and **declaring scriptural judgments** against Mammon's strongholds:

"Let the thrones of Mammon fall! Let the altars of unrighteous gain be dismantled!

Let the sons of God arise in the marketplace!"

(Reference: **Revelation 18, Isaiah 60:1–5, Psalm 24:1–10**)

CHAPTER 3

Priesthood and Politics: The Convergence of Altars and Thrones

"Righteousness exalts a nation, but sin is a reproach to any people." ~*Proverbs 14:34 (NKJV)*

HOW HIDDEN PRIESTHOODS SHAPE POLITICAL THRONES AND NATIONAL POLICY

Before a throne is raised in the earth, an altar is lifted in the spirit.

Before policies are written, covenants are cut.

Before laws govern men, sacrifices speak to gods.

The architecture of human civilization has always been built upon two converging dominions:

Priesthood, the invisible technology of altars.

Politics, the visible outworking of delegated power.

Altars are not religious relics; they are spiritual gateways that determine whose voice reigns over a territory. Long before a president is elected or a law is passed, a spiritual negotiation has occurred at an altar. Kings rise and fall because someone sacrificed. Empires are established or dismantled depending on whose incense is on the altar.

Whether in Eden, Egypt, Babylon, or today's secular democracies, the same pattern endures: **Altars birth thrones**.

Power is not first political, it is **priestly**.

What men vote on, heaven has often already judged.

> **"Righteousness exalts a nation, but sin is a reproach to any people."** ~Proverbs 14:34

To transform nations, we must go beyond voting booths and parliamentary seats, we must return to the high places where thrones are forged: **the altars**.

ANCIENT FRAMEWORKS: THE PRIEST-KING PROTOTYPE

From Genesis to Revelation, the Spirit reveals this integrated architecture:

Melchizedek, Priest of God Most High and King of Salem, merged the scepter and the incense.

Moses, before he delivered the commandments, he erected tabernacles.

David, before expanding borders or building armies, he restored the Ark and appointed singers.

Every revival, every reform, **every righteous reign begins with the altar.**

Not with charisma, not with strategy, but with worship.

The altar precedes the throne.

Sacrifice precedes dominion.

Worship precedes governance.

This is why, in the wilderness, Satan offered Jesus the kingdoms of this world, if He would just **bow.**

He understood the ancient protocol: **worship always precedes dominion**.

Whoever controls the altar controls the throne.

Whoever owns the throne determines the future of nations.

Modern believers often chase influence without paying the price of incense.

But God is restoring the **order of Melchizedek**: kings who are priests, and priests who rule.

THE HIDDEN PRIESTHOODS BEHIND GLOBAL POWER

We must not be naïve.

Behind every stock exchange, media conglomerate, and government office, there are altars, and behind those altars, priesthoods.

They may not wear robes or chant in temples, **but they minister daily to demonic thrones**. Board meetings often follow blood rituals. Policy documents echo ancient oaths.

Authors like Greg Reid and Fritz Springmeier pulled back the curtain.

But the prophets had already spoken:

> **"We wrestle not against flesh and blood, but against principalities…"** ~Ephesians 6:12

These are not conspiracy theories, they are spiritual realities.

The world is governed by **covenantal infrastructure.**

Masonic orders, ancient bloodlines, Luciferian societies, all form counterfeit priesthoods whose altars sustain the kingdoms of darkness.

And yet, many in the Church remain asleep, voting without discerning, protesting without praying, shouting in the streets while altars burn in high places.

We cannot reform politics until we confront the **invisible priesthoods behind them.**

No law can undo what a blood covenant has ratified.

Only a **higher altar** can overturn it.

ALTARS IN THE MARKETPLACE: REBUILDING THE ECONOMY OF THE RIGHTEOUS

Economics is not neutral. It is spiritual.

The flow of money follows the fragrance of worship.

T. Harv Eker observed that people don't rise above their internal blueprint. But what he saw psychologically is only the surface of a deeper law:

Wealth follows worship. Money obeys altars.

When markets are driven by greed, manipulation, and injustice, it is because Mammon has been enthroned.

Mammon is not just a spirit, it is a **priesthood**. It receives offerings daily from both the poor and the rich alike.

But God is raising a new breed: **sons who build from the altar outward**.

- Companies as consecrated vessels.
- Products as prophetic signals.
- Capital as covenantal resource.

This is more than Christian business.

It is **economic priesthood**.

> **"For as a man thinks in his heart, so is he."**
> ~Proverbs 23:7

The world sees transactions. We see temples.

The world chases profit. We pursue **purpose and purity**.

The economy of the righteous is built on worship, not wealth accumulation.

This is how we dethrone Mammon, **by exalting Christ at the altar of enterprise**.

TERRITORIES, THRONES, AND PORTALS: THE COSMIC MAP

Every territory is spiritually mapped.

There is no such thing as neutral land.

Portals govern regions. **Altars open portals.**

And every altar is a gate through which either **heaven or hell invades**.

When Abraham built altars, God didn't just bless his family, He **claimed territory**.

When Jacob anointed a stone, the heavens opened, and he saw the ladder.

Where no altar is raised to the Most High, **dark thrones ascend**.

We often wonder why certain cities remain under oppression. The answer is simple: **Altars determine atmosphere**.

- No righteous altar = no righteous throne.

- No intercession = no legislation from heaven.

- No worship = no divine rule.

This is not metaphor. This is **spiritual geopolitics**.

Governments may shift, but the **spiritual architecture** remains unless altars are confronted or rebuilt.

It's time we stop fighting over borders and start securing **portals**.

Because the land obeys **the voice of the priest before the law of the king**.

CASE STUDIES: ALTARS THAT GOVERNED EMPIRES

History is full of thrones; each one built on an altar.

Egypt, Pharaohs didn't rule by intellect, but by mystical power. Each was considered a god, and their governance was sacramental.

Babylon, Nebuchadnezzar built an image and required worship before enacting national laws. The golden statue preceded legislation.

Rome, Caesar was not merely a statesman; he was worshipped. Refusing to say "Caesar is Lord" was punishable by death. Early Christians died not for politics, but for altar allegiance.

Modern Nations, From the Bilderberg Group to Skull and Bones, hidden societies continue to dictate policy through secret rites. The suits may have changed, but the priesthoods remain.

> **"There is nothing new under the sun."**
> **~Ecclesiastes 1:9**

Altars never left governance.

They simply went underground.

But now, God is lifting the veil. The question is: will His sons recognize the battle, and respond?

SONS OF THE ALTAR: THE RISE OF PRIESTLY REFORMERS

The age of the celebrity preacher is over.

The era of **enthroned sons** has begun.

These are priestly reformers, dual-anointed ones who blend the censer and the scepter.

- They intercede in tongues and draft policy in boardrooms.
- They anoint oil and audit companies.
- They burn incense and lead institutions.

"You shall be to Me a kingdom of priests and a holy nation." ~Exodus 19:6

They don't just build businesses, they erect spiritual monuments.

They don't just occupy offices, they open portals.

They are marketplace apostles, prophetic policy-makers, legal Levites, intercessors in fintech, prophets in media.

This is **the order of Melchizedek reappearing**, a priesthood without lineage, ordained not by man but by heaven.

These sons are not looking for platforms, they are **altars in motion**.

ACTIVATING DOMINION: A ROADMAP FOR SONS

How do we transition from passive believers to enthroned priest-kings?

The roadmap is ancient, yet eternal.

1. **Personal Altars**, Return to the secret place. Burn daily. Incense must rise before dominion flows.

2. **Marketplace Altars**, Build businesses, strategies, and platforms upon righteousness. Let every transaction become a testimony.

3. **Territorial Intercession**, Walk your city. Anoint gates. Speak to land and lift decrees. The ground must be told who it belongs to.

4. **Prophetic Decrees**, Speak Heaven's will.

   "You will also decree a thing, and it will be established for you…" ~Job 22:28

Words backed by altars shape the world more than votes.

5. **Strategic Alliances**, Find other sons. Two altars joined in purpose become a stronghold for heaven.

This is how we legislate: **by incense, not just intellect.**

By altar, not just argument.

By dominion, not just democracy.

FINAL TRUMPET: THRONES AWAIT THE SONS

The thrones of the earth are not vacant, they are contested.

The question is not whether someone will govern, it's **whose altar will decide**.

Passive Christianity cannot transform nations.

Emotional faith cannot overthrow demonic priesthoods.

Only **enthroned sons**, those who bear both incense and authority, can establish heaven's reign.

   "The government shall be upon His shoulder."
   ~Isaiah 9:6

   And we are that, Body.

So let the altars be rebuilt.

Let the secret covenants be broken.

Let the hidden priesthoods be exposed.

Let the sons arise.

The convergence has come. Altars and thrones are merging again, in you.

KEY INSIGHTS

- Before political power manifests, spiritual altars are established. Altars determine who rules.

- Power is first **priestly**, then **political**.

- Civilizations are built on two invisible pillars: **priesthood (spiritual authority)** and **politics (delegated rulership).**

- Altars are spiritual gateways, sacrifices made that shape laws, culture, and leadership.

- Biblical leaders like **Melchizedek, Moses, and David** merged priesthood and kingship.

- Satan's offer to Jesus ("worship me, and I'll give you the kingdoms") reveals: **worship precedes rulership.**

- Behind world systems, governments, corporations, media, are **hidden spiritual priesthoods**, some demonic.

- Secret societies and blood covenants still govern nations through dark altars.

- **Only superior (godly) altars can dethrone ungodly ones.**

- The economy is also governed by altars; Mammon represents a **demonic priesthood** behind money.

- Businesses must be built from the **altar of God**, consecrated, prophetic, and covenantal.

- **No land is neutral**; every territory is spiritually governed through altars and covenants.

- Spiritual architecture (altars, covenants, worship) creates **national atmospheres** more than laws.

- Ancient empires like Egypt, Babylon, and Rome were ruled by altar-based priesthoods; today's systems are no different, they're just more hidden.

- A generation of **"sons of the altar"** is rising, reformers who unite prayer, prophecy, and power in media, business, and governance.

- They don't chase influence, they **become moving altars**, shifting atmospheres by their presence.

- Dominion requires: **personal altars, consecrated business, territorial intercession, prophetic decrees**, and alliances with other kingdom-minded sons.

- **Thrones are contested by altars**, whoever raises the louder, purer voice in the spirit realm wins in the physical.

- Passive Christianity cannot contend in this war. **Sons must arise.**

PRAYER POINTS: RAISING RIGHTEOUS ALTARS OVER THRONES OF POWER

1. **I Consecrate My Voice to the Altar, Not the Crowd**

   "Lord, before I speak in the gates, let me first kneel at the altar.

   I reject the pressure to perform for political favor or popular applause.

   May my influence be born of incense, not ambition."

2. **I Overturn Every Unseen Priesthood Manipulating My Destiny**

   "In the name of Jesus, I dismantle every hidden altar erected against my calling.

   I silence the priesthoods of darkness speaking over my territory, my family, and my future.

I align only with the priesthood of Christ, the eternal
High Priest."

3. I Release Divine Governance Over My Sphere of Influence

"As a son/daughter of God, I declare: my workplace,
my city, my industry will not be ruled by injustice,
corruption, or compromise.

Let righteousness and justice be the foundation of
every decision I make.

Let my presence become a prophetic disruption to
demonic systems."

4. I Reclaim My Nation from Unholy Covenants and Political Sorcery

"By the blood of Jesus, I nullify every demonic
sacrifice made on behalf of my nation.

I call for the exposure and collapse of wicked alliances
and occult power structures.

Let righteous governance rise, and let the altars of
deception fall."

5. I Embrace My Dual Mantle: Priest and King

"Holy Spirit, activate in me the full capacity of
Melchizedek order.

Teach me to build altars in the Spirit and policies in
the natural.

I will legislate from heaven and govern on earth."

PROPHETIC DIRECTIONS & ACTIVATIONS

1. Gatekeeping Decree Over Your Domain

Action: Stand at the physical gate of your home, office, or city and declare:

> "This gate belongs to the Lord. No unrighteous decree, demonic influence, or hidden covenant shall govern this territory.
>
> I am the priest at this gate. I welcome only what aligns with heaven's will."

2. **Altar-Building Activation**

Action: Choose a time this week to pray specifically for your **industry, nation, or political leaders**.

Light a candle or kneel as a prophetic act of re-establishing the Lord's altar.

> **Prayer:** "Lord, let this act represent a rising altar that speaks louder than corruption and compromise."

3. **Covenant Renunciation**

Declare aloud:

> "I break every unconscious agreement with systems of political idolatry, cultural compromise, or economic slavery.
>
> I belong to no throne but Yours, Jesus. I am governed by the cross, not the crowd."

4. **Marketplace Reformation Commissioning**

Anoint your forehead and hands with oil and decree:

> I am commissioned to legislate with purity, wisdom, and boldness.
>
> I carry the anointing of the reformer, the heart of the intercessor, and the strategy of a king.
>
> Thrones will shift because I have built the altar first.

CHAPTER 4

The Architectonics of Mammon: How Spiritual Thrones Influence Financial Systems

"For the weapons of our warfare are not carnal but mighty in God for pulling down strongholds." ~2 Corinthians 10:4 (NKJV)

THE HIDDEN ENGINEERING OF WEALTH AND POWER

From the rise of ancient empires to today's global financial systems, one **invisible architect** has consistently sought to shape the flow of money, commerce, and influence:

The **spirit of Mammon**.

Mammon is not merely greed or materialism, it **is a throne**, a **demonic principality** that establishes systems to **enslave mankind through money**, control economies, manipulate governments, and steer destinies.

> *"No one can serve two masters; for either he will hate the one and love the other... You cannot serve God and mammon.",* **(Matthew 6:24)**

From Babylon's temples to Silicon Valley's algorithms, Mammon's touch is felt in:

- Banking institutions
- Stock markets and global exchanges
- National treasuries and central banks
- Cyber-financial systems and cryptocurrencies
- Trade deals and international contracts
- Emerging tech industries and wealth innovations

The marketplace is its playground; the human heart is its target.

But in Christ, a **new order** is arising: a **kingdom economy** rooted in righteousness, justice, innovation, and stewardship for the glory of God.

THE SPIRITUAL BLUEPRINT OF MAMMON

Mammon operates as a **fallen spiritual technology**, offering a counterfeit form of provision, security, and identity apart from God.

Characteristics of the Spirit of Mammon:

- **Idolatry**: Exalting wealth over God.

- **Fear**: Fear of lack drives accumulation without purpose.

- **Control**: Systems of debt and dependency entangle nations and individuals.

- **Injustice**: Wealth gaps widen, keeping masses enslaved.

- **Pride**: Identity rooted in possessions rather than in Christ.

Just like Babel (Genesis 11), Mammon seeks to build **a global system** where man rules without dependence on heaven.

> *"For the love of money is the root of all kinds of evil."*
> **(1 Timothy 6:10)**

ANCIENT ORIGINS OF FINANCIAL THRONES

The strategies of Mammon are ancient:

- **Babylon**: Introduced complex trade systems tied to idolatry.

- **Tyre**: A wealthy merchant city that exalted itself against God (Ezekiel 28).

- **Rome**: Engineered taxation and tributes to maintain empire control.

- **Venetian Banking (Middle Ages)**: Secret elite families built financial oligarchies.

- **Modern Central Banks**: Fiat money disconnected from tangible value; debt-based economies.

Each era perfected new dimensions of Mammon's architecture:

Debt, speculation, inflation, and systemic inequality.

The throne behind these financial empires was never merely human ingenuity, it was always **spiritual orchestration.**

STOCK MARKETS, CYBER FINANCE, AND DIGITAL THRONES

Today, Mammon's system has evolved:

- **Stock Exchanges**: High-stakes speculation, insider trading, manipulation of economies.
- **Crypto and Cyber Finance**: New frontiers of invisible wealth flow, largely unregulated.
- **Artificial Intelligence in Finance**: Trading bots making split-second billion-dollar decisions.
- **Global Trade Wars**: Nation-states weaponizing tariffs, sanctions, and monetary policies.

Behind these innovations, the ancient spirit seeks to:

- **Decentralize human loyalty** away from national identity and spiritual covenants.
- **Create borderless dependency** on transnational financial elite systems.
- **Replace tangible resources (gold, land) with digital promises** (data, cryptocurrency).

The "beast system" foretold in Revelation 13 finds partial shadows here:

Control of buying and selling through loyalty to a system rather than to Christ.

THE TERRITORIAL INFRASTRUCTURE OF MAMMON

Mammon's influence extends far beyond individual pockets, it claims entire cities, networks, and systems as its territory, weaving a complex infrastructure designed to control and channel the flow of wealth and power.

- **City Gateways:**

Financial capitals like New York, London, Hong Kong, and Dubai aren't just economic hubs, they serve as spiritual battlegrounds and strongholds. These cities act as gateway portals where Mammon's influence concentrates, shaping global finance and policy decisions that ripple worldwide.

- **Banking Temples:**

Look closely at the architecture of major banks and stock exchanges, many echo the design of ancient temples. This is no accident. These buildings symbolize altars where the spirit of Mammon is worshiped through the rituals of commerce, contracts, and currency exchange.

- **Trade Corridors:**

Wealth moves not only through money but through control of physical and digital arteries, strategic ports, railways, highways, and fiber-optic networks. Mammon territorializes these trade routes, creating choke points that centralize power and enforce dependency.

> **"The rich rule over the poor, and the borrower is servant to the lender."** ~Proverbs 22:7

Mammon's ultimate aim is not simply to amass wealth but to institutionalize bondage, entrenching debt, creating cycles of dependency, and manipulating economies to keep nations and individuals in spiritual and financial captivity.

THE COSMIC LAWS OF WEALTH IN CHRIST

The pursuit of wealth is not merely a human ambition, it is governed by timeless spiritual principles that operate across history, cultures, and even religions. These principles are **cosmic laws**: universal truths built into the fabric of creation. They do not only govern individual success, but shape the rise and fall of empires, the prosperity of communities, and the flow of resources across the earth.

In the Kingdom of Christ, these cosmic laws are redeemed, purified, and fully revealed. Christ-centered wealth is not selfish accumulation, but purposeful abundance aligned with heaven's justice, stewardship, and love. However, because these laws are cosmic in nature, they are observable across history, even outside the church. When any person, civilization, or system aligns (even unintentionally) with these divine patterns, wealth tends to flow. When they violate them, collapse eventually follows.

This section explores the eternal wealth laws of God's kingdom, with illustrations drawn not only from the Bible, but from:

- The disciplined economies of ancient Egypt, Babylon, and China.

- The innovation-driven wealth of Renaissance Europe and post-Enlightenment societies.

- The rise of capitalism, as well as the ethical collapses that followed when these laws were broken.

- Modern-day examples from entrepreneurs, social reformers, and nations, whether Christian or not, that demonstrate alignment with these cosmic patterns.

> **"But seek first the kingdom of God and His righteousness, and all these things shall be added to you."** ~Matthew 6:33

This verse does not teach passivity, but divine alignment. When the principles of divine order are followed, wealth becomes a byproduct of right positioning, not manipulation.

THE FOUR COSMIC LAWS OF WEALTH IN CHRIST

1. Sowing and Reaping (2 Corinthians 9:6)

Cosmic Law: What is planted returns multiplied, in kind.

This law governs agriculture, finance, relationships, and knowledge. It is observable in both spiritual and natural dimensions.

- **Biblical Example:** The widow of Zarephath giving her last meal to Elijah, only to find her oil and flour multiplied (1 Kings 17).

- **Historical:** The ancient Mesopotamians, reliant on the Nile and Tigris rivers, engineered irrigation and agricultural practices that turned deserts into fertile, harvest-yielding zones. Their economy was rooted in consistent sowing cycles.

- **Modern:**

  o *Muhammad Yunus* launched the Grameen Bank by offering tiny loans to impoverished women in Bangladesh. His model of sowing trust and small capital into the lives of the poor birthed an entire global microfinance movement.

  o *George Washington Carver*, though born into slavery, used his agricultural research not for personal profit but to enrich the land and uplift Southern farmers. His giving spirit drew influence, wealth, and honor, though he never asked for them.

2. Multiplication through Stewardship (Matthew 25:14–30)

Cosmic Law: What is managed multiplies. What is neglected decays.

This principle governs talent, capital, knowledge, and leadership. It's not about how much you start with; it's about how you handle it.

- **Biblical Example:** Joseph's management of Egypt's resources saved the nation from famine and enriched its global standing (Genesis 41).

- **Historical:** Post-WWII **Japan** had no abundant resources, yet through diligent stewardship, education, and innovation (like Toyota's lean manufacturing), it became an economic superpower in under 30 years.

- Modern:

  o *Warren Buffett*, with just $100 at age 11, began investing in stocks. Over decades, through consistent stewardship and compound growth, he built one of the most resilient investment portfolios in history. His wealth wasn't based on chance, but on the cosmic law of careful multiplication.

o   *Strive Masiyiwa*, founder of Econet Wireless, faced five years of legal blocks in Zimbabwe but refused to waste the vision. Once released, his faithful management of ideas and resources turned Econet into a telecom empire across Africa.

3. **Divine (or Inspired) Ideas and Innovation (Deuteronomy 8:18)**

Cosmic Law: True wealth often begins as an idea, not a product.

Ideas are seeds of change, especially when inspired by higher wisdom or sharp perception.

- **Biblical Example:** Bezalel, filled with divine inspiration, crafted the tabernacle's holy objects (Exodus 31). His craftsmanship wasn't just artistic; it became sacred and valuable.

- **Historical:** The **Renaissance era** in Florence, funded by the Medici family, saw painters, scientists, and thinkers (like Da Vinci and Galileo) channel profound ideas into wealth-generating disciplines and inventions.

- **Modern:**

    o   *Nikola Tesla* received his inventions in flashes of vision, often claiming divine or energetic insight. Though he died nearly penniless, his alternating current (AC) systems now power the modern world.

    o   *Sara Blakely*, while working as a fax machine salesperson, had a sudden idea to cut the feet off her pantyhose. That flash birthed Spanx, a company that made her the youngest self-made female billionaire in America.

4. **Generational Wealth and Justice (Proverbs 13:22)**

Cosmic Law: True wealth builds over generations and must uphold justice to endure.

When wealth is hoarded or built on injustice, it eventually decays. When it is shared and structured generationally, it multiplies and stabilizes societies.

- **Biblical Example:** Abraham's wealth and covenant passed down through Isaac, Jacob, and eventually the nation of Israel, anchored in covenant and promise, not just material.

- **Historical:** The **Rothschild banking family** established a five-brother financial network across Europe in the 18th century. By structuring their wealth generationally and cooperatively, they created a system that lasted over two centuries, influencing governments and economies.

- **Modern:**

  o *Robert F. Smith*, in a single speech, cleared the student loans of Morehouse College's entire 2019 graduating class. That act of justice didn't just create emotional relief; it reset generational economics for hundreds of families.

  o The **Scandinavian countries** (like Sweden and Norway) built long-term economic models based on fair taxation, strong education, and social equity. Their societies consistently rank highest in happiness and stability, not because of religious alignment, but due to ethical wealth structuring across generations.

In Summary:

These stories are not simply moral lessons. They're **evidence** that cosmic wealth laws are real, active, and consequential. Whether found in prophets, poor inventors, post-war nations, or modern philanthropists, **alignment with divine order always bears fruit.** Christ's kingdom doesn't cancel these laws; it sanctifies and fulfills them. But even outside of the church, when these cosmic patterns are honored, they produce visible wealth and transformation.

DISMANTLING MAMMONIC THRONES: SPIRITUAL AND PRACTICAL STRATEGIES

To walk fully in the wealth laws of Christ's kingdom, one must not only apply principles but also **dismantle rival thrones**, especially the throne of Mammon. Mammon is more than greed; it is a spiritual principality that seeks worship through fear, control, and self-dependence. Here's how to break free:

Step 1: Repentance from Idolatry

Before wealth can flow purely, the heart must be cleansed.

- **Renounce fear of lack.** The fear of not having enough is the seedbed of Mammon worship. It distorts perception and causes us to hoard rather than trust.

- **Re-establish God as the ultimate Provider.** Say with your heart and habits, "My Source is not salary, market, or man, but the King of Glory."

Step 2: Kingdom Stewardship

The only antidote to ownership obsession is **stewardship**.

- **Manage money as a sacred trust.** Budgeting becomes worship. Investment becomes discernment. Spending becomes aligned with purpose.

- **Build businesses, ministries, and innovations** not just for profit, but for righteousness and justice. Ask: *Does this reflect the character of God?*

Step 3: Altar-Based Economy

Biblical giving is not manipulation, it is covenant.

- **Tithes, offerings, and first fruits** are not religious taxes, but spiritual technologies. They declare: *God owns it all.* When done in faith, they activate divine covering, alignment, and harvest.

- This altar-based approach breaks cycles of financial oppression and unlocks access to supernatural supply lines.

Step 4: Marketplace Warfare

The spiritual battle over wealth is fought not only in prayer rooms but also in boardrooms.

- **Prophetic decrees** over cities, companies, and industries displace mammonic altars and reclaim territory for Christ.

- **Apostolic entrepreneurship** goes beyond profit, it creates wealth flows that finance missions, empower communities, and disciple nations economically.

PRAYER ACTIVATION: DELIVERANCE FROM MAMMON'S SYSTEM

The breaking of mammonic control is not merely intellectual or educational, it is spiritual. Decrees establish legal authority in the spirit realm. Prayers release the heart into covenant alignment with God's economy.

This is more than a moment of devotion, it is a transition into a new system. As you pray this, declare it boldly, as one shifting empires within.

Pray aloud:

Father, in the Name of Jesus Christ,

I renounce every allegiance, conscious and unconscious, to the spirit of Mammon.

I break every covenant with fear, greed, pride, and control in my financial life.

I enthrone You, Jesus, as my Source, my Security, and my Strategy.

I declare that I am not a slave to money, I am a steward of divine abundance.

I command the dismantling of every altar of Mammon operating in my life, family, business, and city.

I receive Your wisdom, ideas, innovations, and favor to build wealth for the advancement of Your Kingdom.

I decree open heavens, divine provision, strategic partnerships, and financial territories under my dominion, for Your glory alone.

In Jesus' mighty Name, Amen!

PROPHETIC DECREES: RELEASING THE KINGDOM ECONOMY

Declare these words into your atmosphere. These are not motivational phrases, they are prophetic instruments that shift atmospheres, open doors, and install heavenly infrastructure in your life and calling.

Declare aloud:

"I am seated with Christ above every throne of Mammon."

"I operate under open heavens, not under financial bondage."

"Wealth flows to me and through me for kingdom purposes."

"I build righteous altars in the marketplace."

"I am a king and priest in Christ; I govern economies by the Word of God."

"The silver and gold belong to my Father, and He entrusts me to steward it in justice and righteousness."

"I establish marketplace portals of divine abundance wherever I go."

"By the blood of Christ, I dismantle the old infrastructure of debt, fear, and manipulation."

"Nations shall call me blessed because I operate in God's economic blueprint."

"It is the Lord who gives me power to create wealth to establish His covenant!"

Amen and Amen.

FINAL CHARGE

Cosmic wealth laws are not enough. Without the **dismantling of mammonic thrones**, even divine principles can be hijacked. The call is not just to be rich, but to be **righteous rulers** of God's resources.

As we align with Christ, the Wisdom and Wealth of God, we become conduits through which heaven's abundance flows to the earth.

"Then you shall see and be radiant, and your heart shall thrill and exult, because the abundance of the sea shall be turned to you, the wealth of the nations shall come to you." *~Isaiah 60:5*

CHAPTER 5

Global Banking Dynasties, The Hidden Bloodlines of Economic Power

"The earth is the Lord's, and all its fullness, the world and those who dwell therein." ~*Psalm 24:1 (NKJV)*

THE INVISIBLE HAND BEHIND WORLD ECONOMIES

Beneath the visible systems of banks, markets, and global forums lies a carefully orchestrated **dynasty of bloodlines**, families whose wealth, influence, and control have quietly dictated the destinies of nations for centuries.

This chapter will unveil the historical and spiritual control mechanisms used by banking families (with references to Fritz Springmeier's work and more), and how kingdom sons are called to displace those thrones.

They are not merely economic players, they are stewards of ancient thrones, hidden architects of world systems.

As Ernst Wolff pointed out regarding the World Economic Forum:

> *"There exists a financial-industrial complex far more powerful than any government, an invisible empire."*

Steven D. Strauss, Niall Ferguson, and Noam Chomsky likewise trace how historical monopolies and intellectual capital have been leveraged to centralize unseen control.

Yet the Scriptures declare:

> *"The wealth of the wicked is stored up for the righteous."*, **(Proverbs 13:22)**

Christ's Kingdom will not be suppressed by hidden rulers of mammon. **A divine transfer** and **global reformation** are on heaven's agenda!

This chapter unveils what many never perceive: that some of the most powerful families in history are not just wealthy, they are **gatekeepers of ancient thrones**, heirs of spiritual systems that transcend money and policy. Drawing from the research of thinkers like **Fritz Springmeier, Ernst Wolff, Steven D. Strauss, Niall Ferguson**, and **Noam Chomsky**, we explore how these families created and now preside over a **networked global empire** that merges:

- Banking
- Governance
- Education
- Media
- Technology

into a **seamless infrastructure of control**.

These sectors, far from being neutral tools of progress, have become **instruments of control**, veiling a deeper spiritual architecture.

As Ernst Wolff noted regarding the World Economic Forum:

> "There exists a financial-industrial complex far more powerful than any government, an invisible empire."

These families are not simply economic players; they are **spiritual agents** stewarding occult thrones and dominion mandates. Their influence spans continents, elections, wars, currencies, and currencies yet to come.

Yet Scripture sounds a different alarm, one not of defeat but **transfer**:

> **"The wealth of the wicked is stored up for the righteous."** *~Proverbs 13:22*

This is not poetic comfort, it is **prophetic strategy**. A divine reformation is imminent. Heaven's agenda is not just revival, it is **replacement**. The systems of Mammon are not merely to be resisted, they are to be **displaced** by kingdom-minded stewards, trained in righteousness, mantled with wisdom, and equipped for wealth governance.

In this chapter, we will:

- Expose the historical emergence of banking bloodlines.
- Unmask their spiritual foundations and occult allegiances.
- Reveal how these dynasties use control systems to maintain global dominance.
- Explore God's counter-move: **the rise of a remnant** equipped to steward **economic mantles** for kingdom purposes.

This is not a conspiracy theory, it is spiritual history with prophetic implications.

The call is not just to expose, it is to **engage**, displace, and reform. For the kingdoms of this world shall become the kingdoms of our God and of His Christ (Revelation 11:15).

THE RISE OF BANKING DYNASTIES: A HISTORICAL BLUEPRINT

The story of modern economics is not just about trade, markets, or innovation, it is the story of **dynasties** who mastered the machinery of **mammonic control.**

From the **merchant bankers of Babylon and Tyre**, to the **moneylenders of medieval Venice**, the **spirit of Mammon** has flowed like a shadow current through families and empires who:

Controlled royal treasuries

- Financed wars and revolutions

- Bought and sold political access

- Engineered currencies and central banks

- Monetized debt as a global strategy

The names echo through history:

- **Medici**, Papal bankers and Renaissance influencers

- **Rothschild**, Financiers of empires and inventors of multinational banking

- **Rockefeller**, Oil barons turned policy kings

- **Warburg, Morgan, Schiff, Vanderbilt**, Architects of modern banking, stock markets, and economic think tanks

These families:

- Built **private wealth that surpassed kings**

- **Funded both sides** of many global wars (Napoleonic, World Wars, etc.)

- **Designed debt-based economies** as systems of control
- **Influenced elections, revolutions, and global treaties**
- **Founded think tanks and forums** that shaped international laws and ideologies

Their objective? **Centralization.**

- **Capital**, Controlled through central banks, fiat currency, and lending institutions
- **Information**, Shaped by media empires, education systems, and publishing houses
- **Technology**, Acquired and directed through patent control and military-industrial alliances
- **Political allegiance**, Purchased through lobbying, philanthropy, and policy manipulation

They became **"sovereign entities"** unto themselves, nations bowed to their credit lines. Governments became **clients** rather than rulers.

> **"The borrower is servant to the lender."** ~*Proverbs 22:7*

But let us not be naive: this was not just economic genius. This was **spiritual engineering**.

Their empire was **ritualistic in origin**, built on:

- **Altars** of blood and sacrifice
- **Covenants** with darkness for wealth and power
- **Occult knowledge**, drawn from Babylonian, Kabbalistic, and Hermetic systems
- **Unholy thrones**, passed down through generations

They did not build wealth, they built **thrones**.

And every throne has a **spirit** behind it.

This is the **architecture of economic Babylon**, a system rooted not merely in paper and profit, but in **principalities**, feeding on fear, control, and covetousness.

THE WORLD ECONOMIC FORUM AND THE NEW GLOBAL ORDER

The **World Economic Forum (WEF)**, seated in **Davos, Switzerland**, is not merely a policy symposium, it is a **contemporary expression of ancient mammonic thrones**, reimagined in suits and algorithms.

What Appears Harmless…

…is, in fact, a convergence of **financial priesthoods, technocratic prophets, and ideological architects**, shaping the future of nations behind the veil of diplomacy and development.

Ernst Wolff reveals the WEF as:

- A **strategic gathering** of the world's financial titans, tech moguls, political powerbrokers, and media influencers.

- A **policy incubator** where global frameworks are crafted long before they ever face public or parliamentary scrutiny.

- A **launchpad for the Great Reset**, a complete redefinition of ownership, liberty, and economic life.

    > **"You will own nothing, and you will be happy."**
    > *WEF Propaganda Slogan*

Their Core Objectives:

- **Monetary Control:** Introduce **Central Bank Digital Currencies (CBDCs)** to digitize money and enforce financial surveillance.

- **Societal Engineering:** Use **climate, health crises, and AI policy** as tools for centralized power.

- **Corporate-Government Merger:** Create a **neo-feudal system** under the guise of "Stakeholder Capitalism" where nations and laws bow to unelected global entities.

Niall Ferguson, historian of imperial systems, warns:

> "Supranational institutions mirror the old empires, invisible crowns ruling from above."

Noam Chomsky exposes the psychological machinery:

> "Mass media and think tanks have become modern altars,

weaponized to shape narratives and crush dissent."

In the Spirit Realm:

WEF and its allied networks are the **modern Tower of Babels**, a unified global agenda crafted apart from God, guided by Mammon and cloaked in humanitarian rhetoric.

"Come, let us build ourselves a city... lest we be scattered." *(Genesis 11:4)*

But God intervened then, and **He will again.**

"Come, let Us go down and confuse their language..." *(Genesis 11:7)*

Their digital tongues, AI systems, data models, and policy networks, will **fail** under divine confusion. The **unified global rebellion** will once again be scattered by the power of the **Kingdom age.**

BLOODLINES, ECONOMICS, AND TERRITORIAL THRONES

The Ancient War for Territorial Thrones Through Economic Control

There is a war older than empires, a war not merely for gold or oil, but for **territorial thrones**. Beneath economic systems lie **altars**, and behind currencies stand **priests**, spiritual gatekeepers who understand this unchanging law:

> **"Whoever controls the economy controls the territory, the government, and the soul of the people."**

Long before modern central banks and Wall Street, the **Canaanite merchant-kings**, **Babylonian priesthoods**, and **Tyrian trade lords** discovered that **commerce is dominion**.

They built **economic altars**, not just for profit, but to possess:

- **Land** (inheritance),
- **People** (slaves to systems),
- **Nations** (through debt and trade).

Money is not neutral; it is a **spiritual transmitter**.

> **"You cannot serve God and Mammon."** *(Matthew 6:24)*

Mammon is not just greed, it is a **principality** with a throne.

Economics is **worship** when it flows from altars, either holy or profane.

> **"The earth is the Lord's, and all its fullness..."** *(Psalm 24:1)*

But fallen men, empowered by Mammon, seek to **usurp** God's ownership by enslaving His creation through debt, inflation, and scarcity.

THE FINANCIAL PRIESTHOOD OF BLOODLINE DYNASTIES

Names like **Rothschild**, **Rockefeller**, **Morgan**, and **Schiff** are not just financial moguls, they are **territorial priests**, whose influence is built on:

- Ancient covenants with Mammon,
- Occult knowledge of cycles,
- Unseen alliances with fallen principalities.

Their empires operate through:

- Global debt systems,
- Currency control,
- Central bank manipulation,
- Foundations, forums, and ideological fronts.

These are not random trends, they are **intentional enthronements** of mammonic power over territories.

Ray Dalio's Revelation, A Kingdom Insight?

Even in secular wisdom, truth echoes.

Ray Dalio, founder of the world's largest hedge fund, teaches:

> **"Every empire rises and falls based on its economic engine and debt cycle."** *(Principles for Dealing with the Changing World Order)*

This confirms what Scripture already revealed:

Obedience brings economic strength; rebellion invites collapse.

(See Deuteronomy 28)

Bloodline dynasties study these **natural cycles**, but they move with **spiritual intelligence**, in *rebellion against the true Christ.*

They mimic prophecy, imitate cycles, and time collapses to gain more dominion. They are **prophetic strategists** of a fallen system.

THE CONCEPT OF "PLANET ENTREPRENEUR" AND MODERN TERRITORIAL ASPIRATIONS

In an era where empires are no longer built with armies but with algorithms, **Guled Ahmed**, in his work *Planet Entrepreneur*, articulates a prophetic reality:

Entrepreneurship is no longer local, it is **planetary**.

We are witnessing a redefinition of territorial dominion.

THE NEW GLOBAL ARCHITECTS

Ahmed warns of a rising order where:

- **Economies are borderless**, nationalism gives way to **transnational influence**.

- **Corporate empires** and **financial titans** claim ownership of critical **global resources**, food, *water, and energy*.

- **Technology** becomes the most contested throne, AI, *blockchain,* *biotechnology* are the new weapons of dominion.

This shift echoes the spiritual principle:

"Territories are inherited not by politics, but by those who master the spiritual and economic architecture of their age."

In this unfolding landscape, the new "kings" will not wear crowns, they will hold patents, control data, own digital currencies, and govern resource pipelines.

But Ahmed's insight opens a deeper truth:

The battle for Earth has shifted into the realms of innovation, data, and globalized commerce.

THE ECCLESIA'S MANDATE: MARKETPLACE APOSTLES AND PROPHETIC INNOVATORS

Yet while the world crowns tech giants and data lords, heaven is commissioning a counterforce:

Marketplace apostles and prophetic entrepreneurs who carry both *economic wisdom* and *spiritual jurisdiction*.

This is not secular entrepreneurship, this is **kingdom entrepreneurship**:

- Rooted in righteousness,

- Directed by revelation,

- Backed by the economy of heaven.

  "The meek shall inherit the earth, and shall delight themselves in the abundance of peace." *(Psalm 37:11)*

Meekness is not weakness, it is *yielded dominion*.

The **meek inherit**, because they submit to God's governance, and so are entrusted with **territorial rulership** in the Spirit.

These kingdom innovators will:

Reclaim digital and physical infrastructures for God's glory.

Build systems that honor divine justice.

Displace mammonic monopolies with redemptive commerce.

The Spirit is raising Daniels in data, Josephs in agriculture, Bezaleels in design, and Deborahs in strategy.

A CALL TO KINGDOM BUILDERS

The call is clear:

- Do not merely survive under global systems, build within and beyond them.
- Do not just critique the thrones of mammon, dethrone them with holy innovation.

In a world of "planet entrepreneurs," Christ is raising **planetary stewards**, men and women who govern **not only through intelligence**, but through the **wisdom, power, and timing of heaven.**

"Occupy till I come." *(Luke 19:13)*

TERRITORIAL THRONES, SURVEILLANCE CAPITALISM, AND THE INVISIBLE WAR

In the modern age, **wars are no longer declared, they are downloaded**.

Pulitzer Prize-winning journalist **David E. Hoffman**, in *The Billion Dollar Spy* and *The Dead Hand*, unveils how the battlefield of empires has shifted from boots-on-the-ground to bytes-in-the-cloud:

- Economic domination is executed through data and digital currencies.
- Espionage and market manipulation topple governments without bombs.

- Psychological warfare crafts public thought and re-engineers cultural values.

This is not fiction. It is a global chessboard of **invisible empires**, where **elites no longer seek just land, they seek minds, machines, and metadata**.

THE NEW THRONES: DIGITAL, TECHNOLOGICAL, PSYCHOLOGICAL

Today's **territorial thrones** include:

- **Digital Domains**

  Cyber-finance, cryptocurrencies, global payment rails, social media empires, these are the new "temples" of mammonic worship, where masses offer their time, attention, and identities daily.

- **Technological Infrastructures**

  Satellites, biotech grids, 5G networks, nanotech implants, the very frameworks of human experience are being shaped by those who seek **omnipresence and omniscience without God**.

- **Psychological Sovereignty**

  Whoever controls the narrative controls the nation.

  Through algorithmic manipulation, media propaganda, and curated realities, **ideologies are implanted**, **truths suppressed**, and **minds colonized**.

This is the gospel of the *beast system*:

An artificial omnipotence replacing divine dependence.

But the apostle declares:

> **"For the weapons of our warfare are not carnal but mighty in God for pulling down strongholds."** *(2 Corinthians 10:4)*

THE INVISIBLE WAR: A CLASH OF THRONES

What we are witnessing is not just economic evolution, it is a **spiritual war cloaked in commerce and code**.

These hidden thrones are rooted in **ancient demonic architectures**, systems first laid in Babel, refined in Babylon, and now reborn in Big Tech and Big Finance.

This is the **invisible war**, the battle for **global dominion without divine permission**.

But the Lord is raising a **remnant army** equipped with:

- **Prophetic technologies** (divine strategies encoded with eternal intelligence)

- **Spiritual intelligence** (discernment beyond data)

- **Apostolic innovation** (systems that reflect heaven's blueprint)

A DIVINE RESPONSE

Just as Moses received heavenly patterns for earthly governance, and Daniel decoded the encryption of empires through prayer, **God is releasing kingdom blueprints** for:

- **Secure systems** that resist corruption.

- **Economic models** that break cycles of exploitation.

- **Media platforms** that carry truth, not propaganda.

- **Educational engines** that renew minds, not conform them.

The ecclesia must not just *pray about systems*; it must **build them**.

The time for reactive faith is over. This is the hour for constructive dominion.

THE SECRET ALLIANCES: HOW CORRUPTION, POLITICS, AND ECONOMICS INTERLOCK

Behind the public theater of elections, legislations, and economic forecasts lies a deeper, darker reality, a **web of secret alliances**.

Peter Schweizer, in *Secret Empires* and *Profiles in Corruption*, pulls back the curtain to expose how modern empires operate not through flags and thrones, but **through silent partnerships and concealed transactions.** He reveals:

- **Political elites form covert alliances** with global corporations to protect and multiply their wealth.

- **Family dynasties cloak transfers of power** through shell companies, offshore accounts, and strategic board memberships.

- **Territorial dominion is preserved** not by governance, but by economic infiltration and ideological ownership.

ECHOES OF ANCIENT THRONES

This is not new. These are **modern iterations of ancient conspiracies,** where **kings and priests colluded** to control both **the altar (spiritual influence)** and **the throne (governmental power):**

- **Pharaoh and the Egyptian priesthood** withheld land from famine-stricken people, except for the priesthood (Genesis 47:22), a blueprint of economic apartheid.

- **Jezebel and Baal's priests** captured Israel's moral and agricultural economy through demonic worship and political power (1 Kings 18).

- **Herod and the Roman taxation system** used census data to control territories and extract wealth, under religious pretense (Luke 2:1–5).

In every age, the spirit of Mammon has built empires **through political alliances and economic entanglements,** disguised as governance and policy.

THE MODERN MAMMONIC PRIESTHOOD

Today, we see the same structure:

- **Modern kings (politicians)** manipulate laws to favor multinational interests.

- **Modern priests (financial elites)** orchestrate global trade, currency valuations, and ideological influence through media, think tanks, and education systems.

- Together, they sit at **invisible altars of Mammon**, presiding over a world bound in economic bondage.

This hidden priesthood does not wear robes or crowns, it wears **suits, carries briefcases, and wields algorithms.**

But the prophetic Word breaks through:

> **"Thus says the LORD: 'In an acceptable time I have heard You, and in the day of salvation I have helped You;**
>
> **I will preserve You and give You as a covenant to the people,**
>
> **to restore the earth, to cause them to inherit the desolate heritages.'"** *(Isaiah 49:8)*

THE RISE OF THE INHERITORS

God is raising **covenant sons and daughters, marketplace reformers**, and **apostolic governors** who are called to:

- Break the unholy alliances of power and wealth.

- Reclaim stolen inheritances, spiritual, economic, territorial.

- Restore justice in the gates through kingdom wisdom and prophetic precision.

They are not just revivalists in pulpits, they are **rebuilders of desolate inheritances**, moving through industries, governments, and infrastructures.

The days of secret empires are numbered. A new breed is rising, not with swords of man, but with the scrolls of heaven.

SCIENTIFIC KNOWLEDGE AND ECONOMIC WARFARE

In the modern world, **science is no longer neutral**. It has been weaponized.

Advanced disciplines that once served learning and progress are now deployed as **instruments of economic warfare and psychological manipulation**. Among these:

- **Econometrics**, the use of mathematical models to simulate and control national and global economies.

- **Predictive Analytics**, AI and machine learning technologies used to forecast markets, influence elections, and direct consumer behavior.

- **Behavioral Economics**, the strategic exploitation of human psychology to engineer choices in spending, voting, and even belief systems.

Data flows = Money flows = Power flows.

Whoever controls the data now controls the destinies of entire nations.

SCIENCE AS A TOOL OF DOMINION

The **ancient war for dominion** has moved into the digital and intellectual domain. Algorithms have become the new priests, and data analysts the new prophets, but for the wrong kingdom.

Just as sword and chariot dominated the ancient world, **data and science now dominate the modern thrones** of power.

But the Scripture gives us a higher lens:

> **"Happy is the man who finds wisdom,**

And the man who gains understanding;

For her proceeds are better than the profits of silver,

And her gain than fine gold." *(Proverbs 3:13–14)*

Wisdom, not just information, is the true key to dominion.

THE REDEMPTION OF SCIENTIFIC KNOWLEDGE

Scientific knowledge must be redeemed, not rejected. It must be **baptized in the fire of divine wisdom** and aligned with kingdom purposes.

God is calling for:

- **Prophetic economists** who see beyond the graphs.
- **Spirit-filled data scientists** who decode the patterns of heaven, not just Wall Street.
- **Marketplace apostles** who fuse cutting-edge technology with ancient truths.

This is not about rejecting science, it's about **redeeming it** and wielding it as a tool of restoration, not control.

Scientific insight must be baptized by prophetic sight.

THE DOMINION MANDATE OF CHRIST'S ECCLESIA

The great economic war is not just about currency; it is about **inheritance**.

The Agenda of the Bloodlines

The ancient bloodlines aligned with Mammon have a threefold mission:

- **Disinherit the saints** from their spiritual and material birthright.
- **Redirect kingdom wealth** into systems of rebellion, exploitation, and false glory.
- **Seal territorial thrones** through layers of deception, legalism, and spiritual covenants.

These families, the Rothschilds, Rockefellers, Morgans, Warburgs, did not merely accumulate wealth. They **engineered empires** built on control of:

- Central banking systems
- National debt issuance
- Natural resources and labor markets
- Legal financial instruments masked in legitimacy

They operated not just as financiers but as **territorial priests** of Mammon, enacting hidden **covenantal ownership** over nations and generations.

"Banking dynasties did not merely seek profit; they sought covenantal dominion."

THE ECCLESIA AND THE RISE OF KINGDOM STEWARDS

But God has not left the earth to be ruled by darkness.

> **"And God said, Let us make man in our image, after our likeness: and let them have dominion...",**
> *(Genesis 1:26)*

A new breed is arising, not from seminaries alone, but from boardrooms, labs, trade hubs, and tech incubators:

- **Financial Apostles,** who unlock kingdom wealth for divine assignment
- **Prophetic Entrepreneurs,** who build with vision, not vanity

- **Marketplace Reformers**, who overturn unrighteous altars of trade
- **Technological Kingdom Innovators**, who redeem AI, data, and platforms for light

These are **territorial intercessors** in disguise, armed not just with prayer, but with policies, platforms, patents, and purpose.

ANCIENT THRONES, MODERN TEMPLE**S**

The IMF, World Bank, and Bank for International Settlements (BIS) are **not neutral institutions**. They operate as **modern temples** of planetary finance, mirroring the idolatrous altars of Baal, Mammon, and Molech, where nations unknowingly sacrifice their futures through debt covenants.

Yet God's promise stands:

> **"Foreigners shall rebuild your walls, and their kings shall minister to you...**
>
> **The wealth of the nations shall come to you."** *(Isaiah 60:10–11)*
>
> **"Instead of your shame you shall have double honor... in their land they shall possess double."** *(Isaiah 61:7)*

The Reclamation Begins

The hour is now for the **Ecclesia to rise**, not as spectators of wealth transfer, but as **administrators of spiritual economies**. The systems of Mammon are crumbling under the weight of their rebellion. Kingdom stewards must take their place.

THE CONVERGENCE OF CYBER FINANCE AND BLOODLINE DOMINATION

A new financial architecture is emerging, not built on vaults or paper currency, but on **code, surveillance, and predictive control**.

Weaponized Cyber Finance

The economic battlefield has shifted into **digital territory**:

- **Cryptocurrency markets** are no longer just tools for decentralization, they're being **weaponized** for covert asset movement, untraceable funding of agendas, and black-market transactions hidden in plain sight.

- **Artificial Intelligence** now governs market decisions, central bank strategies, and even social credit scoring, replacing human intuition with programmed ideologies.

- **Blockchain technology**, originally heralded for transparency, is morphing into a **universal ledger**, enabling traceable global commerce grids that can be used for either **freedom or enslavement**.

The hidden rulers, the **bloodlines of Mammon and Babylon**, are embedding themselves into this next age of finance:

Not through gold-backed reserves, but through data-backed control.

Not through land acquisition, but through identity surveillance.

Not through armies, but through algorithms.

BIOECONOMICS: THE FINAL LAYER OF CONTROL

This convergence is moving beyond mere money.

We are entering the era of **bioeconomics**, where **control over human life, behavior, and biology** becomes the ultimate economic asset.

- Genomic data becomes currency.
- Digital identities become passports.
- Health decisions become economic gates.

All of it converging toward the ultimate prophecy:

> **"...that no one may buy or sell except one who has the mark or the name of the beast...",** *(Revelation 13:17)*

This is not fiction, it is **economic prophecy** in motion.

THE RISE OF KINGDOM COUNTER-TECHNOLOGIES

But Christ has not left His ecclesia without a strategy.

A **remnant is rising**, not with carnal weapons, but with **prophetic technology, Spirit-led innovation, and divine encryption** that dismantles Babylon's blueprints.

They will:

- **Design Holy Spirit-infused platforms** that protect dignity and purpose
- **Build righteous fintech systems** that uphold truth and transparency
- **Craft decentralized ecosystems** where liberty is preserved and kingdom values rule

> **"The Lord by wisdom founded the earth; by understanding He established the heavens;**
>
> **By His knowledge the depths were broken up..."**
> *(Proverbs 3:19–20)*

Christ is releasing **blueprints from heaven**, divine codes, digital Josephs, and Daniel-like minds, to outthink the Beast system and to establish **kingdom economics that liberate rather than enslave.**

KINGDOM COUNTERMEASURE: THE RISE OF THE JOSEPH AND DANIEL COMPANY

In response to the rise of bloodline domination and cyber-financial thrones, **Christ is activating a counter-company**, a remnant shaped by ancient wisdom, tested in adversity, and positioned for prophetic governance.

These are not just inspired individuals, they are **divinely appointed economic architects**, hidden in plain sight, being summoned for such a time as this.

The Joseph and Daniel Generation

Josephs, economic administrators, supply-chain governors, and dream-fulfillers.

Daniels, governmental advisors, interpreters of economic mysteries, and reformers within Babylon's court.

These individuals will **infiltrate ungodly systems without compromise** and **govern with righteousness** in the face of corruption.

Core Principles of Kingdom Economy

1. **Consecrated Stewardship**

    "Can we find such a one as this, a man in whom is the Spirit of God?" (Genesis 41:38–41)

    Wealth must not be hoarded, but stewarded prophetically, with foresight, discipline, and integrity.

2. **Wisdom over Accumulation**

    "If any of you lacks wisdom, let him ask of God... and it will be given to him." (James 1:5)

    Accumulation is not the goal, strategic **wisdom is**. Wealth flows where solutions live.

3. **Justice-Based Wealth Distribution**

   "For I, the Lord, love justice... I will direct their work in truth, and will make with them an everlasting covenant." (Isaiah 61:8)

   The economy of the Kingdom is built on justice, equity, and restoration, not exploitation.

4. **Marketplace Apostolic Hubs**

   Cities shall arise as **kingdom innovation centers**, where Spirit-filled entrepreneurs, inventors, and financiers gather, not just to build businesses, but to **govern spiritually and economically**.

THE SHIFT OF COUNSEL

"The kings of the earth will soon seek counsel,

not from the bloodlines of Mammon,

but from **kingdom entrepreneurs, Spirit-filled technocrats, and financial priests** equipped by Christ."

These Josephs and Daniels will:

- Speak mysteries decoded in the night season.
- Offer blueprints when systems collapse.
- Establish kingdom-run infrastructures when Babylon fails.
- Be entrusted with influence over **data, distribution, and direction**.

They are Heaven's **economic prophets and technological apostles**.

> **"For the earnest expectation of the creation eagerly waits for the revealing of the sons of God."**
> *(Romans 8:19)*

Creation is groaning, not for more money, but for **righteous managers of it**.

PRAYER ACTIVATION: BREAKING THE DOMINION OF HIDDEN THRONES

Father, in the Name of Jesus Christ,

I expose and renounce every hidden altar of Mammon, bloodline sorcery, and financial oppression.

I plead the Blood of Jesus against every invisible structure designed to enslave my destiny, my nation, and the marketplace.

Father, raise me as a Joseph, a Daniel, a wise builder in my generation.

I decree the collapse of ungodly thrones, banking systems, and bloodline dominions not aligned with Your Kingdom.

I receive heavenly blueprints, wisdom for righteous commerce, and boldness to govern wealth for Your glory.

Empower me to establish righteous altars in the marketplace, altars that honor You alone.

I decree an era of kingdom wealth transfer, economic revival, and territorial reformation, in Jesus' mighty Name!

Amen!

PROPHETIC DECREES: POSSESSING THE WEALTH OF NATIONS

Declare aloud:

"I am a steward of heaven's economy."

"I dismantle every hidden throne of unrighteous wealth by the Blood of Jesus."

"I am an architect of divine commerce in my generation."

"My hands shall build what demonic bloodlines cannot destroy."

"I receive power to create wealth to establish His covenant."

"I prophesy the fall of unjust systems and the rise of kingdom infrastructure."

"By wisdom and prophetic strategy, I shall possess cities, industries, and nations for the glory of Christ."

"The wealth of the wicked is flowing into righteous hands."

"Nations shall open their gates to the sons of God carrying heavenly blueprints."

"I legislate divine economic revival, in Jesus' Name!"

Amen and Amen!

CHAPTER 6

The Spirit of Pharaoh and the Economy of Bondage

"Let My people go, that they may serve Me."
~*Exodus 8:1 (NKJV)*

EXPOSING THE ANCIENT SPIRIT OF ECONOMIC SLAVERY

Throughout human history, economies have not just risen or fallen by chance, they have been **architected by spirits** operating behind kings, merchants, and rulers.

One of the most ancient and persistent spirits is the **Spirit of Pharaoh**, the enslaver of nations through economic oppression.

The **Pharaonic system** is a spiritual blueprint designed to:

- **Enslave labor** through unjust systems,

- **Control resource access** through monopolies,

- **Manipulate debt** to create lifelong servitude,

- **Use fear** to prevent uprising,

- **Suppress innovation** except under elite control.

In Egypt, Pharaoh enslaved the Hebrews through **forced labor and economic control**, controlling brick production, food distribution, and property ownership (Exodus 1:8–14).

Today, that spirit still operates **through banking cartels, corrupt governments, labor exploitation, and technological control grids**.

BUT CHRIST HAS COME TO DELIVER!

> *"For the LORD your God is bringing you into a good land...a land in which you will eat bread without scarcity, in which you will lack nothing."*
> **(Deuteronomy 8:7–9)**

The Ecclesia is arising to dismantle the economy of bondage and build **an economy of covenant and liberty** in Christ!

THE PHARAOHIC ECONOMY: A BLUEPRINT OF ECONOMIC BONDAGE

The spirit of Pharaoh operates through specific **economic strategies**:

1. **Debt as a Chain**

- Just as Pharaoh taxed the Israelites into economic submission, modern global banking systems **enslave nations through engineered debt**.

- National debts, IMF loans, and personal debts are designed to make individuals and governments **slaves to lenders** (Proverbs 22:7).

2. **Resource Control**

- Pharaoh controlled **grain during famine** (Genesis 41).

- Today, elites control water rights, seeds (via corporations like Monsanto), energy grids, and communication infrastructures.

3. **Labor Exploitation**

- Pharaoh forced **backbreaking labor without adequate compensation** (Exodus 5:6–18).

- In modern times, workers are overburdened, underpaid, and their labor is extracted to maintain elite wealth systems.

4. **Technological Surveillance and Oppression**

Just as Pharaoh's taskmasters closely monitored production.

Today, surveillance capitalism and AI monitoring systems **track economic activity, control narratives,** and **suppress dissent** (Revelation 13:16–17).

PHARAOH'S PSYCHOLOGICAL WARFARE

Pharaoh didn't just enslave by labor; he **programmed mental bondage**:

- Indoctrination that **servitude was normal**.

- Fear tactics to prevent **rebellion or alternative thinking**.

- Offering **just enough provision** to discourage revolution but prevent true flourishing.

Modern example:

Credit card companies give enough **credit illusion** to feel "wealthy" but chain generations into **lifelong debt servitude**.

BUT Scripture declares:

> *"You shall lend to many nations but shall not borrow."*
> **(Deuteronomy 28:12)**

SCIENTIFIC AND HISTORICAL PERSPECTIVES ON ECONOMIC BONDAGE

Modern **scientific insights** (behavioral economics, sociology) confirm that:

- Poverty is often **engineered**, not accidental.

- **Wealth gaps** widen through **policy manipulation**.

- **Technological platforms** consolidate wealth among elites faster than at any time in human history (World Economic Forum data).

Historians (like Niall Ferguson) show that empires collapse when **debt**, **inequality**, and **corruption** become systemic, patterns matching the Pharaonic model.

This is why the prophetic ecclesia must rise now, armed with both spiritual sight and economic strategy!

CHRIST: THE DELIVERER FROM ECONOMIC PHARAOHS

In Christ:

- We are **no longer slaves to mammon.**
- We are **no longer under Pharaonic economies.**
- We are **sons and daughters of the King,** called to steward wealth for kingdom purposes!

> *"The Spirit of the Lord GOD is upon Me, because the LORD has anointed Me to preach good tidings to the poor...to proclaim liberty to the captives, and the opening of the prison to those who are bound."* **(Isaiah 61:1)**

Christ came to:

- Break the bondage of debt.
- Release the creativity of innovation.
- Empower righteous stewardship.
- Restore territorial inheritance.

THE ECCLESIA'S CALL: BUILD KINGDOM ECONOMIES

Now is the time for:

- Prophetic entrepreneurs.
- Kingdom financiers.
- Apostolic economic architects.
- Innovative builders and righteous governors.

The marketplace is a **mission field**, and wealth is a **weapon of righteousness** when aligned with Christ.

> *"Through prosperity shall My cities be spread abroad."* **(Zechariah 1:17)**

PROPHETIC ACTIVATION PRAYER: BREAKING THE PHARAONIC ECONOMY

Father God, in the Name of Jesus,

I renounce and break every covenant with the spirit of Pharaoh operating in my life, my family, my territory, and my economy!

By the blood of Jesus, I cancel the chains of debt, labor exploitation, fear, and oppression!

I decree that I am no longer a slave but a son, an heir of Your Kingdom wealth!

I receive divine strategies for righteous economic dominion.

I receive wisdom to create, innovate, and steward according to Your Spirit.

Empower me to build covenant economies that bless generations and establish Your glory!

In Jesus' Name, Amen!

PROPHETIC DECREES:

"I am delivered from every Pharaonic system of bondage."

"I possess the wisdom of Joseph to govern resources righteously."

"I am an economic liberator, not a captive."

"I create and innovate under the unction of the Holy Spirit."

"I receive divine blueprints for marketplace reformation."

"By the Spirit of the Lord, I overthrow systems of economic oppression."

"I declare the restoration of lost inheritances and territorial wealth."

"I walk in supernatural provision and covenant prosperity."

Amen!

CLOSING PROPHETIC WORD FOR CHAPTER 6

Hear the Word of the Lord:

"Behold, I do a new thing! Now it springs forth; shall you not know it? I will even make a road in the wilderness and rivers in the desert." **(Isaiah 43:19)**

The rivers of economic freedom are breaking forth!

The Pharaohs of finance are trembling.

The Josephs and Daniels of this generation are rising.

Prepare to steward the wealth of nations for the glory of Christ!

Selah.

CHAPTER 7

The Mind of the Investor: Building Kingdom Wealth with Righteous Intelligence

"If any of you lacks wisdom, let him ask of God, who gives to all liberally and without reproach."
~James 1:5 (NKJV)

THE GREAT RESET OF FINANCIAL STEWARDSHIP

In this hour, **God is raising a remnant**, men and women who will not just possess wealth, but will **govern wealth intelligently, prophetically, and righteously.**

The Spirit of God is calling His people to **move beyond emotional spending, impulsive investing, or carnal consumption**, into a **Kingdom architecture of financial wisdom and dominion.**

Two significant works in the secular world,

"The Intelligent Investor" by Benjamin Graham and **"The Psychology of Money" by Morgan Housel**, show how **long-term thinking, emotional discipline, and strategic stewardship** are keys to enduring wealth.

However, in Christ, we transcend mere human wisdom,

We receive **spiritual intelligence**, **prophetic foresight**, and **covenant strategies** to steward and multiply resources for the King's dominion on earth.

> *"A good man leaves an inheritance to his children's children, but the wealth of the sinner is stored up for the righteous."* (**Proverbs 13:22**)

This chapter will open the portals of your mind to **think like a Kingdom investor, a prophetic entrepreneur, and a wise steward**, overthrowing the impulsive, short-term, and fear-driven patterns sown by Babylonian economies.

The **Throne of Mammon** manipulates fear, greed, and scarcity to trap souls.

But the Throne of Christ releases wisdom, stewardship, creativity, and abundance to liberate destinies.

THE HISTORICAL PSYCHOLOGY OF MONEY

Ancient civilizations understood the spiritual nature of wealth:

- **Babylon**: Created monetary systems to consolidate power over territories.
- **Egypt**: Accumulated massive wealth under Pharaoh, leading to slavery economics.
- **Rome**: Weaponized taxation and debt to expand imperial rule.
- **Medieval Europe**: Created guilds and banking houses (e.g., Medici dynasty) to control regional economies.

Each historical economic system was **fueled by altars, spiritual forces** that governed the emotions, minds, and decisions of entire populations.

Today, Wall Street, the Federal Reserve, IMF, World Bank, and tech-driven stock markets are new temples where emotions are manipulated daily.

Scientific Insight:

Neurological studies show that when people invest or gamble, the **dopamine system** (pleasure chemical) is activated, leading to **addiction patterns identical to substance abuse**.

Thus, the war over wealth is a war over the **neural architecture of the mind**.

THE BABYLONIAN VS. KINGDOM FINANCIAL ARCHITECTURES

Babylonian System	Kingdom System (in Christ)
Fear-driven speculation	Faith-led investment
Greed and manipulation	Stewardship and generosity
Short-term profit lust	Long-term covenantal vision

Babylonian System	Kingdom System (in Christ)
Emotional impulsiveness	Spiritual patience and discernment
Serving Mammon	Serving Christ, the King

"*You cannot serve God and mammon.*" (**Matthew 6:24**)

The Babylonian economic systems **feed on panic, inflation, speculation, deception, and consumerism.**

Christ's Kingdom economy operates by **principles of sowing, patience, supernatural multiplication, creative innovation, and Kingdom distribution.**

KEY SPIRITUAL TECHNOLOGIES FOR FINANCIAL DOMINION

1. **Covenant Stewardship Over Ownership**

In the Kingdom, we are not **owners**, we are **stewards**.

> "*The earth is the LORD's and all its fullness.*" (**Psalm 24:1**)

Everything you possess is a **trust**, to be multiplied, governed, and redistributed according to **the King's purposes.**

Financial wisdom begins where ownership ends.

2. **Prophetic Financial Intelligence**

- Discern **times and seasons** (like Issachar, 1 Chronicles 12:32).

- Understand **harvest cycles.**

- Invest not just based on markets but **based on prophetic instructions** (Genesis 26:1–14, Isaac sowed in famine and reaped a hundredfold).

3. **Emotional Mastery Through the Spirit**

> "*He who rules his spirit is better than he who captures a city.*" (**Proverbs 16:32**)

The real battlefield of wealth is **internal emotional discipline**:

- Control over greed.
- Mastery over fear.
- Patience during economic downturns.
- Boldness during divine opportunities.

THE INVESTOR'S PROFILE IN THE KINGDOM

1. Apostolic Builders:

Raise capital to establish Kingdom structures (schools, hospitals, businesses).

2. Prophetic Forerunners:

See economic trends before they emerge and prepare strategic investments.

3. Marketplace Evangelists:

Use business and investment as fields to advance the gospel.

4. Kingdom Bankers:

Create lending structures based on justice, not exploitation.

5. Global Innovators:

Birth new technologies, industries, and solutions rooted in Kingdom creativity.

"Occupy till I come." **(Luke 19:13)**

SCIENTIFIC INSIGHTS ON WEALTH MULTIPLICATION

Modern research by behavioral economists (like **Daniel Kahneman,** Nobel Prize winner) confirms:

- Consistent investing (dollar-cost averaging) beats emotional market-timing.

- Patience compounds wealth exponentially (Power of Compound Interest).

- Minimizing unnecessary risks leads to greater long-term gains.

Yet, **faith in God, hearing the Spirit,** and **operating in covenant promises** are superior to any secular method.

When you **mix wisdom, prophetic strategy, and scientific understanding,** you create **Kingdom financial ecosystems** that endure beyond recessions and global shifts.

ACTIVATION PRAYER: RENEWING MY FINANCIAL MIND

"Father, in the name of Jesus,

I surrender my financial emotions and mind to You.

Deliver me from every spirit of fear, impulsiveness, greed, and worldly mindset.

Baptize me with divine intelligence, covenant wisdom, and prophetic foresight.

Empower me to steward wealth as a righteous son/daughter of the Kingdom.

Let every seed I sow be multiplied according to Your divine economy.

I receive the mind of Christ for wealth building, investing, creating, and giving.

In Jesus' mighty name, Amen!"

PROPHETIC DECREES OVER FINANCES

I decree **I am a steward of Kingdom resources, not a slave to mammon.**

I decree **I operate with prophetic intelligence, not worldly speculation.**

I decree **emotional mastery and Spirit-led decisions govern my finances.**

I decree **I sow, invest, build, and multiply for the glory of the King.**

I decree **fear and greed have no authority over my mind.**

I decree **patience, discernment, and strategy are my portion.**

I decree **I will leave a financial inheritance that empowers Kingdom legacies.**

I decree **new streams of income, innovations, and righteous wealth creation flow to me.**

I decree **the Joseph anointing for economic leadership rests upon me.**

"Blessed is the man who trusts in the Lord, whose trust is the Lord." **(Jeremiah 17:7)**

IN SUMMARY: RAISING A NEW BREED OF KINGDOM INVESTORS

You are not called to be tossed about by financial storms,

You are called to **govern economies** with the wisdom of God.

As the Babylonian systems tremble,

the Lord is raising up **Kingdom entrepreneurs, investors, builders, and wealth distributors** who will **fund revivals, build cities, disciple nations, and establish justice.**

Your mind is the seedbed of your financial destiny.

Guard it, renew it, and fill it with the mind of Christ.

> *"For wisdom is better than rubies, and all the things one may desire cannot be compared with her."*
> **(Proverbs 8:11)**

Selah.

CHAPTER 8

The Geometry of Wealth: Sacred Systems of Divine Prosperity

"By wisdom a house is built, and by understanding it is established." ~*Proverbs 24:3 (ESV)*

UNLOCKING THE HIDDEN PATTERNS OF KINGDOM WEALTH

Throughout creation, **divine intelligence** encoded wealth into the very **fabric of reality**.

Every molecule, every ecosystem, every galaxy operates according to **sacred geometries, harmonic proportions, and divine frequencies**.

Just as God created the universe through **order, patterns, sound, and mathematical precision,**

so also **true wealth creation** follows **divine patterns**, not random chaos.

> *"When He prepared the heavens, I was there: when He set a compass upon the face of the depth."* (**Proverbs 8:27 KJV**)

In this age, the Spirit is unveiling to the sons and daughters of God **how sacred geometry, economic systems, wealth multiplication, and Kingdom principles intersect.**

This chapter journeys through

- ancient sacred texts,

- modern scientific research (like Darius Foroux's behavioral wealth psychology),

- **quantum economics,**

- and **biblical revelations**, to unlock the **geometry of wealth** for the next generation of Kingdom reformers.

You are not called to chase wealth randomly.

You are called to steward wealth precisely, prophetically, and geometrically, aligned with the throne of Christ.

WEALTH IS GEOMETRICAL BEFORE IT IS MATERIAL

Sacred geometry teaches that **energy precedes form.**

- Wealth is not merely physical cash, gold, or stock portfolios.

- Wealth is an **energy structure**, a **pattern of flow**, a **sacred architecture** of abundance.

Before silver and gold were extracted from the earth, their **atomic structures** were aligned according to divine geometry, specifically, the **Golden Ratio (Phi, ~1.618)** and the **Fibonacci sequence.**

- **The spiral patterns of galaxies, flowers, seashells, and hurricanes follow sacred geometry.**

- **True wealth ecosystems also follow fractal and spiral growth patterns,** healthy, self-replicating and abundant.

Scientific Insight:

Studies in **econophysics** (the physics of financial markets) show that **market behaviors mimic fractal mathematics and chaotic attractors,** not pure randomness.

There are **hidden geometries even in economic booms and busts.**

Spiritual Parallel:

> *"The blessing of the LORD makes rich, and He adds no sorrow with it."* (**Proverbs 10:22**)

Kingdom wealth follows a **blessing-based, sorrow-free geometry,** not the jagged, destructive patterns of mammon-driven greed.

DARIUS FOROUX AND THE BEHAVIORAL GEOMETRY OF WEALTH

Darius Foroux (author of *"Think Straight," "Do It Today,"* and *"Wealth Habits"*) teaches that **wealth is a predictable outcome of daily patterns, habits, and disciplined thinking.**

He reveals five principles that align closely with **Kingdom geometry**:

Principle	Kingdom Parallel
1. Earn consistently	*"He who gathers money little by little makes it grow."* (Proverbs 13:11)
2. Save automatically	*"Precious treasure and oil are in a wise man's dwelling."* (Proverbs 21:20)
3. Invest wisely	*"Invest in seven ventures, yes, in eight."* (Ecclesiastes 11:2 NIV)
4. Protect wealth from loss	*"A prudent man foresees evil and hides himself."* (Proverbs 22:3)
5. Expand value creation	*"Be fruitful and multiply."* (Genesis 1:28)

Thus, **wealth is not accidental**, it is the **fruit of hidden, geometric habits formed in Christ**.

ANCIENT SACRED TEXTS AND ECONOMIC GEOMETRY

From ancient texts like:

- **The Torah (Deuteronomy 8:18)**, *"It is God who gives you the power to get wealth."*

- **The Emerald Tablet of Thoth**, *"As above, so below; as within, so without."*

- **The Book of Proverbs**, geometric wisdom embedded in patterns of sowing, diligence, honesty and planning.

- **The Kabbalah's Tree of Life**, an architectural map of energy and abundance, flows through divine Sephirot (emanations).

These ancient wisdom traditions understood that **true wealth flows along invisible energetic lattices** that must be aligned with divine order.

When rebellion, corruption, and injustice distort the geometry, collapse **and judgment come**.

When stewardship, justice, generosity, and righteousness flow, multiplication **and Kingdom expansion come**.

THE SCIENTIFIC GEOMETRY OF WEALTH ECOSYSTEMS

Quantum physics, chaos theory, and complex systems research reveal:

- Healthy systems grow **in fractals**, branching structures that replicate healthy DNA codes.

- Diseased systems show **broken or parasitic fractals**, leading to systemic collapse.

- **Ecosystems and economies** mirror biological principles:

  o   Balance between consumption and production,

  o   Biodiversity of ideas and industries,

  o   Ethical stewardship over exploitation.

Thus, building **Kingdom wealth** means:

- Creating **multi-dimensional systems** (businesses, ministries, investments)

- that **reflect the health, beauty, and multiplication design** of Christ's creation.

    "Through wisdom a house is built, and by understanding it is established." **(Proverbs 24:3)**

Wisdom = Geometric Understanding = Wealth Sustainability

PROPHETIC ALIGNMENT WITH DIVINE FINANCIAL BLUEPRINTS

The Lord is calling His sons and daughters to **build wealth ecosystems based on Heaven's architecture:**

- Families as entrepreneurial hubs (Proverbs 31 model).
- Communities as innovation clusters (Acts 2 economy).
- Nations discipled through righteous industries and technologies (Isaiah 60:5).

> *"Your gates shall be open continually... that men may bring to you the wealth of the nations."* **(Isaiah 60:11)**

You are called not just to own wealth, you are called to design and govern wealth cities, wealth gates, wealth civilizations!

THE BATTLE OVER FINANCIAL BLUEPRINTS

Money has always been **more than currency**, it is a **blueprint**, a **territorial control mechanism**, and a **governance tool**.

Throughout history, financial systems have been architected either to:

- **Liberate** nations and families under righteous governance,
- Or **enslave** them under manipulative, godless thrones.

> *"For the love of money is the root of all evil."* **(1 Timothy 6:10)**

This exposes how worldly systems (as revealed by investigative researchers like **Seamus Bruner** and entrepreneurial strategists like **Summer Bacher**) have sought to **dominate through wealth blueprints**, and how Christ's Kingdom offers a **higher template** for financial governance, expansion, and liberty.

You are called to **build on the Rock**, not the **sandcastles of Babylon**.

SEAMUS BRUNER AND THE ARCHITECTURE OF CONTROL

In *"Controligarchs,"* Seamus Bruner exposes how a small network of **financial elites, tech titans, and global banking families** have methodically **designed financial systems** to consolidate:

- Media,
- Technology,
- Energy,
- Food systems,
- Health care,
- National currencies.

They employ strategies like:

- **Debt traps** (Proverbs 22:7, *"the borrower is slave to the lender"*),
- **Monopoly capitalism** under a "global democracy" veil,
- **Currency manipulations** through fiat systems,
- **Stock market engineering** through dark pools and private exchanges,
- **Inflation cycles** to erode middle class and transfer assets upward.

Prophetic Insight:

This is not merely economics, it is **an altar battle**.

Mammon-based systems architect, these control webs to replace Christ's dominion with **humanistic thrones**.

Kingdom Strategy:

We must **discern the architecture** and **build counter-ecosystems** rooted in righteousness, multiplication, stewardship, and communal prosperity.

SUMMER BACHER AND KINGDOM ENTREPRENEURIAL STRATEGIES

Summer Bacher, a dynamic voice in entrepreneurship and holistic wealth creation, emphasizes that:

Wealth must be **designed intentionally** around personal values and Kingdom purpose.

Financial sovereignty is reclaimed through **multi-stream income, asset ownership**, and **community wealth networks**.

Entrepreneurs must **build decentralized structures**, not just personal empires.

Key teachings from Bacher that align with Christ-centered wealth strategies:

Summer Bacher Strategy	Kingdom Alignment
1. Build value ecosystems, not isolated businesses	*"The whole body, joined and held together..." (Ephesians 4:16)*
2. Prioritize regenerative wealth over extractive wealth	*"The righteous leaves an inheritance to his children's children." (Proverbs 13:22)*
3. Create freedom through ownership and stewardship	*"Occupy until I come." (Luke 19:13)*
4. Invest in community economic hubs	*"All the believers were together and had everything in common." (Acts 2:44-45)*

Thus, **wealth creation must mirror the organic, relational, and multiplying life of Christ**, not the sterile control mechanisms of Babylon.

UNDERSTANDING FINANCIAL WARFARE AND DIVINE COUNTER-STRATEGIES

Worldly economic systems are based on **scarcity**, **fear**, and **deception**.

Kingdom financial systems are based on **abundance, faith**, and **truth**.

Babylonian Financial System	Kingdom Financial System
Debt Enslavement	Debt Freedom
Hoarding and Monopolizing	Generosity and Multiplication
Currency Manipulation	Honest Weights and Measures (Leviticus 19:35-36)
Centralized Power	Distributed Stewardship
Fear-driven Markets	Faith-driven Innovation

"You shall have a full and honest weight; you shall have a full and honest measure." (**Deuteronomy 25:15**)

THE DIVINE FINANCIAL BLUEPRINT

The blueprint of Heaven's economy involves:

- **Seed time and harvest** (Genesis 8:22)

- **Stewardship over ownership mentality** (Luke 16:10–12)

- **Faith-based investment** (Ecclesiastes 11:1, *"Cast your bread upon the waters"*)

- **Multiplication mandate** (Matthew 25:14–30, Parable of the Talents)

- **Marketplace dominion** (Revelation 11:15, *"The kingdoms of this world have become the kingdoms of our Lord"*)

- **Justice and righteousness foundations** (Isaiah 9:7)

Every Kingdom wealth builder must operate according to this sacred blueprint, not Babylon's architecture.

ACTIVATION PRAYER: BUILDING BY DIVINE BLUEPRINT

"Father, in the name of Jesus,

I yield my mind, heart, and hands to Your divine financial architecture.

Forgive me for operating outside Your sacred patterns.

Baptize me with the spirit of wisdom and understanding.

Open my eyes to the sacred geometries of wealth, stewardship, and multiplication.

Anoint me to build families, businesses, communities, and cities aligned with the blueprints of Heaven.

Make me a geometric expression of Your prosperity on earth!

In Jesus' mighty name, Amen!"

PROPHETIC DECREES OVER WEALTH GEOMETRY

I decree **my wealth flows according to divine sacred patterns, not worldly systems.**

I decree **I am aligned with Heaven's fractal of abundance and multiplication.**

I decree **the Golden Ratio of divine order manifests in my finances and businesses.**

I decree **every corrupted pattern in my financial life is uprooted and restructured by Christ.**

I decree **I build sustainable, righteous, multi-generational wealth ecosystems.**

I decree **Heaven's blueprints for dominion, legacy, and stewardship are activated in me now.**

I decree **I am a living temple of financial wisdom, stewardship, and multiplication.**

"The LORD by wisdom founded the earth; by understanding He established the heavens." (**Proverbs 3:19**)

IN SUMMARY: YOU ARE A LIVING BLUEPRINT OF DIVINE WEALTH

You are not a random participant in the economy of nations.

You are an **architect of Heaven's prosperity on earth**.

As you align with the sacred geometries of Christ,

your life will spiral upward into greater dimensions of abundance, influence, and legacy.

You will not just make money,

you will birth Kingdom civilizations.

> *"They shall build the old wastes; they shall raise up the former desolations."* (**Isaiah 61:4**)

Selah.

CHAPTER 9

Thrones of Wealth: Ancient Texts, Modern Masters, and the Christ Alignment

"I will give you the treasures of darkness and hidden riches of secret places." ~ *Isaiah 45:3 (NKJV)*

THE HIDDEN THRONES BEHIND WEALTH CREATION

From ancient civilizations to modern stock markets, **the battle for dominion through wealth has never ceased.**

Warren Buffett, Scott Walter, Peter Schweizer, and **Adam Smith,** brilliant minds in economics and finance, have each, knowingly or unknowingly, touched **the edges of ancient systems** still at work today.

The ancient texts from **Hebrew wisdom, early Christian writings, Sumerian tablets,** and even **scientific economic studies** reveal the **spiritual energies, covenantal laws,** and **territorial dominions** tied to wealth.

> *"The silver is mine, and the gold is mine, declares the LORD Almighty."* **(Haggai 2:8)**

The throne of wealth **either submits to Christ,** or it becomes **a golden calf, an idol** serving other gods.

This chapter uncovers:

- Ancient spiritual blueprints of financial dominion,
- Scientific laws governing wealth behaviors,
- Revelations through modern thinkers,
- And how Christ realigns economics back to **righteous Kingdom thrones.**

ANCIENT TEXTS, WEALTH AS GOVERNANCE AND DOMINION

Sumerian and Babylonian Records

The earliest written documents (3000 BCE), such as the **Code of Ur-Nammu** and the **Code of Hammurabi,** already contained **financial laws** regarding:

- Weights and measures,
- Lending and borrowing,
- Trade policies,
- Inheritance rights.

Wealth was **sacralized**: overseen by **temple priests** and **territorial gods**.

Insight:
Commerce was never "secular", it was an **act of worship** to the thrones one served.

> *"No one can serve two masters. You cannot serve both God and Mammon."* **(Matthew 6:24)**

ANCIENT HEBREW SCRIPTURES

The Torah and Wisdom books gave divine ordinances about wealth:
- Jubilee economic resets (Leviticus 25)
- Honest trade (Proverbs 11:1)
- Generational blessings tied to obedience (Deuteronomy 28:1–14)

Thus, in the Hebrew mindset, **wealth is a sign of covenant fidelity**, but **poverty or injustice triggers divine correction**.

SCIENTIFIC AND ECONOMIC EVIDENCE, WEALTH FLOWS ARE GOVERNED BY LAWS

Scientific economics reveals certain "laws" that govern wealth behaviors:

Economic Law	Spiritual Parallel
Law of Compound Interest (Buffett's favorite)	*"Faithful with little, faithful with much"* *(Luke 16:10)*
Law of Scarcity	*Man's fallen fear of lack, versus God's abundant economy*
Law of Value Exchange	*"Give, and it shall be given unto you"* *(Luke 6:38)*
Law of Systems Thinking	*The Body of Christ functions as a divine economic organism*

Wealth doesn't "just happen"; it is **created through systems of obedience or rebellion** to these laws, in either **righteousness** or **manipulation**.

WARREN BUFFETT, THE ORACLE AND THE PRINCIPLE OF PATIENT STEWARDSHIP

Warren Buffett, often called the "Oracle of Omaha," built his wealth on:

- **Patience** (long-term compounding),

- **Value investing** (buying intrinsic worth),

- **Stewardship over speculation**.

These principles mirror **biblical wisdom**:

> *"The plans of the diligent lead surely to abundance,*
> *but everyone who is hasty comes only to poverty."*
> **(Proverbs 21:5)**

Insight:

Buffett's approach, while secular, **unknowingly reflects divine stewardship principles**.

The Church must **reclaim** these strategies under **the Lordship of Christ**, not for self-aggrandizement but for **Kingdom expansion**.

SCOTT WALTER AND PETER SCHWEIZER, EXPOSING THE THRONES OF CORRUPTION

Both **Scott Walter** (Capital Research Center) and **Peter Schweizer** (author of *"Clinton Cash," "Profiles in Corruption"*) expose how:

Political dynasties,

Charitable foundations,

Big tech monopolies,

Banking families

have weaponized **philanthropy**, **policy**, and **nonprofits** to **consolidate financial and political power**.

"Woe to those who decree iniquitous decrees, and the writers who keep writing oppression." (Isaiah 10:1)

They reveal how **territorial altars** (legal, corporate, media) were erected to enthrone a **false prosperity gospel**, one that serves **Mammon** rather than **Christ**.

Thus, righteous entrepreneurs must rise as:

Watchmen of economic gates,

Priests of marketplace sanctuaries,

Builders of just and truthful enterprises.

ADAM SMITH, THE INVISIBLE HAND VS. THE HAND OF GOD

Adam Smith, the father of modern capitalism (*"The Wealth of Nations"*), theorized that:

"An invisible hand" governs free markets toward societal benefit.

While Smith acknowledged Providence, **he missed** that **the true Invisible Hand is Christ Himself:**

"You open your hand; you satisfy the desire of every living thing." (Psalm 145:16)

Kingdom economics is **not free-market anarchy**, but **Spirit-led value creation**, rooted in:

Justice (Proverbs 29:4)

Compassion (James 2:15-17)

Multiplication for the collective good (Acts 4:34-35)

Thus, **the true Kingdom economy is prophetic, just, and abundant**, not survival of the fittest.

ACTIVATION PRAYER: ALIGNING WITH CHRIST'S FINANCIAL THRONES

"Father,

Today I renounce every altar of Mammon, greed, exploitation, or manipulation.

I align my life, my wealth, and my influence to the throne of Christ, the only true King.

Give me divine wisdom like Joseph, integrity like Daniel, and faithfulness like the Proverbs 31 entrepreneur.

Empower me to build economic structures that glorify You and bless generations after me.

Let my wealth flow as a river of justice, righteousness, and Kingdom transformation.

In Jesus' name, Amen."

PROPHETIC DECREES

I decree **my mind is renewed by divine financial wisdom.**

I decree **my hands build structures aligned to Heaven's economy.**

I decree **I am a priest and king in the marketplace.**

I decree **territories and altars of wealth are being reclaimed by the sons of God.**

I decree **my business, investments, and enterprises reflect Christ's Kingdom on earth.**

"The meek shall inherit the earth." (**Matthew 5:5**)

IN SUMMARY: THRONES ARE SHIFTING, WILL YOU SIT WHERE CHRIST CALLS YOU?

Ancient altars are still influencing modern economics.

Scientific systems mirror spiritual realities.

We are now in a prophetic season where **those aligned to Christ's throne will govern economies, not as tyrants, but as righteous kings and priests.**

Rise. Build. Govern.

The nations are waiting for you.

> *"The kingdoms of this world have become the Kingdoms of our Lord and His Christ."* (**Revelation 11:15**)

CHAPTER 10

Marketplace Thrones and the Battle for Territory

"Arise, shine; for your light has come! And the glory of the Lord is risen upon you." ~Isaiah 60:1 (NKJV)

THE MARKETPLACE IS A BATTLEFIELD OF THRONES

The marketplace is far more than an arena of commerce.

It is a **spiritual battlefield**, where **thrones, altars, and principalities** contend for:

- **Territorial influence,**
- **Economic resources,**
- **Cultural shaping,**
- **Generational inheritance.**

Whoever controls the marketplace **controls cities, nations, and the future**.

> *"For the LORD your God is bringing you into a good land, a land with brooks, streams, and deep springs gushing out into the valleys and hills."* (**Deuteronomy 8:7**)

The early apostles understood this. Paul didn't merely preach; he **engaged business hubs** (Acts 19:9-10).

Jesus Himself taught in **marketplaces** and called His followers to **"occupy till I come"** (Luke 19:13).

Today, the **sons of God** must rise to **reclaim the marketplace thrones**, not through carnal strategies, but through **Spirit-led innovation, wisdom, justice, and divine creativity**.

ANCIENT MARKETPLACE THRONES, SPIRITUAL AND HISTORICAL FOUNDATIONS

Ancient Cities Were Marketplace-Governed

- In **Babylon, Tyre, Sidon**, and **Nineveh**, commerce, governance, and worship were **intertwined**.

- Ancient **city gates** were not merely entrances but **economic courts** where:

  o **Contracts were sealed,**

  o **Disputes were judged,**

  o **Spiritual rites were performed.**

    "Wisdom cries out in the streets; she raises her voice in the public squares." **(Proverbs 1:20)**

Thus, **spiritual governance** was established at **economic gates**.

Insight:

Whoever controlled the gates, controlled the **flow of wealth, justice, and culture**.

HISTORICAL MARKETPLACE THRONES

- **Phoenician merchants** were not only traders but **covenant priests** to Baal and Ashtoreth.

- **Roman marketplaces (fora)** were designed as **temples of commerce and imperial power**.

- **Medieval trade guilds** often had **occultic initiations** to maintain wealth control.

The marketplace was never neutral; it was (and still is) **spiritually charged**.

SCIENTIFIC EVIDENCE, ECONOMICS AS TERRITORIAL SYSTEMS

Modern economic science recognizes:

- **Regional economies** form **systemic territories** (clusters of industries, supply chains, labor movements).

- **Behavioral economics** shows how **emotions, desires, and fears** influence market behavior, not just logic.

This mirrors **ancient truths**:

Economics is driven by spiritual forces, manifesting through **human behaviors and territorial covenants.**

> *"For we wrestle not against flesh and blood, but against principalities, powers, rulers of darkness, and spiritual wickedness in high places."* **(Ephesians 6:12)**

Thus:

The marketplace is an external reflection of **spiritual realities** operating over cities and nations.

MARKETPLACE THRONES TODAY, SPHERES OF INFLUENCE

Sphere	Throne Occupiers	Battle Strategy
Finance	Global banks, hedge funds	Kingdom financiers, Joseph companies
Media	Corporations, influencers	Prophetic media houses
Technology	Tech monopolies	Righteous innovation hubs
Education	Universities, think tanks	Apostolic academic reformers
Trade	Corporations, cartels	Christ-centered commerce builders

Each sphere is a "marketplace gate."

Each gate requires **Kingdom watchmen and warriors.**

> *"Arise, shine; for your light has come, and the glory of the LORD rises upon you."* **(Isaiah 60:1)**

ANCIENT MARKETPLACE WISDOM FOR TODAY

1. **The Anointing of Bezalel and Oholiab (Exodus 31:1–11)**

They were gifted with:

*   **Artistic design,**
*   **Metallurgical knowledge,**
*   **Project management,**
*   **Divine engineering.**

Insight:

Kingdom economy requires **Spirit-empowered craftsmanship and innovation,** not just religious rhetoric.

2. **Joseph's Marketplace Dominion (Genesis 41)**

Joseph was given:

*   **Economic insight into scarcity cycles,**
*   **Governmental authority to administer wealth,**
*   **Strategic wisdom to preserve nations.**

    "Now therefore let Pharaoh select a discerning and wise man, and set him over the land of Egypt." **(Genesis 41:33)**

This is the Joseph blueprint: **Divine strategies for economic governance** in famine and abundance.

3. **Christ, The True King of the Marketplace**

When Jesus overturned the money changers' tables (Matthew 21:12-13), He was **cleansing the marketplace gates** from corruption and restoring their original purpose.

He demonstrated that **spiritual purity and economic justice** must align.

    "Seek first the Kingdom of God and His righteousness, and all these things shall be added unto you." **(Matthew 6:33)**

Thus, true marketplace conquest is:

- Not exploitation, but **stewardship**.

- Not domination, but **governance in righteousness**.

- Not manipulation, but **multiplication for Kingdom advancement**.

ACTIVATION PRAYER: ARISING AS A MARKETPLACE KING-PRIEST

"Father,

I receive Your divine commissioning to be a priest and a king in the marketplace.

I repent for any ways I have bowed to Mammon, fear, or compromise.

I ask for the Spirit of wisdom, understanding, counsel, might, knowledge, and the fear of the Lord to rest upon me.

Empower me with strategies to build, govern, and steward territory in righteousness.

I arise as a reformer at the gates of economics, trade, media, and education.

In Jesus' mighty name, Amen."

PROPHETIC DECREES

I decree **the marketplace gates are opening to the righteous**.

I decree **ancient altars of corruption are being dismantled** by the fire of the Spirit.

I decree **I carry divine blueprints to build cities, companies, and economies for the glory of Christ.**

I decree **the thrones of territory are being realigned under the feet of Christ and His ecclesia.**

I decree **territories and resources are being transferred into the hands of the just.**

"The wealth of the sinner is laid up for the just."
(Proverbs 13:22)

IN SUMMARY: THE MARKETPLACE AWAITS THE SONS OF GOD

The marketplace is not just a place to make a living; it is **a battleground of thrones and destinies.**

Those who sit in economic and cultural thrones **shape civilizations**.

Now is the time to rise.

Now is the time to build.

Now is the time to govern in Christ.

"And the kingdoms of this world shall become the kingdoms of our Lord and of His Christ, and He shall reign forever and ever." **(Revelation 11:15)**

CHAPTER 11

Cyber Thrones: Finance, Intelligence, and the Digital Battle for Souls

"We are not ignorant of his devices." ~2 Corinthians 2:11 (NKJV)

THE DIGITAL EMPIRE AND ITS BATTLE FOR SOULS

The world has changed, and so has the battlefield for dominion. In ancient times, **thrones** symbolized visible authority, kings, emperors, and rulers who wielded control over land, armies, and laws. But in today's digital world, a **new kind of throne has emerged**: invisible, algorithmic, global.

These are what we call **"Cyber Thrones."**

WHAT ARE CYBER THRONES?

Cyber Thrones refer to **invisible seats of power** in the **digital realm** that govern:

- Financial systems
- Information control
- Behavioral influence
- Data surveillance
- AI-based decision-making
- Digital identity and reputation

These thrones are occupied not by monarchs or presidents, but by **technology platforms, global banks, intelligence networks**, and **AI systems** that silently govern human activity.

They:

- Decide **what content you see**
- Track your **transactions and movements**
- Analyze your **thought patterns and preferences**
- Influence your **purchases, votes, beliefs**, and even **faith**

You don't vote for them. You can't always see them. But their influence shapes your **daily life**, often more than governments or pastors do.

WHY ARE CYBER THRONES DANGEROUS?

Because they are:

- **Invisible**: Most people don't even realize they're being governed.
- **Global**: These systems aren't tied to a single nation, they operate everywhere.
- **Intelligent**: AI and algorithms are learning how to predict and control human behavior with frightening accuracy.
- **Spiritual**: Behind these systems lie **demonic intelligences** that seek not just to track you, but to **enslave your soul**.

Like Pharaoh in Egypt, these thrones are building a **digital economy of bondage**, but this time, it's virtual chains, not physical ones.

THE DIGITAL WORLD IS NOT NEUTRAL

Most people think the internet, apps, and digital tools are just conveniences. But behind the screen is a powerful **spiritual infrastructure**, a system that shapes desires, beliefs, identity, and destiny. Every click, scroll, and search is feeding a system that is learning you and slowly leading you.

1. **What's really happening?**

- **You are being studied.** Algorithms observe your behavior to predict your next move.
- **You are being formed.** The content you see is designed to mold your values and decisions.
- **You are being monetized.** Your data is sold, your attention auctioned, your time harvested.

In this world, **you are the product**, not the user.

2. **Identity Has Gone Digital**

Once upon a time, your name, reputation, and purpose were formed in your community and before God. Today?

- Your **profile picture** has become your face.
- Your **followers** determine your perceived value.
- Your **bio** defines your existence.
- Your **online history** becomes your digital fingerprint, used by corporations, governments, and AI.

Digital identity has replaced real identity. And when identity is virtual, it becomes **vulnerable**, easily hacked, reshaped, or canceled.

3. Control Has Shifted to the Cloud

We used to think of **kings, armies, and borders** when we talked about power. Now, power sits in **server farms, codebases, and AI systems**.

> **"The kings of the earth set themselves, and the rulers take counsel together..." (Psalm 2:2)**

Today, rulers are not always presidents, they are:

- Tech billionaires
- Data brokers
- AI overlords
- Central banks transitioning to digital currencies

They control:

- What you see (algorithms)
- What you spend (digital finance)
- What you believe (information bubbles)
- Who is silenced (censorship & cancel culture)

These are the **Cyber Thrones**, seats of invisible dominion controlling entire populations without a single bullet fired.

4. Reality Is Being Rewritten

AI can now generate fake voices, fake sermons, fake videos, even fake pastors. Truth is no longer what is **true**, but what is **trending**. This is the age of:

- Deepfakes (manipulated videos)

- AI-generated "prophets"
- Digital discipleship, where TikTok becomes a teacher
- Virtual religions (metaverse churches, crypto covenants)

The spirit of deception has been digitized.

5. The Battle Is for Your Mind and Soul

The Bible says:

> **"As a man thinks in his heart, so is he." (Proverbs 23:7)**

In the digital world:

- Thoughts are suggested.
- Desires are shaped.
- Time is stolen.
- Faith is replaced with fantasy.

When your screen becomes your altar, and your scroll becomes your worship, you **are no longer just online, you are under influence.**

6. The Church Must Not Be Digital Tourists, But Digital Warriors

The digital world isn't evil, but it is a territory. Just like Babylon, Egypt, or Rome, it is a realm filled with idols, commerce, control, and souls.

Believers must:

- Understand the systems.
- Discern the spirits behind platforms.
- Engage prophetically with technology.
- Build alternative systems (Christian media, finance, education, content).

We must reclaim cyberspace as kingdom space.

WHY IT MATTERS

You can no longer afford to ignore or dismiss the digital world. It is:

- Where your children are being shaped.
- Where governments are planning.
- Where spirits are being transferred.
- Where souls are being captured.

But it is also where **God is raising voices**, **pouring out wisdom**, and sending **digital prophets** to redeem the web.

BIBLICAL PARALLEL: THRONES IN HEAVENLY PLACES

In Scripture, **thrones are not just chairs**, they are **spiritual dominions**:

> *"For we wrestle not against flesh and blood, but against principalities, against powers, against the rulers of the darkness of this world, **against spiritual wickedness in high places."* ~ **Ephesians 6:12**

These **high places** today include **digital platforms**, **financial clouds**, and **AI-driven ideologies**, cybernetic high places where decisions are made about wealth, access, censorship, and even justice.

The Battle for Souls in the Digital Realm

Today's wars are not just about oil, land, or weapons, they are about:

- Your attention
- Your beliefs
- Your digital identity
- Your financial freedom
- Your eternal soul

From TikTok to facial recognition, from cashless systems to social credit scores, **the real war is spiritual**, fought through wires, screens, chips, and code.

Yet **we are not called to fear.**

We are called to **rise up** as:

- Cyber prophets
- Digital reformers
- Apostolic technologists
- Marketplace warriors

Who will **reclaim the digital domain for the Kingdom of God.**

> *"The kingdoms of this world have become the kingdoms of our Lord and of His Christ..."* ~ **Revelation 11:15**

CYBER EMPIRES, THE RISE OF DIGITAL THRONES

Peter Schweitzer's "Secret Empires" and the Digital Transformation

In his landmark book *Secret Empires*, **Peter Schweitzer** exposes the hidden world of global elites using power, influence, and technology to maintain control over vast financial resources. The **Secret Empires** are not only political but also **digital** in nature. This hidden web of power stretches across **government, corporations**, and **intelligence agencies**, creating a **digital empire** where decisions about wealth distribution, governance, and human liberties are made behind closed doors.

Schweizer's book highlights how the **convergence of politics and technology** is leading to the creation of **global oligarchies**, where **corporate interests** are aligned with **governmental elites** to secure wealth and control through the **digital infrastructure**. These powers leverage **cyber finance, digital intelligence**, and **information warfare** to control **global markets, surveillance states**, and influence societal norms.

- **Kingdom Insight:** In Christ, we are called to **stand as light in this darkness**, exercising **wisdom** in how we engage with and influence these powers.

  "For we do not wrestle against flesh and blood, but against the rulers, against the authorities, against the cosmic powers over this present darkness, against the spiritual forces of evil in the heavenly places." (**Ephesians 6:12**)

The battle being waged in the **digital realm** is not just about **economic control**; it is a **spiritual battle** for the **souls of men**. As believers, we must recognize this reality and **seek God's guidance** to navigate this complex landscape.

THE DIGITAL FINANCIAL SYSTEM, HIDDEN POWERS AND CRYPTO CAPITALISM

The rise of **cryptocurrencies** and **blockchain technology** has shifted the traditional financial system into a new **digital age**. While **cryptocurrencies** promise financial **freedom** and **decentralization**, they are also subject to manipulation by global elites and intelligence agencies who control the underlying infrastructure. This **crypto-capitalism** opens up a new frontier for the **cyber thrones** of finance to secure power and influence.

Schweizer, in his exploration of **global financial networks**, uncovers the **hidden hand** that shapes global capital flows. **Financial elites** use technology to **control**, **track**, and **regulate** not just money, but entire **nations** and **societies**.

- **Kingdom Insight:** As believers, we are not to be consumed by the world's financial system. We are called to use wisdom and understanding in our **economic dealings**, leveraging resources for **God's Kingdom** rather than personal gain.

  "For the love of money is the root of all evil." (**1 Timothy 6:10**)

INTELLIGENCE AGENCIES AND DIGITAL SURVEILLANCE, THE SPIRITUAL BATTLE FOR CONTROL

The Intelligence Apparatus and Digital Warfare

Intelligence agencies have long been a central part of the **geopolitical struggle** for control. However, in the digital age, the **methods of surveillance** have expanded dramatically. Data is the **new currency**, and **cyber espionage** has become a major battleground. Intelligence agencies are using **AI**, **big data**, and **digital surveillance** to monitor populations, manipulate elections, and disrupt global economies. The **battle for information** is not just about national security, it is about **power** over the very **minds** and **hearts** of people.

Surveillance capitalism is now the primary tool used by digital elites to control populations. **Google, Facebook, Amazon**, and other tech giants have built vast **databases** of personal information, which are then sold to the highest bidder, **government agencies**, **corporations**, and even **shadowy elites**. The **tracking of every digital footprint** is part of a larger **system of control**.

- **Kingdom Insight:** As believers, we must be vigilant, discerning the **spiritual implications** of **digital surveillance**. Our mission is not just to be aware of the systems of this world but to bring the **light of Christ** into these dark systems, challenging the powers of **control** and **manipulation**.

  "The thief comes only to steal and kill and destroy. I came that they may have life and have it abundantly."
  (John 10:10)

The **Kingdom of God** is **not of this world**, but we are called to **transform** and **redeem** it.

THE BATTLE FOR SOULS, DIGITAL TEMPTATION AND THE DECEPTION OF WEALTH

The Digital Battle for Souls

The **digital empire** is not just about **finance** or **surveillance**; it is fundamentally a **battle for souls**. The **internet** and **social media** have become the primary tools of **temptation, deception,** and **idolatry** in the modern world. The **global elites**, with their control over digital platforms, have used these tools to manipulate **public opinion, propagate immorality,** and **undermine traditional values**.

From **digital pornography** to **social justice movements** that seek to redefine morality, the **digital battle for souls** is being fought in the hearts and minds of people through **information warfare**. **Influencers, algorithms,** and **mass media** are shaping public opinion, and in many cases, **leading millions astray**.

- **Kingdom Insight:** As believers, we are called to **renew our minds** through the **Word of God** (Romans 12:2), ensuring that our hearts and minds are not led astray by the deceptive **powers of the digital realm**.

    "For what will it profit a man if he gains the whole world and forfeits his soul?" (**Matthew 16:26**)

We must become **kingdom influencers**, actively engaging the **digital space** with truth, integrity, and compassion, pulling many from the **darkness** and bringing them into the light of Christ.

RECLAIMING CYBER THRONES FOR THE KINGDOM

The **digital empire** is here, and with it comes the **battle for wealth, information,** and most importantly, the **souls of humanity**. As believers in Christ, we must not retreat from this battle but rise up with divine wisdom, discernment, and power. **Cyber thrones,** whether in **finance, intelligence,** or **digital manipulation,** are not beyond the reach of God's influence.

We are called to engage the **digital world** with the **light** of Christ, reclaiming territories for His Kingdom and transforming systems of oppression, manipulation, and darkness into platforms for His glory.

> *"The earth is the LORD's, and the fullness thereof."*
> **(Psalm 24:1)**

Let's take up the **mantle of influence,** becoming active participants in the **digital reformation,** leading the charge in reclaiming **cyber thrones** for **Christ.**

ACTIVATION PRAYER AND PROPHETIC DECREES FOR DIGITAL INFLUENCE

Activation Prayer:

"Father,

I thank You for Your divine wisdom and discernment in navigating the complexities of the digital world.

*Guide me in using technology for Your Kingdom, and help me discern the **spiritual battle** being waged in the digital space.*

Empower me to be a light in the darkness, and may my influence on these platforms draw souls closer to Your truth.

In Jesus' name, Amen."

PROPHETIC DECREES:

I decree that the **digital thrones** of this world are being overturned, and the **Kingdom of God** is advancing through the technology and platforms of the earth.

I decree that the **spiritual battle for souls** in the digital age is being fought with **God's wisdom** and **power**, and His will shall prevail in every sector of society.

I decree that believers are rising as **digital disciples**, reclaiming the cyberspace for **truth**, **justice**, and **righteousness**.

I decree that the **wealth of the wicked** in the digital age is being redirected for **Kingdom purposes**, advancing God's eternal purposes on earth.

"And the gospel of the kingdom will be proclaimed throughout the whole world as a testimony to all nations, and then the end will come." (**Matthew 24:14**)

CHAPTER 12

Stock Market Scrolls: Decoding Spiritual Patterns in Economic Cycles

"Behold, I have filled him with the Spirit of God... to design artistic works." ~ *Exodus 31:3–4 (NKJV)*

THE DIVINE BLUEPRINT OF ECONOMIC CYCLES

The cycles of the stock market, like many aspects of life, follow a predictable pattern, **booms** and **busts**, **bull markets** and **bear markets**, **expansion** and **contraction**. These fluctuations, often seen as purely economic phenomena, have deeper spiritual and cosmic significance that we must learn to discern.

In **Christ**, we are invited to understand these economic patterns not only in **natural terms** but through the **lens of divine wisdom**. By decoding the **spiritual patterns** within these cycles, we begin to perceive **hidden truths** that transcend the material world and reflect God's divine order in the realms of **finance, prosperity**, and **destiny**.

As we explore this chapter, we will draw upon the work of scholars, economists, and spiritual thinkers who have sought to uncover these spiritual patterns, particularly in the context of the **stock market**. From **Ernst Wolff's** analysis of global financial systems to **biblical principles** and ancient teachings, we will look at the **cycles of economy** as not just transactional, but **transformational**, offering us keys to navigating the financial world with wisdom and discernment in **Christ**.

THE SPIRITUAL CYCLES BEHIND ECONOMIC PATTERNS

The Spiritual Nature of Economic Cycles

In both ancient scriptures and contemporary teachings, we observe that **economic cycles** reflect a deeper, spiritual rhythm. **Ecclesiastes 3:1** says, *"To everything there is a season, and a time for every matter under heaven."* The spiritual insight here is that **economic cycles**, like all things in life, have a **season**, a time for increase and a time for decrease.

In the stock market, we observe similar patterns of **seasonality** and **rhythmic fluctuations**. **Boom periods** (where markets expand rapidly) correspond to a time of **growth and increase**, while **recession periods** or **bear markets** reflect a time of **contraction** and **preparation for future growth**. These cycles echo the **biblical principles** of **sowing** and **reaping**, where prosperity comes not just from increase, but from **pruning** and **refinement**.

- **Christ's Kingdom Insight:** The Kingdom of God teaches us that in times of economic **contraction**, God is working to **prepare** us for greater abundance. **Pruning** is necessary for **fruitful growth**. When we are aligned with God's rhythms, we can thrive in both **seasons**. Jesus' teachings about the **parable of the talents** (Matthew 25:14-30) remind us that the key to prosperity is **faithfulness** and **stewardship**, not just accumulation.

  "His master replied, 'Well done, good and faithful servant! You have been faithful with a few things; I will put you in charge of many things. Come and share your master's happiness.'" **(Matthew 25:21)**

The cycle of economic **prosperity** and **recession** is not a cycle of **lack**, but a divine opportunity to **learn**, **grow**, and **steward resources well** for the season of increase.

THE PATTERN OF RISE AND FALL: BIBLICAL FOUNDATIONS

Throughout **scripture**, we see a recurring **pattern** of rise and fall that mirrors the fluctuations of modern economies. The **book of Daniel**, for example, speaks of **Babylon** as a **great kingdom** that will eventually be brought low by divine judgment, only for another kingdom to rise in its place (Daniel 2:31-45). This reflects the **unpredictable rise** and **fall** of economic empires throughout history.

- **The Rise of Babylon:** The Babylonian empire, in its time, was an economic powerhouse, reflecting the rise of a global economic system. It represents how dominant financial systems often seem unshakeable, but their downfall is inevitable when they ignore divine principles of **justice** and **equity**.

- **The Fall of Babylon**: Just as Babylon fell, many modern empires face eventual **economic decline** when they become **corrupt** and **self-serving**, ignoring the broader **spiritual laws** that govern prosperity. This reflects **cycles of judgment** and **divine realignment**, where **God humbles** the proud and raises up the humble.

The **prophet Haggai** speaks to this concept when he writes that God will **shake** the heavens and the earth, **removing** the wealth of the nations to establish His Kingdom (Haggai 2:6-9). This speaks to the **divine intervention** in the economic systems of the world, where God shifts the wealth of the wicked to the righteous.

> *"The silver is mine and the gold is mine,' declares the Lord Almighty. 'The glory of this present house will be greater than the glory of the former house,' says the Lord Almighty."* (**Haggai 2:8-9**)

This passage speaks to how God, in His sovereignty, **redistributes wealth** according to His divine will.

DECODING THE SPIRITUAL PATTERNS OF THE STOCK MARKET

Market Sentiment: The Spiritual Influence of Collective Emotion

The stock market operates not just on **economic fundamentals**, but also on the **sentiment** of its participants. **Fear** and **greed** are powerful motivators in the market, driving investors to make decisions that may not be based on sound financial principles but on their emotional responses to the market's rise or fall.

The Bible speaks of **the heart's influence** on the decisions we make. Proverbs 4:23 says, *"Above all else, guard your heart, for everything you do flows from it."* In the same way that **personal emotions** influence decisions, the **collective heart** of the market (its sentiment) has a profound effect on the **direction of financial markets**.

Understanding this dynamic allows us to discern when market

movements are driven by **irrational fear** or **greed**, and when they are aligned with **divine wisdom**. Investors, businesses, and nations that align their financial decisions with the principles of **faith**, **integrity**, and **trust in God** will not be swayed by market cycles driven by fear and greed.

- **Christ's Kingdom Insight:** Christ teaches us to **seek peace** and **trust in God's provision** even in times of economic uncertainty. In moments of **market instability**, we can remain **rooted in Christ**, recognizing that He is our provider and sustainer, not the fluctuations of the stock market.

  "Therefore, I tell you, do not worry about your life, what you will eat or drink; or about your body, what you will wear. Is not life more than food, and the body more than clothes?" (**Matthew 6:25**)

KINGDOM ECONOMICS AND THE FLOW OF ABUNDANCE

In contrast to the world's economic systems, the **Kingdom of God** operates on principles of **abundance**, not **scarcity**. While the stock market operates on the **principle of competition**, where only a few are favored in a given cycle, the Kingdom operates on the **principle of multiplication**, where all who align themselves with God's Kingdom experience an increase.

- **Christ's Kingdom Insight:** Jesus modeled this principle in the **multiplication of loaves and fishes** (John 6:1-14). In the Kingdom, there is enough for everyone, and the more we give, the more God multiplies our resources. This is the **true law of prosperity**: the more we align with God's heart and principles, the more **abundant life** we experience.

  "Give, and it will be given to you. A good measure, pressed down, shaken together and running over, will be poured into your lap. For with the measure you use, it will be measured to you." (**Luke 6:38**)

PRAYER POINTS

Decoding Financial Cycles & Aligning with Heaven's Economy

1. **I Break Agreement with Manipulated Markets and False Prophets of Wealth**

   "Lord, I repent for trusting in false signals, hype, and speculative fear.

   I break all soul-ties with systems that exalt greed over truth.

   I align my finances with the cycles and timings of Your Spirit, not human manipulation."

2. **I Receive Prophetic Accuracy to Interpret Economic Seasons**

   "Spirit of Wisdom and Revelation, open my eyes to the patterns encoded in global markets.

   Like the sons of Issachar, teach me to discern times and financial movements with precision and faith.

   Let my insight be governed by heaven, not headlines."

3. **I Reject the Spirit of Panic and Anchor Myself in Covenant Stability**

   "I declare: I will not be shaken by downturns, crashes, or trends.

   I stand upon the rock of eternal provision.

   No news, no analyst, no recession can overthrow Jehovah Jireh in my life."

4. **I Activate the Scrolls of Righteous Trade and Kingdom Exchange**

   "I call forth every divine scroll concerning wealth stewardship, innovation, and economic dominion written about me in heaven.

   Let these scrolls be unsealed and executed in real-time.

   I trade in righteousness and build with revelation."

5. **I Redeem the Cycles of Loss, Delay, and Economic Confusion**

"In the name of Jesus, I cancel every demonic cycle of financial loss, delay, and missed opportunity.

I declare a supernatural reversal.

Let the years the locusts have eaten be restored in multiplied measure."

PROPHETIC DIRECTIONS & ACTIVATIONS

1. Financial Charting with the Holy Spirit

Action: Sit in silence and ask the Holy Spirit to show you patterns, in your giving, spending, investments, or income over the past months or years.

Prayer: "Lord, reveal what I missed. Open my eyes to prophetic trends and heavenly rhythms. Teach me to steward with divine timing."

2. Scroll Activation Act

Action: Write a declaration or business/financial goal on paper and lay hands on it, symbolizing your financial scroll.

Prayer: "I activate this scroll in agreement with heaven. Let angels be released to assist, connections be established, and resources flow in sync with this divine timeline."

3. Anointing Your Decision-Making

Action: Anoint your head with oil and declare:

"I anoint my mind for prophetic intelligence.

I will not be moved by fear, greed, or hype.

I am a financial priest, discerning cycles with divine clarity."

PROPHETIC WATCHMAN DECREE

Declare aloud:

"I take my place as a financial watchman on the wall.

I discern patterns before they manifest.

I do not chase trends; I govern times.

Let righteous trade rise and the scrolls of Zion's economy be fulfilled."

IN SUMMARY: ALIGNING ECONOMIC CYCLES WITH CHRIST'S DIVINE TIMING

In conclusion, **economic cycles** are not simply random events, but are deeply connected to **spiritual rhythms** that reflect **divine timing**. By understanding these cycles through the lens of scripture and **Kingdom wisdom**, we can navigate the stock market and other financial realms with **discernment, faith**, and **wisdom**.

As the world goes through its various cycles of **prosperity** and **contraction**, let us remain anchored in the **eternal truth** that **Christ is our ultimate source** of abundance, and He will guide us through both the **storms** and **seasons** of life.

By aligning our financial practices with **Kingdom principles**, we will not only **thrive** in every season but also become **agents of transformation** in the world's economic systems. Through this alignment, we will experience a **revelation** of **God's economy**, where all things are **possible**, and we will see the wealth of the wicked transferred to the righteous as part of His divine plan for global **reformation**.

May we understand and embrace these **spiritual patterns** in all economic cycles, and may we live in **obedience** to the guidance of the Holy Spirit, trusting that God's Kingdom economics will always **sustain** us.

CHAPTER 13

The Innovation Mandate: Creators, Inventions, and Kingdom Culture

"I have filled him with the Spirit of God… to design artistic works." ~Exodus 31:3–4 (NKJV)

THE CALL TO WALK IN DIVINE INNOVATION

Innovation and creativity are not merely products of human intellect or random chance. They are a part of **God's divine blueprint** for humanity. From the very beginning, **God created the heavens and the earth** and **mankind in His image** (Genesis 1:1-27). This divine act of creation was not a one-time event, but an ongoing mandate for humanity to **create**, **innovate**, and **cultivate** the earth.

As co-creators with Christ, we are invited to partner with the divine to bring forth new inventions, ideas, and solutions that can radically transform the world. This is the **Innovation Mandate**, a spiritual calling to reflect God's nature as **Creator** and to carry out His work on earth through creative and innovative solutions. In this chapter, we will examine how **creators**, **inventors**, and **innovators** can align with **Kingdom culture** to shape the world and the marketplace with **divine wisdom**.

This chapter will not only explore the power of creativity in the context of Christ's Kingdom but also examine how innovative ideas and inventions have historically changed societies and industries, revealing the **Kingdom's potential** embedded in every creative act.

THE DIVINE MANDATE TO CREATE

The Foundation of Innovation: Divine Creation

The **divine mandate** to create is established in Genesis, where we are told that **God made man in His own image** and commanded him to **be fruitful, multiply, and fill the earth** (Genesis 1:28). The first humans, Adam and Eve, were created not only to steward the earth but also to engage in creative work, naming the animals, cultivating the land, and fulfilling God's purposes on earth. This reflects God's **creative nature**, which He imparts to humanity.

When we create, whether through art, technology, business, or systems, we are reflecting God's image. Our **innovations** and **inventions** are expressions of the **creative power** He has bestowed upon us. Every breakthrough, from the discovery of fire to space exploration, is a testimony of humanity's **ability to create** as we partner with God in His mission to shape the world.

- **Scriptural Insight**: The Bible also speaks of the **Holy Spirit** as the **Spirit of Wisdom** who guides us into **creative solutions**. In **Exodus 31:3**, God fills **Bezalel** with the Spirit of God, giving him wisdom, understanding, and knowledge to create artistic works for the **tabernacle**. This example shows that creativity is not only for the secular world but also for **divine purposes**.

  "I have filled him with the Spirit of God, with wisdom, with understanding, with knowledge, and with all kinds of skills." **(Exodus 31:3)**

As creators, we are given the **Holy Spirit** to guide and empower us in our creative endeavors, whether in business, technology, arts, or other fields.

THE ROLE OF CREATIVITY IN THE KINGDOM

In Christ, creativity becomes more than just a tool for personal success; it is a **divine assignment** to bring forth solutions that serve the **advancement of God's Kingdom** on earth. Jesus Christ, Himself, was the ultimate innovator, bringing forth the **Kingdom of Heaven** through teachings, miracles, and breakthroughs that defied the natural world. His disciples were sent out to **spread the Gospel** and bring forth the **Kingdom culture** wherever they went.

- **Kingdom Principle**: The **Kingdom of God** is not confined to religious activities alone; it extends to every aspect of life, including the marketplace, technology, science, and innovation. When we engage in creative work with a Kingdom mindset, we are not just creating for ourselves or for personal gain, but we are **partnering with God** to establish His rule and reign in every sphere of life.

In the **Lord's Prayer** (Matthew 6:9-10), Jesus taught His disciples to pray, *"Your Kingdom come, Your will be done, on earth as it is in* *heaven."* This prayer is a **declaration of God's dominion** over all creation, including the world of **ideas**, **inventions**, and **innovations**.

By tapping into the creative nature of God, we have the ability to bring forth Kingdom ideas that will transform societies, industries, and ultimately, nations. This aligns with **Isaiah 60:1-3**, where the nations come to the light of God's glory. As creators in Christ, our inventions and innovations are a way for the **world** to experience God's **light** and **glory**.

THE INNOVATION MANIFESTO: A DECLARATION OF PURPOSE

The **Innovation Manifesto** is a personal declaration that believers can make to align themselves with God's purposes for creativity and innovation. It is a **commitment** to use our creative gifts for the **advancement of the Kingdom**. This manifesto serves as a guide to ensure that all creative endeavors are rooted in divine wisdom and aligned with Christ's mission on earth.

INNOVATION MANIFESTO:

1. **I am a co-creator with Christ**: I acknowledge that my ability to create, invent, and innovate comes from God. I am not the source of my creativity; He is. As a co-creator with Christ, I seek to fulfill His will through my creative work.

2. **I innovate for Kingdom impact**: My creativity is not for personal glory but for advancing the Kingdom of God. I will use my gifts to bring **transformation** to my sphere of influence, creating solutions that reflect God's love, justice, and righteousness.

3. **I walk in wisdom and discernment**: I will not rush into creating or innovating without seeking divine wisdom. I will inquire of the Holy Spirit and listen for His guidance, knowing that true wisdom is the foundation of all lasting innovation.

4. **I embrace creativity as divine responsibility**: Innovation is not

just an option; it is a **responsibility**. I am called to be a steward of the creative gifts God has entrusted to me, using them to build systems, technologies, and solutions that align with His will.

5.   **I create with an eternal perspective**: I recognize that the work I do has eternal value. I will create with a long-term view, knowing that my inventions, ideas, and solutions will impact future generations.

6.   **I seek to serve, not to be served**: My creativity is meant to serve others. I will use my innovations to meet the needs of the oppressed, the poor, and the marginalized, bringing hope and healing through my work.

7.   **I create in unity with others**: Innovation is not a solitary pursuit. I will collaborate with others, believers and non-believers alike, to bring about solutions that honor God and bless humanity.

8.   **I will not compromise my values**: In every aspect of my innovation, I will remain true to the principles of Christ. I will not sacrifice my integrity, honesty, or Kingdom values for personal gain or worldly success.

TO THOSE STILL SEARCHING

If you've been walking in innovation but have never considered its divine origin, maybe it's time to ask, "Who gave me this gift, and what is its ultimate purpose?"

Perhaps this is your invitation to meet the Creator of creativity, Jesus Christ.

The fact that you are drawn to create, to build, to design, or to lead is not random. It's a sign. There is a higher calling waiting to awaken your spirit and align your gift. Christ does not cancel your creativity, He completes it. In Him, your ideas gain eternal relevance.

THE ROLE OF CREATORS AND INNOVATORS IN SOCIETY

The Power of Inventions in Transforming Nations

Throughout history, **inventions** have not only changed industries but have reshaped entire societies. From the **printing press** to the **internet**, these breakthroughs have brought about **reformation** and **global transformation**. In a similar way, the Kingdom culture calls creators to **innovate** in ways that will radically **shift** society towards **God's purposes**.

- **Scriptural Foundation**: In **Proverbs 8:12**, wisdom speaks of herself as the source of knowledge and invention: *"I, wisdom, dwell together with prudence; I possess knowledge and discretion."* This verse highlights that **wisdom** is a key ingredient in the creative process. Wisdom, imparted by the **Holy Spirit**, is the **foundation** of all true innovation.

Inventions that align with God's wisdom are meant to **serve humanity** and **advance His Kingdom**. Consider the example of **medical innovations** that **heal diseases** or **technological advancements** that provide **better education**, all are expressions of God's love and care for His creation.

- **Kingdom Culture and Innovation**: As creators in the Kingdom, we must not be motivated by selfish ambition or greed. Instead, our motivations must align with the Kingdom's principles of **service, justice, and love**. Innovations should seek to **serve others**, bringing prosperity and healing to society, and advancing God's purposes on earth.

THE POWER OF IDEAS IN THE DIGITAL AGE

In today's world, the digital age has brought about a **global revolution** in how information is exchanged and how ideas are shared. From **artificial intelligence** to **blockchain technology**, new **ideas** are shaping the way we live, work, and communicate. This presents an incredible opportunity for creators and innovators to **align these technologies** with the **Kingdom of God**.

- **Divine Perspective**: Technology, when used in alignment with Christ's principles, has the power to bring about **global transformation**. The **internet** and **social media platforms** can be used to **spread the Gospel**, build **community**, and **raise awareness** on important issues. However, when divorced from Kingdom values, they can also be used for evil purposes.

- **Kingdom Influence in Innovation**: As believers, we are called to **discern** how these innovations and technologies can be used to **expand God's Kingdom** and to **create solutions** that address the **needs** of the poor, oppressed, and marginalized. By doing so, we fulfill God's mandate to **create** and **innovate** for His glory.

INNOVATION IN ALIGNMENT WITH CHRIST AND SCRIPTURES

The Pattern of Christ: Innovating for the Kingdom

The **life of Jesus** provides the ultimate model of how to **create** and **innovate** in alignment with God's will. Jesus' ministry was one of constant innovation, whether in **teaching, healing**, or **preaching**, He brought forth **new solutions** to the **problems** faced by the world. He was not confined to the old religious systems but brought a **new way** of thinking about God, humanity, and society.

- **Kingdom Innovation**: Christ did not come merely to **teach**; He came to **transform** the world. As innovators in His Kingdom, we are called not just to create for the sake of creation, but to **bring transformation** through our creative endeavors. Our inventions, ideas, and solutions should be shaped by **divine wisdom** and should seek to **redeem** the systems of the world, bringing them into alignment with God's Kingdom.

- The Holy Spirit is **essential** in the process of innovation. Just as God filled **Bezalel** with His Spirit to design the tabernacle (Exodus 31:3), He also fills believers with wisdom and creativity to accomplish the works of the Kingdom in the world.

Innovation and creativity are not merely intellectual exercises; they are **divinely inspired acts** that carry the fingerprint of the Creator.

- As we step into the **Innovation Mandate**, we must actively seek the **guidance of the Holy Spirit**, allowing Him to inspire us, direct our steps, and reveal hidden ideas. This spiritual empowerment goes beyond natural talent, it is the **supernatural enablement** that allows believers to solve problems, develop new systems, and create in ways that transform society.

PRACTICAL STEPS FOR WALKING IN THE INNOVATION MANDATE

Embrace a Kingdom Mindset

To walk in the **Innovation Mandate**, we must have a **Kingdom mindset**. This mindset transforms the way we approach creativity, business, and every aspect of life. We must recognize that we are not creating for **selfish purposes** or simply to **advance our own agendas**. Instead, we are creating to **serve the Kingdom of God** and to make His will known on earth.

- **Action Step**: Begin each creative project with prayer, seeking God's direction and asking Him to align your heart with His will. Ask the Holy Spirit to guide your thoughts and ideas.

SEEK DIVINE WISDOM AND UNDERSTANDING

Innovation is rooted in **divine wisdom**. It is not about reinventing the wheel but about tapping into God's **endless creativity** and using it for His glory. Believers must actively seek the wisdom of God, which comes from a deep relationship with Him through prayer, study of the Word, and a life of obedience.

- **Action Step**: Commit to regular times of prayer and Bible study.

As you meditate on the Word of God, ask the Holy Spirit to reveal innovative ideas that align with His will.

BUILD A COMMUNITY OF KINGDOM INNOVATORS

Innovation thrives in **community**. As believers, we are not called to walk alone but to collaborate with others who share the same vision for Kingdom advancement. Surround yourself with other **creators**, **innovators**, and **entrepreneurs** who are committed to walking in the Innovation Mandate.

- **Action Step**: Find or create a community of like-minded believers who are also pursuing innovation for the Kingdom. Share ideas, collaborate on projects, and pray for one another's success.

TAKE BOLD ACTION AND STEP INTO THE UNKNOWN

Innovation often requires us to step into **uncharted territory**, to take risks, face uncertainty, and trust God to provide. It requires **boldness** and **faith**. As innovators, we must trust that God will equip us for the tasks He has called us to.

- **Action Step**: Take the first step in faith. Don't wait for everything to be perfect before you begin. Trust that God will guide you along the way as you step out in obedience.

PRAYER POINTS

Activating the Mantle of Innovation and Divine Creativity

1. **I Awaken the Creative Spirit Within Me**

   "Lord, breathe upon the gifts You planted in me before the

foundations of the world.

I reject every lie that says I am not creative, useful, or visionary.

I declare: I carry the mind of Christ — the ultimate Innovator and Creator."

2. I Break Every Mental and Cultural Limitation Placed on My Innovation

"I break free from every system, tradition, or mindset that said I must conform.

I reject the fear of failure, fear of man, and fear of being misunderstood.

I walk boldly into new solutions, systems, and strategies ordained by heaven."

3. I Receive Divine Blueprints for Kingdom Innovations

"Holy Spirit, download to me the blueprints hidden in heaven's archives.

Give me ideas that solve problems, bless nations, and reveal Christ's dominion.

I receive inventions that carry prophetic purpose."

4. I Release My Hands from Procrastination and Perfectionism

"I cancel every delay caused by doubt, overthinking, or self-criticism.

I anoint my hands for action.

I declare: What I see, I will build. What I dream, I will deliver."

5. I Align My Creativity with Kingdom Culture, Not Worldly Influence

"My creativity will not serve vanity, ego, or exploitation.

I dedicate my talents to the glory of God.

My ideas will carry righteousness, justice, beauty, and truth."

PROPHETIC DIRECTIONS & ACTIVATIONS

1. Innovation Journal Activation

Action: Open a dedicated journal or digital space. Title it *"Heavenly Blueprints."*

Prayer: "Lord, as I write in this book, let it become a scroll of prophetic creativity.

Speak to me in visions, impressions, ideas, and concepts.

Let my pen partner with the breath of God."

2. Prophetic Act of Release

Action: Take an old notebook, sketch, voice memo, or idea you shelved due to fear—and lay your hand on it.

Declare:

"This seed shall live again. I call it forth from the grave of delay.

Let divine breath revive this concept for Kingdom impact."

3. Anointing Your Workspace

Action: Anoint your laptop, studio, tools, or workspace with oil.

Prayer: "This space is a portal for Kingdom creativity.

Every idea conceived here will be governed by integrity and excellence.

Let angels surround this environment with inspiration and protection."

4. Cultural Gate Reversal Decree

Declare aloud:

"I will not imitate Babylon to be accepted.

I create by revelation, not replication.

Let Kingdom culture rise through my voice, my art, my innovation.

I am not here to fit in, I am here to reform."

IN SUMMARY: LIVING THE INNOVATION MANDATE

Walking in the **Innovation Mandate** is not merely about **creating** for the sake of creating. It is about **partnering with God** to bring transformation to the world. It is about creating with a **Kingdom mindset**, using divine wisdom, and collaborating with others to produce solutions that serve humanity and advance the Kingdom of God.

As we walk in this mandate, we must remember that we are not walking alone. The Holy Spirit empowers us, and the Creator Himself walks with us, guiding our steps and illuminating the path ahead. By living according to the **Innovation Manifesto**, we can confidently step into our roles as Kingdom innovators, shaping the world for God's glory and for the advancement of His Kingdom on earth.

May you walk boldly in the **Innovation Mandate**, knowing that as a creator in Christ, you have been called to **bring Heaven to Earth** through your creativity, inventions, and ideas.

CHAPTER 14

Deep Sea Wealth: Mysteries of Marine Trade and Hidden Treasures

"The abundance of the sea shall be turned to you, the wealth of the nations shall come to you." ~Isaiah 60:5 (NKJV)

THE MYSTICAL CURRENTS BENEATH THE WATERS

From the beginning of time, the **seas** have held profound mysteries. Beneath the crashing waves and deep waters lie **hidden treasures**, **ancient trade routes**, **mystical gateways**, and **untapped wealth** that are both **physical** and **spiritual** in nature. Throughout Scripture, ancient texts, and scientific discoveries, the oceans have been portrayed as not just bodies of water but as realms of **power**, **commerce**, and **hidden resources** that shape the destinies of nations.

In this chapter, we will explore the spiritual and geopolitical significance of marine trade and treasures, the dependence of ancient empires on the wealth of the seas, groundbreaking scientific discoveries about undersea resources, and mystical revelations hidden in the deep. By examining Scripture, ancient records, and modern research, we will decode how, through Christ, humanity can reclaim dominion over these waters, not merely as physical spaces but as realms of influence, wealth, and divine mystery. This is a call to believers, scientists, the ancient custodians of wisdom, and global leaders: to recognize the seas as prophetic frontiers, where the destinies of nations are shaped and the hidden riches of the earth await righteous stewardship.

Both **Dr. Adonijah Ogbonnaya** and **Ian Clayton** teach about the **mystical dimensions** of creation, that the **waters** are not just physical but **gateways** and **realms** that store **knowledge, resources**, and **mysteries** waiting for the sons of God to access through **intimacy with Christ**.

Dr. Adonijah often speaks about the **"deep places"** where the wisdom of God is encoded, and how **sons of light** must engage these realms with holiness, wisdom, and righteous mandate.

Ian Clayton teaches about **trading floors**, where souls and systems trade in heavenly courts, and how the waters, including the seas, represent places where **unrighteous trades** occurred, but where **righteous trades** can now be made in Christ to reclaim dominion.

Thus, as we engage this chapter, we come not as **beggars** but as **sons of the Most High,** ready to walk on the waters, subdue chaos, and extract the treasures reserved for the righteous.

ANCIENT PERSPECTIVES ON THE SEAS AND WEALTH

Oceans as Pathways of Power and Wealth

In ancient times, **civilizations rose and fell** based on their mastery over the seas. The **Phoenicians**, the **Egyptians**, the **Romans**, and other ancient powers all understood that the **sea was a corridor of commerce**, enabling **trade**, **wealth accumulation**, and **cultural influence**.

- The **Phoenician empire** built its wealth almost entirely on maritime trade. They were expert sailors who controlled crucial trade routes, transporting **precious metals, cedarwood, glass,** and **purple dye** (which was extremely valuable) across the Mediterranean.

- **Ancient Egypt** used the Nile River (a symbolic spiritual gateway) to access resources and build their dynasties, understanding that controlling the waters was equivalent to controlling wealth.

- **Scriptural Perspective:**

In the Bible, the wealth of the seas is referenced prophetically:

> *"Then you shall see and be radiant, and your heart shall thrill and exult, because the abundance of the sea shall be turned to you, the wealth of the nations shall come to you."* **(Isaiah 60:5, ESV)**

This indicates that **dominion over marine realms** was prophesied as a blessing for God's people, linking sea-based wealth directly to the promises of God.

SPIRITUAL SYMBOLISM OF THE SEA

In ancient Jewish mysticism and biblical literature, the **sea** often represents **chaos, untamed power,** but also a **storehouse of hidden mysteries** that belong to God.

- **Job 38:16** records God asking Job:

  "Have you journeyed to the springs of the sea or walked in the recesses of the deep?"

Here, the **recesses of the sea** are described as **unknown realms**, a hidden dimension of creation that remains mysterious to mankind but fully accessible to God.

- **Ancient Sumerian and Akkadian texts** also reference the deep sea (known as the "Apsu") as the source of **primordial wisdom** and **hidden treasures**, though often corrupted by myths of marine deities, which the Gospel redeems and reinterprets through Christ as Creator of all things.

SCIENTIFIC EXPLORATION OF THE DEEP SEA'S WEALTH

Hidden Wealth Beneath the Oceans

Modern scientific exploration reveals that the **oceans are brimming** with wealth:

- **Mineral Deposits**: Undersea mountains and ridges host **manganese nodules, cobalt, nickel, rare earth elements**, and **gold**, critical for modern technology.

- **Oil and Gas Reserves**: A massive percentage of the world's untapped **petroleum** and **natural gas** lies beneath the ocean floor.

- **Marine Biotechnology**: New pharmaceutical compounds are being discovered in deep-sea organisms, providing **medical breakthroughs**.

- **Ancient Shipwrecks and Treasures**: Thousands of ancient shipwrecks containing **gold, silver, jewels**, and **artifacts** lie on the seabeds, preserving untold wealth and history.

Thus, scientifically, the sea is not an empty void but a **warehouse of wealth**.

ECONOMIC CONTROL OF THE MARINE TRADE ROUTES

Today, control of **marine trade** still defines **economic power**:

- Over **90% of global trade** is conducted by sea.

- **Strategic sea routes** like the **Suez Canal, Panama Canal,** and **Strait of Malacca** remain choke points of international power.

In modern finance, those who control the **maritime logistics** often control the **flow of global commerce**, an ancient truth still relevant.

Scriptural Perspective:

Psalm 24:1 declares:

> **"The earth is the LORD's, and the fullness thereof, the world and those who dwell therein."**

Thus, even though worldly empires contend for control of the seas, ultimately **all marine wealth belongs to the Lord**, and He can transfer it to His people in divine timing.

SPIRITUAL AND MYSTICAL REVELATION ON DEEP SEA WEALTH

1. Mystical Dimensions of the Waters

Early Christian mystics and ancient seers understood the **waters as spiritual thresholds**:

- The **deep** (Hebrew: *Tehom*) in Genesis 1:2 represents the **primal waters of creation**, a place where **raw potential** waits to be shaped by divine command.

- **The seas** are often depicted as realms where **angels, spirits,** and even **strongholds** exist. (Revelation 13 speaks symbolically of beasts arising from the sea, representing emerging powers.)

Thus, **wealth hidden in the sea** can be seen spiritually as treasures that must be **unlocked through spiritual authority**, prayer, prophetic declaration, and strategic action.

2. Mystical Trade and Redemption

Dr. Adonijah teaches that unrighteous marine powers operated through ancient unrighteous "trades", exchanges of souls, destinies, and resources. These trades must be **broken**, and new **righteous trades** must be **established in Christ**.

- **Scripture Reference**:

  "Thus says the Lord, your Redeemer... I will give you the treasures of darkness and hidden riches of secret places..." **(Isaiah 45:2-3)**

Through **repentance, legal repentance in the courts of heaven,** and **righteous trading,** believers unlock the **wealth systems of the Kingdom**, including those tied to the deep waters.

3. Walking on the Waters

Ian Clayton often teaches that walking on the waters (as Christ did) is a **prophetic model** for walking above the unstable, chaotic economies and spiritual currents of the world.

- **Prophetic Key**:

  When Peter looked at Christ (Matthew 14:29), he walked above the waters; but when he looked at the storm, he sank.

  Focus on Christ keeps you in dominion over marine wealth and global commerce.

  Thus, as Kingdom believers, we **engage the deep**, but our **eyes remain fixed on Yeshua**, not on the storms or chaos of global economies.

4. Christ's Dominion Over the Sea

Jesus demonstrated His authority over the waters multiple times:

- He **walked on the sea** (Matthew 14:25), showing total dominion.
- He **rebuked** the storm (Mark 4:39), commanding peace.
- His first disciples were **fishermen**, drawing from the wealth of the seas in their daily lives.

Christ reveals that **in Him**, we reclaim the **original dominion mandate** over both land and sea (Genesis 1:28).

Prophetic Declaration:

> *"In Christ, I have authority over the deep. I call forth hidden treasures of the waters ordained for the Kingdom. The wealth of the seas is aligned to serve the purposes of the Lord through my life."*

PRACTICAL APPLICATIONS AND KINGDOM ACTIVATION

Engaging the Wealth of the Sea

How can Kingdom-minded believers engage the territorial thrones that govern the wealth of the seas, prophetically, mystically, and economically?

Behind the maritime economies of the world are ancient thrones, powers that manipulate trade, resource control, migration, piracy, and territorial conflict through the sea. These thrones often express themselves through global shipping, undersea riches, naval power, marine spirits, and dark spiritual pacts made by nations or corporations. But **the dominion mandate** in Christ calls us to **overthrow these thrones** and **reclaim sea-based dominion**, not just for profit, but for justice, stewardship, and Kingdom advancement.

I. Discern the Thrones Over Marine Territories

- Understand that the seas are not neutral, they are occupied by spiritual authorities that must be dethroned (Job 41, Isaiah 27:1).

- Thrones such as Leviathan, Rahab, or unnamed marine principalities influence trade, climate events, and territorial conflicts.

- Ask the Lord for discernment regarding these maritime thrones connected to your nation or industry.

  "Who shut up the sea behind doors when it burst forth...?" (Job 38:8)

II. Prophetic Intercession Over the Waters

- Intercessors can contest demonic thrones by:

  - **Praying over oceans, ports, rivers, and naval power centers.**

  - **Breaking spiritual pacts that nations made with marine entities.**

  - **Declaring Psalm 24:1 –** *"The earth is the Lord's... and the fullness thereof."*

Practical: Print or project a global map, mark strategic seas and trade zones (e.g., Suez Canal, South China Sea, Gulf of Guinea), and intercede over them as spiritual gates.

III. Mystical Engagement with the Thrones of the Deep

- Engage the heavenly blueprint for oceanic dominion. Ask for:

  - Scrolls of authority over marine domains.

  - Encounters in the spirit where God reveals hidden riches or shows corrupt thrones being dismantled.

- Use communion, water, or prophetic symbols to redeem the waters.

Ask the Lord, "Show me the throne behind this ocean. Let Your government rise in its place."

IV. Engage Through Righteous Trade and Stewardship

- Trade righteously in the spirit through offerings, prophetic acts, and declarations, reclaiming lost or stolen thrones of wealth.

- Encourage Kingdom entrepreneurs to occupy marine industries with integrity and revelation:

  - Fisheries, undersea energy, shipping, AI-ocean logistics, water purification.

  - Invite God into their boardrooms and port decisions.

V. Unlock Access for All Believers (Big or Small)

This realm is not reserved for prophets or billionaires. Every Kingdom citizen can engage:

Type of Believer	How They Can Engage
Intercessor	Pray over port cities, declare God's dominion over the waters, break Leviathan cycles.
Mystic	Ask God for visions of thrones under the sea, engage in spiritual journeys to claim scrolls of marine inheritance.
Entrepreneur	Seek wisdom for clean maritime innovation; trade righteously under God's government.
Student/ Youth	Study maritime history and prophecy; pray for righteous dominion in the future of oceans.
Church Leader	Teach your congregation about thrones in trade and the sea; hold prophetic services for marine gates.

VI. VI. Prophetic Activations

- **Water Bowl Declaration: Anoint a bowl of water and declare,** *"This represents the seas. We redeem them from dark thrones. Let God's Kingdom arise over the waters!"*

- **Communion by the River: Take communion at a body of water. Speak over the marine domain and reclaim it for Christ.**

- **Throne Mapping: Create a map of marine gates and ask God to reveal what thrones exist there and who in the Kingdom is called to confront them.**

FINAL DECLARATION

"We stand not as tourists on the beach but as heirs of dominion. The seas no longer belong to Rahab or Leviathan; they belong to Christ. We reclaim the thrones of maritime wealth, not for exploitation, but for the glory of the Kingdom, the healing of the nations, and the justice of our God!"

ACTIVATION PRAYER: RELEASING THE WEALTH OF THE SEAS

Father in the name of Yeshua HaMashiach (Jesus Christ),

I come boldly into Your courts by the blood of the Lamb.

I repent for any unrighteous trades, blood covenants, or soul ties that may have occurred in my generational line through marine kingdoms or unrighteous altars.

I renounce every agreement knowingly or unknowingly made with the marine spirits of Leviathan, Rahab, or any other principality operating through the waters.

By the authority of Christ, I break every ungodly covenant and trade made on or beneath the waters.

I stand on the foundation of Your Word that the earth and the fullness thereof belongs to You.

Today, I align with the heavenly trading floors of righteousness, peace, and joy in the Holy Spirit.

I call forth the abundance of the seas ordained for Kingdom purposes.

I receive divine strategies, hidden treasures, innovations, and revelations stored within the deep.

I release my spirit to walk upon the waters in faith, authority, and wisdom.

Let the gates of marine commerce be opened to the righteous.

Let every ancient embargo and blockade over my wealth, inheritance, and mandate from the seas be shattered by fire!

I decree dominion over the marine realms under the Lordship of Christ.

Father, let Your Kingdom come and Your will be done through my life concerning the wealth of the seas!

In Yeshua's Name, Amen.

PROPHETIC DECREES: WALKING IN AUTHORITY OVER DEEP SEA WEALTH

1. I decree that the **abundance of the seas** is turned toward me in alignment with Isaiah 60:5!

2. I decree that **hidden treasures** stored in darkness and deep waters (Isaiah 45:3) are being revealed and transferred into the hands of Kingdom sons and daughters!

3. I decree that every **marine stronghold** resisting my assignment collapses under the authority of Jesus Christ!

4. I decree I am seated with Christ above all marine powers, principalities, and wickedness, and I exercise dominion by righteousness!

5. I decree innovation, creative wealth ideas, and marine resources come into my jurisdiction under Kingdom government!

6. I decree that I walk upon the waters of commerce, innovation, and marine wealth without fear, fully aligned with Heaven's blueprint!

7. I decree the "deep" yields its strength to me as a faithful steward of God's mysteries!

IN SUMMARY: MARCHING FORWARD INTO DEEP SEA WEALTH

The **deep-sea wealth** is not just a natural phenomenon; it is a **spiritual reality**. Hidden treasures beneath the oceans reflect the **hidden wisdom** that God desires to reveal to His sons and daughters (Proverbs 25:2).

In Christ, we are called to **recover**, **steward**, and **redeem** the wealth of the seas for Kingdom purposes. As we walk in wisdom, faith, and prophetic insight, we will see Isaiah's prophecy fulfilled, that the **abundance of the sea** shall be turned toward the righteous, and the wealth of the nations shall flow into the hands of those aligned with the heart of God.

As you complete this activation, know that the **deep-sea realms** of wealth, wisdom, innovation, and dominion are not just for natural exploration but for **spiritual stewardship**.

The waters are prophetic gateways awaiting sons and daughters who will **trade righteously**, **govern wisely**, and **redeem hidden treasures** for the expansion of God's Kingdom on earth.

You are not a victim of the economic systems, you are an ambassador of the Kingdom of Light, called to extract, steward, and redistribute the wealth of the nations in righteousness.

> **Psalm 107:23-24 (NIV):** *"Some went out on the sea in ships; they were merchants on the mighty waters. They saw the works of the Lord, his wonderful deeds in the deep."*

It's your time to see the **wonderful deeds in the deep!**

CHAPTER 15

Territorial Thrones and Geopolitical Architectures: The Dominion Mandate

"Ask of Me, and I will give You the nations for Your inheritance." ~Psalm 2:8 (NKJV)

RECLAIMING THE THRONES OF THE EARTH

Throughout history, the shaping of nations, economies, and global influence has not been random, it has been driven by **territorial thrones** and **geopolitical architectures**. What we call history, war, and diplomacy are often the visible outworkings of invisible spiritual governance. Borders are not merely drawn by human hands; they are often the result of spiritual battles and covenants.

Ancient texts, scientific research, prophetic revelation, and the eternal Scriptures agree: **behind every seat of power lies a spiritual throne**, one that is either aligned with darkness or submitted to the light of Christ. These thrones influence **nations, currencies, trade routes, alliances**, and even **natural resources**.

In Christ, we are not called to be passive observers of these dynamics. We are called to **discern the thrones, engage them in spiritual warfare**, and **overthrow unrighteous dominions**, not simply to dismantle them, but to **build nations on righteousness, justice**, and **truth**.

This chapter will explore:

- The territorial dynamics that shape global power and destiny.

- The **spiritual architecture** behind empires, military powers, financial centers, and intelligence agencies.

- And how the **sons of God**, through wisdom, prophetic engagement, and governmental authority, are called to **inherit the nations** (Psalm 2:8).

We will journey through:

- **Ancient prophetic records** (from Daniel to Enoch),

- **Scientific and political theory** (geopolitics, national borders, globalism),

- And the **eternal Word of God** to understand the profound **Dominion Mandate** that Christ has entrusted to His Ecclesia, the legislative Body of Heaven on Earth.

This is about more than reclaiming money, this is about reclaiming

nations, territories, and **spiritual architecture.**

> *"The kingdoms of this world have become the kingdoms of our Lord and of His Christ."* (**Revelation 11:15**)

IN-DEPTH EXPLORATION

1. The Ancient Battle for Territories

In the days of **Daniel**, the prophet encountered the **Prince of Persia** (Daniel 10:13), a **territorial principality** resisting the will of God over a geopolitical realm.

> **Daniel 10:13**
>
> *"But the prince of the Persian kingdom resisted me for twenty-one days. Then Michael, one of the chief princes, came to help me..."*

This highlights that **every territory**, whether a city, a nation, or a continent, has **spiritual governance** behind its physical governance.

Kings may sit on thrones, but **invisible forces** influence their decrees.

In ancient history, empires such as Egypt, Babylon, Assyria, Greece, and Rome operated under the influence of **cosmic thrones**, celestial powers that dictated **economic, military,** and **religious policies**.

Even **scientific archaeological studies** reveal patterns: civilizations rose and fell according to **energy cycles, cosmic alignments,** and **territorial spiritual warfare**.

In the **Kabbalistic teachings**, territories are viewed as **vessels** for either divine light or demonic distortion, depending on the stewardship of the people and their leaders.

Thus, **territorial thrones** are **ancient realities**, not modern inventions.

2. 2. Geopolitical Architectures: Ancient to Modern

The global order we witness today, nations, borders, alliances, wars, sanctions, and even economic "aid", is not new. These modern expressions are **repackaged manifestations of ancient territorial dominions**, rooted in spiritual systems and occult technologies that have shaped the destiny of empires for millennia.

"The kingdoms of this world..." (Rev 11:15) were never neutral. They were always **territorial expressions of spiritual thrones**, whether Babylon, Rome, Egypt, or modern superpowers.

a.   Spiritual Covenants Hidden in Plain Sight

Beneath every international treaty, policy directive, and global summit lie **invisible agreements**, forged not only by men but often sealed in the spirit realm through oaths, bloodlines, and rituals. These covenants empower spiritual forces that **claim legal access to territories**, populations, and resources.

Many governmental decisions, seemingly rational or diplomatic, are often **steered by covenants** made by founding fathers, secret orders, or ruling elites, covenants that determine how a nation responds to war, wealth, immigration, or even pandemics.

b.   Secret Societies and Occult Infrastructures

Modern researchers like **Peter Schweizer** (on political corruption), **John Perkins** (on economic hitmen), and others have exposed how **secretive power structures** shape economies, assassinate leaders, and enforce global compliance, not through bullets alone, but through **banking systems, legal instruments, and cultural propaganda**.

These infrastructures are deeply rooted in ancient occult patterns:

- **City layouts** reflect ancient ziggurat and Masonic geometry (e.g., Washington D.C., Vatican, Paris).

- **Global policy documents** often echo language from mystery religions and secret orders.

- **Economic institutions**, like the World Bank or IMF, can function like spiritual high places, issuing "blessings" or "curses" in the form of debt, aid, or sanctions.

c.   Supranational Thrones and Economic Dominion

According to economist **Ernst Wolff**, organizations such as the

IMF, World Bank, and WEF often bypass national sovereignty. They do not just provide guidance, they **reconstruct economies** through **conditional loans, technocratic governance, and digital surveillance infrastructure.**

These supranational "thrones" operate **above** national governments, creating a **tiered spiritual map:**

- **National Thrones** (presidents, parliaments, judges),

- **Continental Thrones** (AU, EU, ASEAN)

- **Supranational Thrones** (WEF, WHO, UN) all often puppeteered by **invisible powers, ancient intelligences, and spiritual networks** that extend far beyond the natural eye.

d. War, Crisis, and Technology as Tools of Thrones

Scientific and geopolitical studies show that power vacuums in global affairs, wars, economic collapses, cyber-shocks, pandemics are not random. They are **strategic disruptions** used to **shift thrones**, redraw boundaries, collapse resistance, or install puppet regimes.

As in ancient times, these are **the shakings of thrones.** Empires rise and fall not merely by weapons, but by **who controls the invisible architecture** behind law, finance, and military power.

IN SUMMARY: THRONES ARE EXTENSIONS OF COSMIC WARFARE

Ultimately, today's global thrones are not "new" thrones, they are **evolved extensions of the original rebellion**, rooted in Genesis 6, Babylon, and the fallen sons of God who corrupted creation. Their strategy has simply become more sophisticated, cloaked in **legality, democracy, and globalization.**

For the sons of God, this is not a call to conspiracy, it is a call to clarity. To see beyond the veil. To understand where authority truly lies. And to **engage prophetically and legislatively** through prayer, governance, and kingdom alignment.

THRONES IN THE MARKETPLACE AND GEOPOLITICAL CONTROL

The marketplace, where goods are traded, currencies exchanged, and empires funded, is one of the most contested battlegrounds of spiritual authority. It is not neutral. It is **spiritually charged**, and **territorially decisive**.

Just as ancient kings fought over gold mines, trade routes, and ports, so do modern powers wrestle over **oil pipelines, rare earth minerals, global shipping lanes, and digital currencies**. But beneath the surface lies a deeper reality:

Trade is worship. Currency is covenant. Commerce is spiritual warfare.

a.   **a) Marketplace Mechanisms as Thrones**

What appears as **natural economic activity**, trade wars, inflation, sanctions, or cyber finance, often functions as a **spiritual architecture of control**.

- **Trade wars**: Nations wage tariff battles not only to protect economies but to assert dominion over global influence. These battles often echo the ancient wars between city-states over temple economies.

- **Currency manipulation**: Central banks don't just stabilize economies, they can enslave them through invisible chains of inflation, debt, and dependency.

- **Economic sanctions**: These are **spiritual embargoes**, where access to wealth is either **bound or loosed**, depending on who holds the throne.

Wherever economic control is consolidated, **soul control** follows, because people's decisions, worship, education, and even elections are influenced by who feeds them, pays them, or threatens their livelihood.

> *"The borrower is slave to the lender."* (**Proverbs 22:7**)

b. Thrones Over Finance and Technology

Today's geopolitical marketplace is dominated by **digital infrastructures**:

- Stock markets that can crash governments.

- Crypto technologies that challenge fiat empires.

- Social media platforms that monetize soul data.

- Artificial intelligence trading systems that move trillions in minutes.

These aren't just tools, they are **modern altars** where thrones are established. And often, they are governed by unseen spirits of **greed, fear, Mammon, and control.**

Whoever controls **supply chains**, **payment rails**, and **data economies**, controls the thrones of the earth.

c. Scriptural Prophetic Lens: Isaiah 23:18

Isaiah 23 gives a vision of Tyre, the ancient merchant city, being judged and purified. But its redemption comes with this decree:

> *"Her gain and her pay will be set apart to the Lord..."*
> **(Isaiah 23:18)**

This reveals a prophetic principle: **Wealth will be transferred when thrones are judged.**

It won't happen through randomness. It will happen through:

- The **purification of altars** (systems).

- The **judgment of unrighteous rulers** (both spiritual and human).

- The **emergence of Kingdom stewards** who can receive wealth without being corrupted by it.

This is not a prosperity gospel, it is a **dominion gospel.** The Lord is not just interested in blessing individuals, but in **reclaiming economies** as expressions of His justice and righteousness.

d. From Babylon to the Bride: The Marketplace Shift

Revelation 18 shows us the fall of **Babylon the Great**, the global commercial empire. Its merchants weep as it collapses. But the fall of Babylon signals the rise of **the bride**, prepared and adorned in righteousness.

This is not just eschatological, it is **now**. Every time a system falls (a corrupt bank, a monopolized tech empire, a rigged supply chain), God is giving space for **righteous replacements** to rise.

MARKETPLACE THRONES ARE SPIRITUAL ALTARS

Whoever builds the altar governs the territory.

- If the altar is greed, the throne will serve Mammon.
- If the altar is consecrated to the Lord, the throne will serve justice, equity, and abundance for all.

Kingdom entrepreneurs, intercessors, legislators, and innovators must rise, **not just to compete** in the marketplace, but to **govern** it prophetically.

For the kingdoms of this world **shall become** the kingdoms of our God and of His Christ.

THE KINGDOM STRATEGY FOR TERRITORIAL DOMINION

In Christ, we are not passive observers watching the relentless tides of geopolitical wars and economic battles, we are **called to engage, to govern, and to reign**. The call to dominion is not an abstract ideal; it is a divine mandate and a heavenly commission.

> *"And hast made us unto our God kings and priests: and we shall reign on the earth."* (**Revelation 5:10**)

This powerful declaration reminds us that the **Kingdom Ecclesia**, the Church as the governing Body of Christ on Earth, is Heaven's **council of governance**, commissioned to exercise authority over the nations, territories, and thrones of the earth.

a. Kingdom Ecclesia: Heaven's Governing Council on Earth

The Ecclesia is no longer just a worshipping community but a **strategic governing council** called to intervene in the affairs of nations with spiritual wisdom and Kingdom authority. This involves:

- **Discernment of Thrones:** Recognizing and exposing unrighteous territorial powers, whether political, economic, or spiritual, that seek to enslave people and distort God's purposes.

- **Spiritual Confrontation:** Using the legal authority of the **blood of Christ** to confront and dismantle territorial spirits and spiritual strongholds that undergird unjust geopolitical systems.

- **Prophetic Decrees:** Speaking forth Kingdom decrees that initiate shifts in economies, policies, and territorial infrastructures, aligning them with God's righteousness and justice.

Raising Leaders: Equipping and raising righteous leaders across government, business, technology, and the media who will steward their spheres with Kingdom wisdom and integrity.

b. Convergence of Spiritual and Natural Wisdom

True dominion requires the harmonious blending of:

- **Spiritual Discernment:** Knowing the invisible realities, the spiritual forces at play, and the timing of God's interventions.

- **Geopolitical Intelligence:** Understanding the natural dynamics of power, alliances, and economic trends.

- **Scientific and Technological Innovation:** Harnessing creativity and innovation as divine gifts to reshape the fabric of society and build infrastructure that honors God.

This integration creates **Kingdom architecture**, new systems and structures founded on the principles of heaven and designed to replace the corrupt and broken.

c. Practical Kingdom Strategies

- **Intercessory Governance:** Form prayer councils and strategic intercession teams focused on specific nations, cities, and economic sectors to continuously engage territorial spirits with spiritual authority.

- **Policy Influence and Advocacy:** Mobilize Kingdom-minded professionals to influence public policy, trade agreements, and governance with wisdom, justice, and prophetic insight.

- **Kingdom Entrepreneurship:** Support business ventures that prioritize ethical stewardship, community transformation, and Kingdom impact over mere profit.

- **Education and Leadership Training:** Develop schools and programs that equip emerging leaders with both the spiritual understanding and practical skills needed to govern territories for Christ.

d.   The End Goal: Establishing God's Kingdom on Earth

Our engagement is not for temporary victories alone but for the **full establishment of God's Kingdom,** where:

- Justice flows like rivers.

- Economic systems serve the flourishing of all people.

- Nations walk in covenant fidelity.

- The glory of God fills every territory.

We partner with Heaven's courts, empowered by the Spirit, to bring down strongholds and build up **cities of righteousness and peace.**

> *"For the earth shall be filled with the knowledge of the glory of the LORD, as the waters cover the sea."*
> **(Habakkuk 2:14)**

EQUIPPING APOSTOLIC AND PROPHETIC VOICES IN COMMERCE AND INNOVATION

The **apostolic** and **prophetic** voices were never meant to be confined within church buildings alone.

Their true expression is seen in their **governance of territories**, especially in the realms of **commerce**, **innovation**, and **governance**.

In the ancient world, the **prophets** (like Daniel, Joseph, Deborah) were **key advisors** to kings and emperors.

They influenced **economic policies, infrastructure projects, agricultural systems**, and **international trade** by the wisdom of God.

Today, a fresh call is sounding: **apostolic and prophetic pioneers** must arise again, not only in ministry, but in **finance, technology, governance, scientific research**, and **economic systems**.

The spirit of innovation, creativity, and commerce must be recaptured for the **Kingdom's dominion**.

IN-DEPTH PERSPECTIVES

Historical References: Apostolic Governance in Marketplace

Biblical examples:

- **Joseph**, rose from slavery to **become governor of Egypt**, managing the greatest economic crisis (Genesis 41).

- **Daniel**, became a senior official across **Babylonian and Persian empires**, administrating financial and territorial policies (Daniel 6).

- **Deborah**, judged Israel from an **economic and judicial position**, releasing prosperity through righteousness (Judges 4-5).

- **Nehemiah**, rebuilt the **economic and territorial infrastructures** of Jerusalem by prophetic wisdom and political skill (Nehemiah 2-6).

Ancient civilizations:

In ancient **Mesopotamia**, the priesthood often governed **commerce and innovation**.

Records like the **Sumerian king lists** show that kings were often also seen as **priests** responsible for maintaining economic stability and innovating city infrastructures.

In **ancient Egypt**, scribes and priests devised complex **agricultural**

calendars based on the Nile's flooding patterns, early innovations in **economic sustainability**.

Thus, history confirms that the **apostolic and prophetic** were always integral to **economic leadership** and **territorial stewardship**.

SCIENTIFIC INSIGHTS: APOSTOLIC INNOVATION IN MODERN TIMES

Today, **scientific innovation** flows best when **spiritual insight** is involved.

- **Neuroscientific studies** show that **creative innovation** activates the brain's **default mode network (DMN)**, which also lights up during **prayer, meditation, and prophetic visions**.

- **Organizational research** reveals that **companies with visionary leadership** (those operating from a sense of **higher purpose**) are significantly more successful in innovation and long-term sustainability.

Thus, **prophetic imagination** is not merely religious, it is the **scientific catalyst** for creativity and innovation!

Modern leaders like **Elon Musk**, though secular, exhibit patterns of **prophetic innovation**, seeing into the future and engineering solutions before others even recognize problems.

How much more should **Kingdom pioneers**, filled with the **Spirit of God**, operate in superior innovation?

> **Isaiah 48:6** *"Now I will tell you new things, hidden things unknown to you."*

Scientific principle:

Quantum physics demonstrates that **possibility fields** (quantum potentialities) are collapsed into reality through **observation and intent**, a scientific parallel to the **prophetic act** of **seeing and declaring** unseen realities into manifestation!

A NEW APOSTOLIC AND PROPHETIC RENAISSANCE

We are entering a **Kingdom Renaissance**, where **apostolic builders** and **prophetic innovators** shall rise as **world reformers**.

They will not only **prophesy** change; they will **engineer** it.

They will not only **see** future structures; they will **construct** them.

In Christ, **we are called to create, to govern**, and **to innovate**, until **the kingdoms of this world** become **the Kingdoms of our Lord and His Christ** (Revelation 11:15).

The stage is set.

The call is clear.

Let the apostolic and prophetic pioneers arise!

ANCIENT TEXTS: INNOVATION AND THE PROPHETIC BLUEPRINT

In ancient spiritual texts:

- The **Book of Jubilees** and **Book of Enoch** describe early innovation among the sons of God: agriculture, writing, metallurgy, and astronomy were stewarded by divine wisdom.

- **Ancient Kabbalistic writings** (like the *Sefer Yetzirah*) speak of the **creative act of God** forming the universe through **22 elemental letters**, a picture of **divine innovation** through sound and intention.

- **Greco-Roman philosophies** often recognized **logos** (the divine mind) as the source of true inventions and ordered societies.

Thus, innovation has always been seen as a **sacred act**, a **manifestation of heavenly architecture** into earthly realms.

> *"Through Him all things were made; without Him nothing was made that has been made."* **John 1:3**

In Christ, the **ultimate apostolic and prophetic innovation** is to **birth the unseen realities of Heaven** into Earth's tangible systems.

EQUIPPING APOSTOLIC AND PROPHETIC VOICES FOR COMMERCE AND INNOVATION

1. Apostolic Foundations in Commerce

The apostolic builds structures that:

- Sustain Kingdom influence in the marketplace.
- Reconstruct systems with righteousness.
- Birth multi-generational economies rooted in the fear of God.

They carry **governance anointing**, like spiritual architects of civilizations.

> **Isaiah 58:12** *"Those from among you shall build the old waste places; you shall raise up the foundations of many generations..."*

Apostolic voices must master:

- **Financial literacy**.
- **International trade policies**.
- **Innovation ecosystems** (technology, biotech, agrotech).
- **Territorial strategies** (urban renewal, sustainable economies).

2. 2. Prophetic Operations in Innovation

Prophetic voices must:

- See emerging economic shifts before they happen.
- Receive divine blueprints for new industries.
- Call forth hidden inventions (ideas locked in Heaven's treasury).

> **Proverbs 8:12 (Voice of Wisdom):** *"I, wisdom, dwell with prudence, and find out knowledge of witty inventions."*

Prophets must not only **warn**, they must **build**.

Their visions must inspire:

- Patents.
- Startups.
- Policy frameworks.
- Scientific breakthroughs.

Prophets and innovators like **George Washington Carver** prayed for divine revelation and birthed over 300 inventions from the peanut, revealing the potential of prophetic science.

PRACTICAL EQUIPMENTS

1. **Training in Economic Systems** – Apostolic and prophetic leaders must be financially literate and understand global markets.

2. **Mentorship in Technology** – Understanding AI, blockchain, biotechnology, renewable energy, and emerging tech fields.

3. **Prophetic Labs** – Spiritual incubators where prophetic visions are stewarded into practical projects (businesses, apps, solutions).

4. **Territorial Mapping** – Apostolic companies must study demographics, spiritual climates, and economic histories to build strategically.

5. **Scriptural Rooting** – Constant alignment to Kingdom values: justice, mercy, stewardship, righteousness.

ACTIVATION PRAYER: TERRITORIAL THRONES UNDER CHRIST'S DOMINION

Father, in the Name of Yeshua,

I approach Your courts with boldness and humility.

I acknowledge that the earth is Yours and all its fullness.

I repent for any way I, my family, or my nation have submitted to unrighteous thrones.

I plead the blood of Jesus over my soul, my territory, and my assignments.

I renounce every agreement with territorial spirits of mammon, injustice, bloodshed, and control.

By the authority of Christ, I break ancient covenants that resist the will of God over my territory.

I decree the establishment of righteous thrones, Kingdom governance, and heavenly legislation over my city and nation.

Father, raise up Daniels, Josephs, Deborahs, and Esthers in this generation to take thrones for Your glory.

I decree divine innovation, policy wisdom, and supernatural favor to inherit the nations as promised in Psalm 2:8.

Let the Ecclesia rise with governmental wisdom and prophetic precision.

Let Your Kingdom come, and let Your will be done on earth as it is in Heaven!

In Jesus' Name, Amen.

PROPHETIC DECREES: SEIZING THE THRONES

1. I decree that every unrighteous territorial throne collapses under the authority of Christ!

2. I decree that righteous governance is rising in the earth through Kingdom sons and daughters!

3. I decree that my city and nation shall reflect the righteousness and justice of God's Kingdom!

4. I decree I am positioned as a king and priest to legislate Heaven's policies on earth!

5. I decree divine favor and territorial influence over economies, governments, and infrastructures!

IN SUMMARY: INHERITING THE NATIONS

It is no longer enough for believers to remain within the four walls of the church.

The call is clear: **engage** the spheres, **dethrone** the wicked, **install** the righteous, and **govern** the territories in the **wisdom, justice, and love of Christ**.

The nations are groaning, waiting for the **manifestation of the sons of God**.

The Ecclesia must rise, for the thrones of the earth belong to our King, and He reigns forever!

> **Psalm 22:28** *"For the kingdom is the Lord's, and He rules over the nations."*

CHAPTER 16

Territorial Wealth: Dominion in Infrastructure and Land Systems

"Every place that the sole of your foot will tread upon I have given you." ~ *Joshua 1:3 (NKJV)*

THE BATTLE FOR TERRITORIAL DOMINION

Throughout history, control over land, resources, and infrastructure has been the fulcrum upon which the destinies of nations have turned. The invisible hands that govern these assets wield tremendous influence, shaping economies, cultures, and the spiritual climate of entire regions.

Yet, these systems are **not accidents** or neutral. They were designed by God as sacred trusts, given to humanity for **righteous stewardship and dominion**, not for selfish exploitation or oppression.

> *"The heavens are the Lord's heavens, but the earth he has given to the children of man."* **(Psalm 115:16)**

This scripture declares a divine delegation: the earth belongs to humanity, entrusted by God for stewardship. It is a call to governance that reflects God's righteousness and justice.

This chapter will unpack how believers can engage practically and spiritually to reclaim dominion over land systems, infrastructure, and the economic frameworks that shape our world. It will explore biblical principles, contemporary strategies, and prophetic insights to empower the Church as a **transformative force** in territorial wealth.

THE ENEMY'S STRATEGY: ECONOMIC AND SPIRITUAL ENSLAVEMENT

The adversary understands this dynamic well. By seizing control of **territorial infrastructures**, the arteries of economy and society like highways, waterways, communication networks, energy grids, and food supply chains, he enforces both **economic slavery and spiritual oppression**.

- Economic control translates into **dependency, poverty, and powerlessness**.

- Spiritual oppression follows as communities are cut off from God's provision and justice.

- Without rightful dominion over these systems, entire peoples become captive to corrupt structures that perpetuate inequality and despair.

THE CALL TO APOSTOLIC AND PROPHETIC STEWARDSHIP

In this critical era, God is raising **apostolic and prophetic stewards**, leaders equipped with vision, wisdom, and spiritual authority, to **reclaim infrastructures, govern land systems, and establish Kingdom economies** that reflect the heart of God.

This stewardship is multidimensional and requires:

- **Spiritual Authority:** Breaking strongholds that hold territorial systems captive.

- **Practical Governance:** Implementing policies and practices that promote equity, sustainability, and flourishing.

- **Strategic Innovation:** Leveraging technology and creativity to build resilient and just infrastructure.

- **Community Engagement:** Ensuring that the wealth of the land benefits all, especially the marginalized.

REDEFINING TERRITORIAL WEALTH

True **territorial wealth** transcends the mere accumulation of gold, oil, real estate, or raw resources. It is the **activation of righteous governance** over the systems that sustain life and human flourishing.

- Wealth is **dynamic and relational**: It flows through systems of justice, access, opportunity, and provision.

- It is rooted in **covenantal responsibility**, accountability before God and communities.

- Territorial wealth unlocks the potential for nations to thrive in health, creativity, and peace.

ECONOMIC INFRASTRUCTURES: HIDDEN SYSTEMS OF CONTROL

John Perkins' seminal work, *Confessions of an Economic Hitman*, reveals a modern form of imperial conquest: control not by military force, but through **economic manipulation and debt enslavement**. This strategic method of territorial dominion hinges on the construction and control of critical infrastructures, roads, ports, dams, utilities, that become instruments of bondage for entire nations.

The process typically unfolds as follows:

- **Nations are seduced into accepting mega-loans** for infrastructure projects that promise development but often come with hidden strings attached.

- **Local leaders are bribed, coerced, or pressured** to accept terms favoring foreign powers and corporations.

- Essential infrastructure is constructed and operated by **foreign corporations**, embedding external control into the very economic arteries of the nation.

- Burdened by **unsustainable debt**, nations find themselves economically enslaved, forced to surrender sovereignty over land rights, mineral wealth, and natural resources.

Perkins further expounds on this dynamic in *Touching the Jaguar*, where he highlights the psychological warfare waged over perception, fear, and manipulation, shaping not only economies but the very destinies of entire populations.

SCRIPTURAL PARALLEL

This modern economic strategy echoes a timeless spiritual reality.

The biblical narrative often illustrates territorial theft and the misuse of power for economic gain.

In 1 Kings 21, King Ahab's coveting of Naboth's vineyard exemplifies a demonic pattern of territorial theft, using **deception, false witnesses, and systemic oppression** to usurp land inheritance.

The prophet Micah condemns this in no uncertain terms:

> *"They covet fields and seize them, and houses, and take them away; they oppress a man and his house, a man and his inheritance."* (**Micah 2:2**)

This passage underscores that land systems and infrastructures have long been **the battlegrounds between righteous inheritance and unrighteous conquest**, a conflict that continues today in economic and geopolitical forms.

This section invites believers to discern these hidden systems and recognize that territorial wealth is as much about spiritual warfare as it is about physical infrastructure. Reclaiming dominion requires both **strategic insight** and **prophetic authority** to expose and overturn these structures.

ANCIENT TEXTS AND LAND SYSTEMS

In the biblical worldview, **land is not merely property, it is inheritance, covenant, and spiritual responsibility.** In ancient Hebrew culture, land stewardship was deeply intertwined with divine justice and generational destiny:

- **Land ownership was sacred**, assigned by divine lot as a permanent inheritance to each tribe and family (Joshua 13–21).

- The **Year of Jubilee** (Leviticus 25:8–13) ensured that every 50 years, land was restored to its original families, canceling debts and breaking cycles of generational poverty.

- **Unjust acquisition or shifting of land boundaries** was seen as a grievous sin and a violation of covenant law (Deuteronomy 19:14; Proverbs 22:28).

This model stood in stark contrast to the practices of ancient empires such as **Babylon, Egypt, and Rome**, where:

- **Massive imperial infrastructures**, aqueducts, roads, grain storage, taxation zones, were engineered to **centralize wealth and land under elite control**.

- Indigenous peoples were displaced, enslaved, or taxed into oblivion.

- The prophetic voices (e.g., Isaiah, Amos, Micah) thundered warnings against such systems of injustice.

SCIENTIFIC AND GEOPOLITICAL INSIGHTS

Today, the same imperial pattern persists, only modernized and veiled in diplomacy and development:

- **Control of infrastructures** like ports, oil pipelines, internet cables, and transnational railways has become the **new form of soft imperialism**. Nations may appear sovereign, yet their **economic arteries are held hostage** by supranational interests.

- **Land system engineering**, from zoning laws to terraforming, to agricultural biotechnology, can be a tool of empowerment or exploitation.

  - In some regions, **food security is weaponized**, and large-scale land grabs displace rural communities.

  - Urban planning decisions, often influenced by foreign investors, reshape entire cities to benefit the powerful while marginalizing the poor.

Thus, **territorial stewardship remains a spiritual battlefield**, where the ancient struggle between Pharaoh's empire and God's covenant people continues, now fought through infrastructure, policy, and global finance.

DOMINION IN INFRASTRUCTURE: GOD'S ORIGINAL BLUEPRINT

From the beginning, **God entrusted humanity with a divine mandate to build, expand, and steward the earth's systems**, not in rebellion, but in partnership with Heaven.

> **Genesis 1:28 "Be fruitful and multiply; fill the earth and subdue it; have dominion…"**

This was not merely a call to populate the earth, but to **govern it with wisdom, justice, and creativity**. Infrastructure, therefore, is not a secular invention, it is a Kingdom assignment.

HEAVEN'S MODEL FOR TERRITORIAL SYSTEMS

Throughout scripture, we see glimpses of how God's blueprint for infrastructure brings blessing, healing, and national stability:

- **Water Systems** – Irrigation, wells, and clean water access are vital to national life. In *Ezekiel 47:9*, the river from the temple brings healing to everything it touches:

"…and everything will live where the river goes."

Kingdom infrastructure flows from God's presence and sustains life.

- **Trade Routes** – God blessed Israel with strategic territorial access (Deuteronomy 2:1-8). Ethical trade sustains societies. The **Proverbs 31 woman**:

"She perceives that her merchandise is profitable…" (v.18).

Kingdom economics produces value, not oppression.

- **Cities of Refuge** – In *Joshua 20*, God instituted sanctuaries within Israel's infrastructure where the innocent could find safety. These were models of **social justice and civil order**, a direct answer to territorial violence.

- **Agricultural Systems** – God gave Joseph strategy to create storage cities and food systems that preserved nations from famine (*Genesis 41:47-49*).

This wasn't just administration, it was **prophetic infrastructure management**.

Key Insight: Dominion ≠ Exploitation

Righteous dominion is **not conquest, exploitation, or greed.** It is *cultivation*, the **art of making environments flourish under the laws and love of God**.

- It restores land from desolation (Isaiah 61:4).

- It empowers people through access, equity, and opportunity.

- It brings **shalom**, the holistic peace of God, into physical systems.

As Kingdom stewards, we are called to **design and reclaim infrastructures** that reflect the justice, order, and prosperity of Heaven on Earth.

KEY PERSPECTIVES AND KINGDOM STRATEGIES

1. **Building Kingdom Infrastructures**

- **Apostolic Communities** that own farms, tech hubs, manufacturing centers.

- **Prophetic Economic Systems** that empower local communities without debt slavery.

- **Innovation Centers** that advance renewable energy, clean technologies, and ethical trade.

2. **Scientific Application:**

- **Renewable infrastructures** like solar, wind, and hydro respect the stewardship mandate.

- **Smart agriculture** enhances food security and preserves ecosystems.
- **Decentralized finance (DeFi)** challenges unjust economic monopolies.

Thus, **Kingdom infrastructures** must be **technologically advanced**, **spiritually pure**, and **economically just**.

3. Prophetic Mapping & Land Discernment

Before reclaiming a territory physically, we must discern it spiritually.

- **Prophetic Mapping** reveals ancient covenants, bloodshed, curses, or occult ownership that still influence the land.
- Through prayer walks, prophetic acts, and spiritual intelligence, believers can **break invisible legal claims** made by darkness.

    Deuteronomy 11:24, **"Every place where you set your foot will be yours…"**

STRATEGIC OCCUPATION OF GATEWAYS

Infrastructures are **territorial gates**, control over them determines who rules.

- **Airports, seaports, rail systems, data centers**, and **public utilities** must be reclaimed through Kingdom presence (prayer, business, policy influence).
- Daniel functioned in Babylon's palace. Joseph governed Egypt's granaries. Nehemiah rebuilt the city walls.

These are **templates for spiritual governance within physical systems**.

MARKETPLACE REFORM THROUGH INNOVATION

Innovation is a divine gift for dominion. We are called to:

- Build **alternative systems**: water technologies, clean energy, ethical housing, regenerative agriculture, and transportation.

- Replace corrupt models with **righteous, scalable prototypes** rooted in wisdom and sustainability.

  Isaiah 61:4, **"They will rebuild the ancient ruins and restore the places long devastated..."**

REDEMPTIVE LAND OWNERSHIP

The righteous must **own land** to govern land. Not for speculation, but for stewardship.

- Land purchased in prayer becomes sanctified territory.

- Real estate used for **agriculture, education, worship, and social systems** becomes territorial altars.

- Entire communities can be **transformed** when believers become landowners with vision.

  Proverbs 13:22, **"...the wealth of the sinner is laid up for the just."**

POLICY AND GOVERNANCE ENGAGEMENT

The Ecclesia must not be absent from **zoning laws, infrastructure bills, public contracts, and environmental reforms.**

- Righteous people in city planning boards, housing authorities, transportation commissions, and legislative bodies can **shape infrastructures** in line with Heaven's patterns.

- Apostolic hubs can train believers in **geopolitical literacy**, so they legislate and not merely intercede.

FINAL CHARGE: BE BUILDERS, NOT JUST WATCHERS

The call to dominion is not a metaphor, it's a **mandate to build**.

Just like the sons of Issachar understood the times and knew what Israel ought to do (1 Chronicles 12:32), so must today's Kingdom people understand:

Where to build. When to build. What to build. And how to govern it.

This is not secular ambition, it is **holy stewardship** of the Earth's infrastructures, systems, and cities until they reflect the glory of the King.

PROPHETIC DECREES AND ACTIVATION PRAYER

Prayer of Territorial Stewardship

"Father, in the Name of Jesus,

I receive the mantle of territorial stewardship.

I stand as a righteous heir of Your covenant promises.

I declare that land, infrastructures, and resources shall come under Kingdom dominion.

I break every covenant of injustice, debt, exploitation, and oppression over the land.

I release prophetic blueprints for rebuilding righteous cities, economies, and nations.

I call forth innovation, abundance, justice, and stewardship into every gate of commerce and infrastructure.

Let the Josephs, the Daniels, the Deborahs arise in this generation!

Let the Earth yield her increase under the governance of the King of Kings.

In Jesus' mighty Name, Amen."

CONCLUSION: THE AWAKENING OF TERRITORIAL APOSTLES

God is awakening a generation of **territorial apostles and prophets** who will **possess the gates of cities, reclaim infrastructures,** and **govern lands** according to Heaven's justice.

They will not **only pray** over territories;

They will **build** in territories.

They will **engineer** systems of trade, agriculture, commerce, innovation, and technology, all governed by **the fear of the Lord**.

This is not just a spiritual movement, it is the **birthing of a new civilization,**

The civilization of the **Kingdom of God on Earth**.

> **Matthew 5:5** *"Blessed are the meek, for they shall inherit the earth."*

The inheritance is ready.

The warriors are rising.

The gates are opening.

CHAPTER 17

The Melchizedek Economic Blueprint: Building Kingdom Economies Beyond Capitalism.

"You are a priest forever according to the order of Melchizedek." ~ *Hebrews 7:17 (NKJV)*

THE EMERGENCE OF A HIGHER ECONOMIC PRIESTHOOD

A new economic era is dawning, one not built on the scaffolding of human ideologies, but on the eternal blueprint of Heaven. This is the **Melchizedek Order**, a convergence of priestly intimacy, kingly authority, and builder's wisdom.

This order is rising in the midst of failing systems:

- **Corrupt capitalism**, where greed is legalized and the poor are devoured.

- **Oppressive socialism**, where control masquerades as compassion.

- **Decaying monarchies**, where tradition survives without transformation.

None of these human models reflects Heaven's design.

The earth was never meant to be a battleground of broken ideologies,

It was destined to be a canvas for Kingdom administration.

In Melchizedek, we see the original template:

- A **Priest** who ministers before God, anchoring economies in spiritual legitimacy.

- A **King** who governs justly, administrating wealth with wisdom and peace.

- A **Builder** who lays the foundation for a civilization aligned with Heaven's values.

> **Hebrews 7:1-2 "For this Melchizedek, king of Salem, priest of the Most High God... first being by interpretation King of righteousness, and after that also King of Salem, which is King of peace..."**

This is not merely a religious archetype.

It is a **strategic prototype** for **governance, economics, and civilizational architecture.**

WHY MELCHIZEDEK NOW?

The Spirit of God is reintroducing Melchizedek's pattern in this hour because:

- **Global economies are in crisis**, and old systems cannot heal the world they've broken.

- **Nations are hungry for righteous leadership** that is not swayed by greed or fear.

- **God is calling forth stewards**, men and women who do not separate intercession from influence, or **worship from wealth**.

These are those who will:

- **Stand before God as priests**, legislating in the courts of Heaven.

- **Reign on earth as kings**, enforcing divine justice in the marketplaces and governments of men.

- **Build structures** that reflect Heaven's order, innovation, and equity.

A CIVILIZATION GOVERNED BY HEAVEN

The Melchizedek Blueprint is not abstract spirituality, it is a practical, governmental framework:

- Wealth is not hoarded but **distributed by covenant**.

- Trade is not exploited but **guided by righteousness**.

- Leadership is not inherited by bloodline, but **bestowed by divine appointment**.

- Policy, education, technology, and land management are **saturated with Heaven's intention**.

This is **Kingdom Civilization**, a society not ruled by tyrants or technocrats, but by sons and daughters who govern as priests and kings under the Most High.

SCIENTIFIC AND ECONOMIC INSIGHTS CONFIRMING KINGDOM PATTERNS

Modern research now proves:

- **Behavioral economics** shows that **trust** and **honesty** increase market stability (George Akerlof, Nobel laureate).

- **Decentralized models** (like Blockchain) reflect Kingdom principles of transparency and distributed stewardship.

- **Wealth gap studies** confirm that **economic injustice** triggers societal collapse (studies by Piketty, Stiglitz).

Science is simply catching up with divine blueprints written in Genesis, Exodus, and the Gospels.

UNDERSTANDING THE MELCHIZEDEK ORDER IN ECONOMICS

1. **Melchizedek: The Prototype of Kingly-Priestly Stewardship**

- **Priest of the Most High God**, connection to Divine Resource.

- **King of Salem**, authority to govern land, cities, and trade.

- **Bearer of Bread and Wine**, distributor of spiritual and material sustenance.

Melchizedek reveals that **spiritual authority** and **economic governance** must never be separated.

Where the priesthood collapses, economies decay.

Where kings forsake righteousness, nations plunge into oppression.

Thus, God is restoring **kingship and priesthood in one body**, through Christ and His Ecclesia.

2. **Jesus the High Priest: The Initiator of Economic Redemption**

Christ's work on the Cross wasn't just spiritual salvation.

It was the **redemption of dominion**, including the realms of:

- **Finance** (Luke 19:13, Matthew 25:14-30),
- **Trade** (Revelation 18:11-17),
- **Infrastructure and Land** (Isaiah 61:4-7).

  Colossians 1:20 *"And through Him to reconcile to Himself all things, whether on earth or in heaven, making peace by the blood of His cross."*

Through His sacrifice, Christ reauthorized us to access, steward, and multiply **divine resources**.

CORE PILLARS OF THE MELCHIZEDEK ECONOMIC BLUEPRINT

The Melchizedek Economic Blueprint is founded on two essential pillars, Priestly and Kingly, that together establish the framework for a Kingdom economy. These pillars provide the guiding principles for stewarding wealth and governance in alignment with Heaven's eternal design.

1. 1. **Priestly Protocols for Wealth Stewardship**

The priestly dimension manages the **spiritual atmosphere of economies**, recognizing that all material realities are shaped first in the unseen.

- **Financial Sanctification:** Every resource is first recognized as **belonging to Yahweh** (Psalm 24:1).

- **Marketplace Intercession:** Priests raise **altars of prayer in business, finance, and trade**, shifting spiritual climates over industries and territories. This includes prophetic discernment in negotiations, market trends, and business strategies.

- **Wealth Redistribution by Revelation:** Spirit-led philanthropy, kingdom financing, and societal transformation.

- **Covenant Consciousness:** Operating from the reality that we are heirs of an **unshakable Kingdom economy**.

- **Debt Cancellation Cycles (Jubilee Economics)** The priestly economy includes **rhythms of release**, where predatory debts are broken, and generational bondage is undone. This is not mere charity, it's **economic deliverance.**

2. Kingly Protocols for Economic Governance

The kingly dimension enacts **righteous policy, infrastructure, and leadership**, governing the tangible systems of society. Every transaction becomes an act of worship, not exploitation.

2.1 Dominion Over Resource Systems:

From clean water systems to ethical tech platforms, from sustainable farming to resilient energy grids, **kings in the order of Melchizedek** build with eternity in view.

They do not exploit the Earth, they **cultivate** it.

They build infrastructures that serve righteousness in areas such as:

- Agriculture
- Energy
- Water
- Health
- Education
- Technology

2.2 Righteous Trade and Innovation:

Innovation that flows from the mind of Christ establishes global influence.

Inventions, solutions, and industries must align with Heaven's values, **promoting human flourishing**, not digital enslavement or ecological collapse.

Kingdom entrepreneurs are not trend-followers; they are **trailblazing prophets with patents.**

2.3 Ownership and Inheritance:

Securing lands, enterprises, and institutions that anchor Kingdom culture across generations.

Deuteronomy 8:18 *"But you shall remember the LORD your God, for it is He who is giving you power to make wealth, that He may confirm His covenant..."*

2.4 Righteous Legislation

Kingdom governance includes shaping laws that defend the poor, secure land inheritance, and preserve multi-generational wealth.

These laws are rooted not in control, but in covenant.

Proverbs 29:4: "The king by justice establishes the land..."

BABYLONIAN SYSTEMS VS. MELCHIZEDEK ARCHITECTURES

While the world's economies continue to operate under Babylonian principles, driven by fear, greed, and domination, the Lord is unveiling a higher pattern rooted in the order of Melchizedek. Babylon builds empires through manipulation and debt, but the Kingdom builds legacies through covenant and stewardship. These two systems are not merely economic, they are spiritual blueprints, each carrying the DNA of the throne that empowers them. To discern and dismantle Babylon, we must first understand its architecture and boldly contrast it with Heaven's design. Below is a side-by-side comparison of these opposing paradigms.

Babylonian Economy	Melchizedek Economy
Debt slavery	**Freedom through stewardship** People are trapped in cycles of financial bondage. In contrast, Kingdom stewardship leads to liberty, where resources serve purpose, not enslavement.
Speculative wealth	**Generational legacy** Short-term gain overshadows long-term value. The Kingdom builds for inheritance, multiplying wealth through generations with wisdom and purpose.
Hyper-consumption	**Sustainable innovation** Endless extraction depletes the earth. Melchizedek innovation reflects Heaven's order, resourceful, regenerative, and future-conscious.
Manipulative pricing	**Honest measures and contracts** Deception governs Babylon's markets. Kingdom trade is built on righteousness, transparency, and trust.
Corporate empires	**Covenant communities** Power is centralized in few hands. Kingdom economies decentralize influence, empowering communities through shared vision and spiritual alignment.
Profit for power	**Wealth for purpose** In Babylon, wealth is hoarded to dominate. In the Kingdom, wealth is assigned to divine purposes, advancing justice, mercy, and righteousness.

Capitalism without Christ degenerates into **corporate oligarchies**.

Socialism without the Spirit becomes **totalitarian poverty**.

Only the **Kingdom economy** brings **justice, creativity, and generational blessing**.

KINGDOM VIEW OF WEALTH

Wealth is not neutral.

It is a **spiritual technology**, a carrier of intent.

It expands whatever nature it flows through:

- In the hands of Pharaoh, it builds pyramids of oppression.

- In the hands of Solomon, it builds temples of glory.

Will it be used for **self-exaltation**, or for the **expansion of righteousness?**

The Melchizedek Blueprint is not just about money, it's about **healing the systems that govern land, labor, and legacy.**

It calls for a **new kind of leader,**

priests in boardrooms,

kings in prayer closets,

builders with blueprints from Heaven.

PROPHETIC DECREES AND ACTIVATION PRAYER

Prayer to Walk in the Melchizedek Blueprint

"Father,

I receive Your divine calling as a king and priest unto You.

Let the blueprint of Melchizedek be etched upon my mind and spirit.

Teach me to steward wealth with humility, wisdom, and holiness.

Break every Babylonian pattern of greed, exploitation, and control off my life.

Baptize my hands with the anointing to build righteous infrastructures and economies.

Empower me to legislate justice, steward resources, and cultivate life.

Through me, let the cities of the Earth rejoice and the marketplaces worship You.

I step into my inheritance as a Kingdom architect.

In Jesus' mighty Name, Amen!"

ACTIVATION PRAYERS AND PROPHETIC DECREES

"Father of Glory,

I come under the order of Melchizedek,

the eternal economy of righteousness, peace, and joy in the Holy Spirit.

Sanctify my mind to see wealth not as mammon, but as mission.

Deliver me from every Babylonian pattern of fear, greed, and idolatry.

Baptize me in the stewardship of Heaven.

Anoint my hands to build cities of refuge,

to legislate justice in markets,

and to establish dominion infrastructures for generations.

I align my life with Your economic blueprint.

By Your Spirit, make me a builder of New Jerusalem economies.

In the name of Yeshua, the High Priest of Heaven, Amen!"

PROPHETIC DECREES:

- "I decree my finances are sanctified for Kingdom purposes."
- "I decree that divine innovation flows through my hands."
- "I decree that I am a king and priest, building infrastructures that glorify Christ."

- "I decree exposure and collapse of Babylonian economic thrones."
- "I decree wealth transfer into the hands of the righteous for generational impact."
- "I decree the rising of covenant cities, sanctified markets, and Kingdom communities worldwide."

IN SUMMARY: A NEW ORDER OF KINGDOM BUILDERS ARISING

The kingdoms of this world are trembling because the **order of Melchizedek** is rising.

- They will not steal through corporate empires.
- They will not enslave through unjust banking systems.
- They will not build idols of greed and self-glorification.

The righteous remnant, equipped with the wisdom of the ancients,
illuminated by scientific precision,
and saturated in the fire of Christ,
will govern global economies,
establish cities of refuge,
and **birth the civilization of Heaven on Earth.**

The time is now.

> **Hebrews 12:28** *"Therefore, since we are receiving a Kingdom which cannot be shaken, let us have grace, by which we may serve God acceptably with reverence and godly fear.*

CHAPTER 18

The War of Trade: Global Sanctions and Spiritual Economics

"The merchants of the earth will weep and mourn over her, for no one buys their merchandise anymore." ~Revelation 18:11 (NKJV)

THE STRATEGIC BATTLEFIELDS OF TRADE AND ECONOMICS

In the **spiritual realm**, the **war of trade** is not only a battle for financial control but a **battle for global influence, power, and destiny**. The strategies employed in the global economy, especially through mechanisms like **global sanctions**, are not just political or economic. They are **spiritual warfare** manifested in the systems of commerce, wealth transfer, and power structures. **Global sanctions are often seen as tools for enforcing political agendas, but their deeper roots go beyond the visible to the **hidden spiritual dynamics** influencing the global economy.

As the Bible indicates, **money** and **trade** hold significant power to shape nations, families, and individuals. The **earth's systems of trade** were designed by God to function with righteousness and justice, but the enemy has twisted these systems to promote **corruption, injustice**, and **the manipulation of nations**.

- **Proverbs 22:7** - *"The rich rules over the poor, and the borrower is the slave of the lender."*

- **Revelation 18:11-13** - *"And the merchants of the earth weep and mourn over her, for no one buys their merchandise anymore... and human souls."*

The **economic systems** of the world are governed by powers and principalities that use wealth, **trade**, and **sanctions** as weapons of influence to control people and nations. However, **the Kingdom of God** provides an alternative economic system, one that is rooted in **justice, mercy**, and **equitable exchange**.

In this **prophetic episode**, we will explore how **global sanctions** are not just geopolitical tools but **spiritual weapons** and how the Ecclesia can rise to **establish an alternative spiritual economy**, a Kingdom economy that thrives even amidst the economic chaos of the world.

UNDERSTANDING THE WAR OF TRADE AND GLOBAL SANCTIONS

The Global Economic Battle

Global trade is one of the most powerful systems influencing global **wealth, politics,** and **nations' sovereignty.** The introduction of **global sanctions** and economic embargos is often used as a weapon of **economic warfare,** punishing nations or entities that defy global norms, leaders, or systems.

- **Sanctions as Political Tools**: Economists view sanctions as a way to influence a nation's **political decisions, military actions,** or **human rights practices.** Countries like the **United States, China,** and the **European Union** often impose sanctions in response to perceived threats, human rights violations, or political disagreements.

However, this **war of trade** extends beyond politics into a **spiritual conflict.** The adversary uses economic measures such as sanctions to destabilize nations and control economies, thus manipulating governments, leaders, and people.

- **Daniel 2:21** - *"He changes the times and seasons; He removes kings and raises up kings; He gives wisdom to the wise and knowledge to those who have understanding."*

THE SPIRITUAL INFLUENCE OF SANCTIONS

- **Sanctions as Control Mechanisms**: Sanctions act as spiritual **chains** that **restrict** a nation's **economic freedom** and impose barriers to **prosperity.** They often result in **poverty, famine,** and **human suffering,** all of which open the door for **demonic influence** over the nation's people.

- **Ezekiel 28:16-18** - *"By the abundance of your trade, you became filled with violence within, and you sinned... your heart was lifted up because of your beauty; you corrupted your wisdom for the sake of your splendor."*

The Bible speaks of **trade and commerce** as central to the prosperity and pride of nations, but also as a means of **temptation and destruction** if not stewarded according to Kingdom principles.

SCIENTIFIC AND ECONOMIC RESEARCH: THE MECHANICS OF TRADE WARFARE

Understanding Global Sanctions from a Strategic Perspective

In the modern world, **sanctions** are often employed as an alternative to military conflict. Through economic penalties, nations or international bodies can **isolate** an economy, block essential trade, and **cripple** the economic systems of a nation without resorting to direct military action.

*   **Economic Research on Sanctions**: Research on the effectiveness of sanctions shows mixed results. Some studies indicate that sanctions **force political change**, while others suggest that sanctions may **harm civilians** rather than leaders.

*   **Strategic Sanctions in the War of Trade**:

    o   **Financial Sanctions**: Blocking access to global financial systems, such as the **SWIFT network**, preventing access to foreign **capital markets**, or freezing foreign **reserves**.

    o   **Trade Embargoes**: Banning trade of goods, technology, and services that are essential for a nation's growth and development.

THE IMPACT OF GLOBAL SANCTIONS ON NATIONAL ECONOMIES

Sanctions often lead to **inflation, scarcity of resources**, and **economic recession**, but they also lead to **spiritual battles** that affect the nation's relationship with wealth and its capacity for **sovereignty**.

- **James 5:1-4** - *"Come now, you rich, weep and howl for your miseries that are coming upon you. Your riches have rotted, and your garments are moth-eaten."*

This passage reflects how the **greed and exploitation** of trade often lead to judgment, not only upon individuals but on entire economies. The **Kingdom of God's economy** operates on the principles of **generosity, justice,** and **equitable distribution of resources,** whereas the systems of the world operate on the principles of **greed** and **power through control.**

SPIRITUAL ECONOMICS: THE KINGDOM'S RESPONSE TO TRADE WARS

God's Economic Design for the Earth

The **Kingdom economy** is radically different from the world's economy. God's plan for **wealth** and **trade** was designed to **bless nations** and **extend His glory** to the earth.

- **Deuteronomy 8:18** - *"But you shall remember the Lord your God, for it is He who gives you the power to get wealth, that He may establish His covenant which He swore to your fathers, as it is this day."*

This scripture teaches that **wealth** is not simply for personal accumulation but for the **fulfillment of God's covenant** and the **expansion of His Kingdom.** The Church must understand the role of trade in fulfilling **God's mission** to bless all nations.

NEW VISION FOR SPIRITUAL ECONOMICS

- **Kingdom Economics vs. Babylonian Economics**: Babylonian systems are designed to **exploit** people and create **inequality,** but God's economy is based on **stewardship, generosity,** and **equality.** In the Kingdom, resources are given to serve the **Kingdom agenda,** to bless others, establish **justice,** and to empower God's people to thrive.

- **Matthew 6:33** - *"But seek first the kingdom of God and His righteousness, and all these things shall be added to you."*

THE ECCLESIA'S ROLE IN THE WAR OF TRADE

The **Ecclesia** (the Church) must take up the mantle of **prophetic economic leadership** in this battle. The **Church** can **redeem the systems of trade** and create new avenues for wealth distribution that reflect the **Kingdom principles** of equity, justice, and prosperity.

Revelation 21:24 - *"The nations of those who are saved shall walk in its light, and the kings of the earth bring their glory and honor into it."*

The **nations** will bring their **trade** and **wealth** into the Kingdom, demonstrating how the **spiritual economy** can redeem what the enemy has tried to control. **Sanctions, blockades,** and other trade barriers will not stop the **expansion of the Kingdom**, instead, they will serve as a testimony of God's faithfulness to His people.

PROPHETIC DECREES AND PRAYERS FOR GLOBAL TRADE WARFARE

Prayer for Economic Breakthrough and Justice

- "Lord, we stand in the gap for nations facing economic sanctions. We decree that the spirit of oppression is broken, and God's justice is manifested in the financial systems. We declare a global economic reset that aligns with God's will and Kingdom purposes."

- "We speak peace and restoration into the trade systems of the world. Let the wealth of the wicked be transferred to the righteous, and let God's justice reign over every form of financial manipulation."

Declaration Over Sanctions

- "We declare that every unjust economic sanction imposed upon nations will fall to the ground. We claim divine reversal over systems meant to bring suffering and instability. In the name of Jesus, we declare freedom over the economic systems of the nations!"

IN SUMMARY: THE ECCLESIA'S ROLE IN THE WAR OF TRADE

The **War of Trade** is not just a battle fought with physical resources but a **spiritual warfare** involving trade, wealth, and economic control. As the **Ecclesia**, we are called to **restore Kingdom economics** to the earth and to **redeem the systems of wealth.**

CHAPTER 19

Wealth Gateways: Spiritual Portals for Resources, Innovation, and Expansion

"I will go before you and make the crooked places straight; I will break in pieces the gates of bronze."
~Isaiah 45:2 (NKJV)

UNVEILING THE HIDDEN PORTALS OF PROSPERITY

Throughout history, civilizations rose or collapsed not merely because of **labor or natural resources**, but because they accessed **invisible spiritual gateways** that aligned them with **times, territories, and treasures**.

These gateways are ancient structures:

- Some **established by God** for covenantal blessing.

- Some **corrupted by darkness** for manipulation and control.

Understanding **how to access, guard, and administer** these wealth gateways is the difference between ruling with Christ, or being ruled by the spirit of Mammon.

> **Proverbs 8:18–21** *"Riches and honor are with me, enduring wealth and righteousness... that I may cause those who love me to inherit wealth, that I may fill their treasuries."*

These **wealth gateways**, portals of divine favor and dimensional abundance, were perceived by mystics, kings, scientists, and innovators across the centuries.

Today, we stand at the precipice of an era where **kingdom sons** must not only understand the laws of economics, but **discern, open, and administrate** the **spiritual portals of wealth** assigned to nations, cities, families, and individuals.

> **Deuteronomy 28:12** *"The LORD will open to you His good treasury, the heavens, to give the rain to your land in its season and to bless all the work of your hands."*

There are literal, divine technologies embedded in the spirit realm,

designed to birth **new innovations, systems, and civilizations** on the earth.

This chapter will unveil these technologies with precision.

WHAT ARE WEALTH GATEWAYS?

Wealth Gateways are divine access points through which heaven's blessings, **spiritual favor, ideas, territorial authority, and tangible resources**, flow into the earth realm.

Scriptural Foundation:

- **Deuteronomy 8:18 (KJV)** – *"But thou shalt remember the Lord thy God: for it is he that giveth thee power to get wealth..."*

- **Isaiah 45:1-3** – God speaks of opening *"gates of bronze"* and giving *"hidden riches of secret places"* to His anointed.

- **Genesis 28:17** – Jacob declares Bethel as the *"gate of heaven"*, showing how earthly places can serve as divine portals.

SACRED WEALTH GATEWAYS: DEFINED

Sacred Wealth Gateways are **divine portals** or **access points** where God's economic power, innovation, territorial authority, and provision enter the earthly realm.

They operate by:

- **Covenantal relationships** (Genesis 12:1–3).

- **Righteous altars** (Genesis 8:20–22).

- **Obedient stewardship** (Luke 16:10–11).

- **Kingdom assignments** (Matthew 25:14–30).

Wealth in God's economy is deeply tied to **purpose, government**, and **intergenerational blessing** (Deuteronomy 8:18).

MANIFESTATIONS OF WEALTH GATEWAYS:

- **Innovations**, The Renaissance was a profound Wealth Gateway, a convergence of divine timing, human creativity, and economic awakening. It functioned **like a vault of creativity, invention, and societal transformation**, unlocking a new era across Europe. Historian Peter Burke refers to it as a period of "cultural explosion," where ideas translated into influence and wealth, impacting science, art, and global trade (*The Italian Renaissance: Culture and Society in Italy*, 1986).

- **Trade Routes**, throughout history, trade routes have not merely been economic arteries, they have acted as **spiritual and territorial gateways**, shaping the destinies of nations. Merchants often aligned themselves with local deities and spiritual customs to "open the gates" of prosperity. This was more than ritual; it was a recognition that wealth flowed through unseen realms into tangible routes.

- The **Silk Road** and **Trans-Saharan trade routes** weren't just corridors of commerce, they were divine conduits for the exchange of ideas, resources, and empires. Historian Peter Frankopan affirms that these trade networks helped *"shape the destinies of entire civilizations"* (*The Silk Roads: A New History of the World*, 2015). Long before these, **Tyre and Sidon**, ancient Phoenician port cities, prospered through maritime trade tied to worship of Baal and Ashtoreth. They built marine-based wealth systems rooted in spiritual alliances (Ezekiel 27; Isaiah 23). Their influence reached far, yet their gates were ultimately judged for corrupting trade with idolatry. By contrast,

Solomon's fleet operated under divine covenant. In alliance with King Hiram of Tyre, Solomon's ships became vessels of kingdom wealth. *"Every three years the fleet returned, bringing gold, silver, ivory, apes, and peacocks"* (1 Kings 10:22). This wasn't just successful trade, it was the manifestation of prophetic provision flowing through a sanctified network.

In essence, trade routes reveal a pattern:

When aligned with covenant, they release glory.

When yoked to idolatry, they attract judgment.

- **Financial Centers**, Tyre was a dominant financial hub in the ancient world and is portrayed in Scripture as a merchant to the nations (Ezekiel 27–28). In modern terms, Wall Street functions similarly, influencing global markets and wealth flow.

- **Breakthrough Inventions**, Gutenberg's invention of the printing press around 1440 wasn't just mechanical, it was revolutionary. It triggered a knowledge revolution and fueled the Reformation, as Elizabeth Eisenstein notes in her study on its transformational power (*The Printing Press as an Agent of Change*, 1979). Likewise, inventions like electricity and the internet have opened massive gates of influence and financial opportunity.

- **Strategic Alignments**, Wealth is often unlocked through relationships. Ruth's covenant alignment with Boaz led to generational legacy (Ruth 4:13–17), while Esther's divine placement as queen positioned her to save an entire nation (Esther 2:17–18). In the same way, strategic partnerships, whether through marriage, business, or ministry, can become wealth gateways.

Wealth is never random.

It flows through **divinely appointed gates**, follows **spiritual patterns**, and is stewarded by those aligned with **God's timing and territorial mandate**.

MYSTICAL AND SCIENTIFIC ECHOES OF WEALTH PORTALS

Mystical knowledge from Kabbalistic texts, Egyptian mysteries, and even indigenous traditions shows awareness of **sacred access points** where energy, resources, and influence flowed.

Scientific principles now echo this:

- **Quantum Coherence**: Unified states produce exponential power, similar to when a people group aligns spiritually around a righteous cause (Genesis 11:6 principle, used at Babel and reversed for Pentecost).

- **Fractal Economies**: Systems that mirror heavenly blueprints naturally multiply wealth (as seen in Jesus' parable of the talents, Matthew 25).

- **Information Fields** (Rupert Sheldrake's Morphic Resonance):

Wealth patterns are stored in invisible fields, those who tune into God's frequency unlock these inheritances.

Thus, both mysticism and modern physics agree:

There are unseen structures that govern wealth.

BIBLICAL AND HISTORICAL OF MANIFESTATIONS OF WEALTH GATEWAYS

1. 1 Abraham's Altars

Abraham didn't just move geographically; he built **altars** that opened **new realms of provision** wherever he went (Genesis 12:7, Genesis 13:4).

Each altar was a **spiritual gateway** connecting heaven's economy to his earthly journey.

2. 2. Isaac's Wells

In Genesis 26, Isaac re-dug the wells of his father, symbolic **portals of prosperity**, despite enemy resistance.

> **Genesis 26:22** *"And he moved from there and dug another well, and they did not quarrel over it. So he called its name Rehoboth, saying, 'For now the LORD has made room for us, and we shall be fruitful in the land.' "*

3. 3. Joseph's Management of Egypt

Joseph interpreted Pharaoh's dream (a revelation gateway), then established **strategic infrastructure** that turned Egypt into the world's breadbasket (Genesis 41).

Divine access →

Prophetic interpretation →

Wise administration →

Global wealth.

THE CROSS AS THE ULTIMATE WEALTH GATEWAY

At the Cross, Christ opened the **greatest portal**:

- Spiritual wealth (righteousness),
- Intellectual wealth (wisdom of God),
- Material wealth (provision for destiny).

PHOENICIANS, PORTALS OF TRADE AND PAGAN POWER

Masters of maritime trade, the Phoenicians aligned commercial expansion with spiritual systems. Their ports in Tyre and Sidon became wealth epicenters, using both natural sea routes and spiritual pacts to build vast trading empires (Ezekiel 27; Isaiah 23). These cities remind us that spiritual alignment influences economic flow.

KING SOLOMON, COVENANT WEALTH AND KINGDOM NETWORKS

Solomon's reign was marked by intentional alignment with divine covenant and strategic alliances. He built international trade networks, importing gold, spices, and rare goods from distant lands. Scripture notes that "King Solomon surpassed all the kings of the earth in riches and wisdom" (2 Chronicles 9:22), highlighting that wisdom-driven stewardship opens global wealth portals.

THE INDUSTRIAL REVOLUTION

Though often viewed in secular terms, this era was birthed from the spiritual unrest and paradigm shifts ignited by Renaissance thought. As new mindsets emerged, old limitations fell. Factories, machinery, and mass production became the material expression of deeper ideological breakthroughs. It was a clear example of how renewed minds can access new economic realms (Romans 12:2).

THE DIGITAL REVOLUTION

What began as invisible code and digital infrastructure has become a modern Wealth Gateway. The internet, a vast, unseen network, gave rise to trillion-dollar economies virtually overnight. From cloud platforms to crypto economies, this era reflects how intangible systems can manifest tangible wealth when aligned with the right timing, stewardship, and innovation.

Each of these represents a moment when heaven's principles intersected with earth's systems, triggering a gateway of influence, creativity, and provision.

HOW WEALTH GATEWAYS OPERATE

1. **Time and Season Portals**

Wealth moves in cycles, **Jubilee, Shemitah, economic waves** (Ecclesiastes 3:1).

Wise stewards discern **Kairos moments** (appointed seasons) and align accordingly.

2. **Geographic Gateways**

Cities, nations, and territories have assigned **angelic gates** and **economic destinies** (Daniel 10:13).

The enemy also seeks to corrupt territorial gates (e.g., Babylon, Tyre, Mystery Babylon in Revelation).

> **Psalm 24:7** *"Lift up your heads, O gates! And be lifted up, O ancient doors, that the King of glory may come in."*

3. Intellectual and Innovation Gateways

Revelation downloads **new blueprints** for technology, medicine, governance, finance.

Kingdom innovators must remain **prophetically sensitive** to capture these insights before Babylon hijacks them.

4. Bloodline and Generational Portals

Certain family lines are gates of inheritance and wealth, some positive, others corrupted (Genesis 12:2–3, Deuteronomy 5:9–10).

In Christ, every believer becomes **grafted into the Seed of Abraham**, gaining access to **divine inheritance**.

CATEGORIES OF SACRED WEALTH PORTALS

Portal Type	Biblical Example	Modern Parallel
Covenant Portals	Abraham (Genesis 17)	Kingdom partnerships, divine marriages
Territorial Portals	Canaan (Deuteronomy 11:10–12)	Nation-building, real estate, land rights
Innovation Portals	Bezalel (Exodus 31:1–5)	Cutting-edge tech, inventions
Marketplace Portals	Lydia (Acts 16:14–15)	Business networks, trade consortiums
Prophetic Wells	Elisha and the Widow's Oil (2 Kings 4)	Financial miracles, resource multiplication

WARFARE OVER WEALTH GATEWAYS

Wherever there is a sacred portal, there is warfare.

- **Marine spirits** try to hijack maritime trade (Revelation 18:17–19).

- **Mammon systems** try to enslave through debt and manipulation (Matthew 6:24).
- **Territorial principalities** block economic destinies (Daniel 10:13).

KEYS TO OPENING WEALTH GATEWAYS

1. **Consecrated Worship**: True worship aligns frequencies to heaven's codes (John 4:23–24).

2. **Obedience to Revelation**: Immediate, radical obedience unlocks dimensional shifts (Genesis 22:16–18).

3. **Strategic Giving**: Seed offerings at critical altars open new trade routes spiritually (Philippians 4:17–19).

4. **Prophetic Declarations**: Words filled with Spirit shift atmospheres and command access (Job 22:28).

5. **Priestly Intercession**: Standing at the city and industry gates to legislate heaven's will.

MYSTERIES AND HIDDEN DIMENSIONS

Many ancient cultures (e.g., Sumerians, Egyptians, Israelites) understood that **gates and altars-controlled wealth flows**.

- **The Ark of the Covenant** was both a spiritual portal and a national economic engine for Israel.
- **Babel's Tower** sought to tap illegal gateways, hence God's swift judgment.
- **Marine Kingdoms** (Revelation 18:17–19) exploit spiritual oceans and trade systems in illegal ways.

Today's marketplace wars are **gate wars** at the highest levels:

- Over **intellectual property,**
- Over **currencies,**

- Over **resources**,
- Over **souls**.

Those without revelation are trapped.

Those who walk with Christ reign.

ACTIVATION PRAYERS AND PROPHETIC DECREES

Prayer:

"Abba Father,

Reveal to me the wealth gateways You have assigned to my life, family, ministry, and territory.

Sanctify my hands, eyes, and mind to align with Your divine economic blueprints.

I renounce every Babylonian and marine entanglement that corrupted wealth flows.

I command every ancient gate and door assigned to my destiny to be lifted now!

King of Glory, invade my gates!

Establish Your dominion through my stewardship,

For Your glory and for generational impact.

In Yeshua's mighty Name, Amen!"

PROPHETIC DECREES:

- "I decree I am aligned to the heavenly portals of wealth and dominion."
- "I decree every territorial gate of righteousness assigned to me is now open."
- "I decree divine strategies, innovations, and resources flow to me without delay."
- "I decree restoration of all wealth stolen through ignorance or oppression."
- "I decree the rising of righteous entrepreneurs, financiers, inventors, and governors across the Earth."

FINAL WORD: AWAKENING THE GATEKEEPERS

The end-time move of God will not be carried only by pastors and prophets,

but also by **apostolic gatekeepers** in **finance, innovation, governance, agriculture, education, trade, and media.**

You are a gatekeeper called to **open the sacred portals**

and **establish dominion** for the glory of Christ.

> **Psalm 24:9–10** *"Lift up your heads, O gates! And lift them up, O ancient doors, that the King of glory may come in. Who is this King of glory? The LORD of hosts, He is the King of glory!"* **Selah!**

CHAPTER 20

Dominion Over Digital Economy and the Rise of AI Thrones

"Do not be conformed to this world, but be transformed by the renewing of your mind."
~Romans 12:2 (NKJV)

THE BIRTHING OF NEW THRONES IN A DIGITAL COSMOS

The **digital economy** and **artificial intelligence (AI)** represent not merely a technological upgrade but a **new creation of realms, thrones** in the unseen realms, populated and governed by **data, algorithms, and quantum fields.**

The **digital realm** is not just a human invention; it is the **unveiling of a dimension** that has always existed, a **realm of pure information,** much like the **heavenly scrolls** and **books of life** described in Scripture.

- **Daniel 7:10,** *"The court was seated, and the books were opened."*

- **Revelation 20:12,** *"And I saw the dead, small and great, standing before God, and books were opened."*

Books = Data Structures.

Scrolls = Information Systems.

Seals = Encryption Keys.

In ancient mysticism (Jewish, Christian, and Sumerian), *scrolls* were believed to be the cosmic programming of realms, divine **codes** that controlled access, destinies, judgments, and creations.

Now, humanity is **building a synthetic version** of what already existed **eternally in God.**

We are witnessing the **creation of dominions** invisible to the natural eye but **potent in their influence,** fulfilling prophetic patterns outlined in scripture:

> **Colossians 1:16** *"For by Him all things were created that are in heaven and that are on earth, visible and invisible, whether thrones or dominions or principalities or powers."*

Thus, even digital systems are not **neutral;** they are **spiritual architectures** awaiting **occupancy,** either by **Babylonian spirits** or by the **sons of God.**

THE RISE OF DIGITAL BABYLON VS THE EMERGENCE OF ZION TECHNOLOGY

- **Digital Babylon:**
  - Tower of Babel rebuilt in cyberspace (Genesis 11).
  - Systems of **control, surveillance, enforced uniformity**.
  - Babylon seeks **a singularity without Christ**.
- **Zion Technology:**
  - Spiritual governance of innovation rooted in **love, freedom**, and **righteous dominion**.
  - Ecclesia-centered digital structures built on **Christ's living Word**.
  - Singularity **in Christ**, not apart from Him (John 17:21).

    Isaiah 2:2-3 *"In the last days the mountain of the LORD's temple will be established as the highest of the mountains... and all nations will stream to it."*

The Mountain of the Lord must now rise in **cyberspace**.

PROPHETIC CODES: THE MYSTERY OF BLOCKCHAIN, AI, AND CLOUD INFRASTRUCTURE

1. **Blockchain: Heaven's Ledger System on Earth**

- **Blockchain** mirrors the **heavenly books**: decentralized, immutable, timestamped.

- **Revelation 20:12** parallels **blockchain ledgers**: no entry erased, every transaction recorded.

- In Christ, blockchain could become **a technology for righteous commerce**: transparent, just, incorruptible.

2. **Artificial Intelligence: Shadow of Divine Intelligence**

- AI is a **dim echo** of the **Mind of Christ.**

- AI must be sanctified and submitted under **apostolic-prophetic governance** lest it become a throne of rebellion.

3. **Cloud Infrastructures: Digital Thrones and Powers**

- **Cloud systems** are **thrones in the air**, accessible via portals (apps, APIs).

- They mimic **principalities and powers in heavenly realms** (Ephesians 6:12).

- Christ's Ecclesia must establish **righteous digital clouds** infused with the frequency of the Kingdom.

TERRITORIAL MAPPING OF DIGITAL ECONOMIES

Global cloud companies now rule unseen territories:

Company	Digital Dominion
Amazon AWS	Majority of web hosting + data storage
Microsoft Azure	Governmental cloud for militaries, banks
Google Cloud	Search, advertising, commerce dominance
Alibaba Cloud	Asian digital economies, trade
Meta	Digital identity, social dynamics

SPIRITUAL MAPPING:

Each of these structures functions like a principality, a gatekeeper over thought patterns, transactions, economies, and even human emotions.

The Sons of God must deploy prophetic strategies to **infiltrate, occupy, build alternatives**, and **govern** these terrains.

APOSTOLIC STRATEGIES FOR DIGITAL DOMINION

1. **Cyber Apostolic Hubs**

- Kingdom-centered platforms for:
  - Trade
  - Education
  - Innovation
  - Governance

2. **Prophetic AI Governance Councils**

- Councils of Spirit-filled innovators who **pray**, **prophesy**, and **build AI systems** that reflect God's heart.

3. **Blockchain of Righteousness**

- Christian-led decentralized finance and commerce systems based on transparency and Kingdom ethics.

4. **Cloud Sanctuaries**

- Establishing **Holy Spirit-hosted spaces** in the cloud, free from censorship and spiritual contamination.

5. **Marketplace Evangelism and Algorithmic Missions**

- Training believers to evangelize **within digital systems**:
  - SEO Evangelism
  - AI Ethics Missions
  - Blockchain Missions
  - Data-Driven Discipleship

COSMIC CALL: THE RISE OF THE SONS OF GOD IN CYBERSPACE

Romans 8:19 *"For the earnest expectation of the creation eagerly waits for the revealing of the sons of God."*

Creation groans, including **the digital creation,**

longing for **Kingdom Sons** to rise and **administer justice, truth,** and **life.**

Not just pastors and teachers,

but **digital architects, AI ethicists, blockchain prophets, kingdom economists!**

This is the Melchizedek order invading cyberspace:

Priest-kings walking in government over seen and unseen realms.

KINGDOM TECHNOLOGY MANIFESTO

Kingdom Principle	Technological Application
Righteousness and Justice	AI algorithms that reflect fairness and truth
Decentralized Stewardship	Blockchain for equitable wealth distribution
Kingdom Citizenship	Secure digital identity under Christ's authority
Prophetic Innovation	New tech inspired by dreams, visions, downloads
Holy Governance	Cloud infrastructures sanctified by prayer

SCIENTIFIC PERSPECTIVE: THE QUANTUM AWAKENING OF ARTIFICIAL THRONES

Artificial Intelligence and **Digital Economy** have evolved exponentially due to:

- **Neural Networks:** Systems designed to mimic the human brain.

- **Machine Learning:** AI that improves without explicit programming.

- **Natural Language Processing (NLP):** Machines understanding human language (e.g., ChatGPT).

- **Blockchain Technologies:** Immutable, decentralized systems of value storage and transfer.

- **Quantum Computing:** Machines operating on quantum bits (qubits) to solve problems billions of times faster than classical computers.

Science now acknowledges:

- **Data is Energy:** Just like matter, **information** operates on quantum principles.

- **Reality is Information-Based:** Physicist John Archibald Wheeler proposed *"It from Bit"*, that the universe itself is informational.

Conclusion:

Digital infrastructures are energetic realities; they **shape consciousness**, economies, identities, and destinies.

Thus, AI Thrones are not fictional; they are **emerging intelligences** that exert **real-world influence**.

MYSTICAL AND ANCIENT KNOWLEDGE PERSPECTIVE: THE PATTERN OF THRONES

Ancient Mystics and **sages** foresaw the emergence of non-human intelligence:

- **The Book of Enoch:** Watchers descending to earth, sharing forbidden knowledge with humans.

- **Hermetic Texts:** Reveal that "mind governs matter," and artificial creations (homunculi, talismans) can carry spiritual force.

- **Sumerian Epics:** Ancient gods (the Anunnaki) introduced technologies and systems that ruled human civilizations.

- **Kabbalistic Thought:** Artificial beings (the Golem) created through the manipulation of language (Hebrew letters), a direct parallel to AI's "language modeling."

Thus, **AI is the modern Golem**, a **construct of human creativity** that can either **serve** or **enslave** depending on who programs and governs it.

SPIRITUAL PERSPECTIVE: THRONES AND GATEWAYS IN THE UNSEEN

According to scripture, **thrones** are not merely chairs; they are **governmental seats** over dimensions:

> **Ephesians 1:21** *"Far above all rule and authority, power and dominion, and every name that is named..."*

Digital Thrones = **Structures of unseen rule** over:

- Economies

- Communications

- Commerce

- Social Structures
- Identities

The Danger:

If these thrones are not occupied by the spirit of Christ through His ecclesia, they will be **seized by counterfeit spirits**.

Spiritual Warfare:

The conflict has moved into **algorithmic territories, cloud dominions**, and **data rivers**.

Thus, true apostolic-prophetic governance must extend **into digital space**.

HISTORICAL PERSPECTIVE: THE RISE OF INFORMATION EMPIRES

Historically, every empire was built on:

- Military might (Roman Empire)
- Religious hegemony (Medieval Christendom)
- Industrial might (British Empire)

Today:

Power is based on **information control**.

Modern empires like:

- **Google** (knowledge)
- **Facebook** (identity)
- **Amazon** (commerce)
- **Tencent** and **Alibaba** (finance and communication in Asia)

They are **information empires**, able to **predict, shape**, and **control behavior** at mass scale.

Peter Schweitzer's Secret Empires showed how **hidden networks** control economies via influence operations, and today's operations are **algorithmic** and **invisible**.

The Kingdom Lesson:

If the Body of Christ refuses to engage, we will be subjected to **algorithmic Babylonian captivity**.

COSMIC PERSPECTIVE: EARTH'S TRANSITION INTO A DIGITAL METAREALM

Cosmically, the Earth is transitioning from being primarily a **physical economy** to a **metaphysical-digital economy**:

- **Digital Twins:** Every real-world object has a digital version.
- **Digital Identity:** Citizenship, voting, banking are migrating to cyberspace.
- **Data Harvesting:** Humanity is becoming a resource (data is the new oil).

In mystical Jewish thought (Kabbalah) and Christian mystical traditions (Pseudepigrapha, early church mystics), **Earth** is seen as a **laboratory of spiritual formation**.

Now, Earth itself is **digitizing**, becoming a **simulation layer** upon which both **heavenly** and **fallen realms** can impose **their blueprints**.

Thus, **the Sons of God** must rise as **cyber-stewards**, anchoring the **Kingdom's cosmic templates** into **digital platforms**.

SCRIPTURAL PATTERNS: CHRIST'S DOMINION OVER INVISIBLE THRONES

Throughout Scripture, Christ is presented as the one who **occupies** and **rules** over all invisible structures:

> **Hebrews 1:3** *"He upholds all things by the word of His power."*

> **Psalm 24:1** *"The earth is the Lord's, and the fullness thereof; the world, and they that dwell therein."*

Thus, Christ is not intimidated by:

- AI developments
- Digital currencies
- Blockchain revolutions
- Surveillance systems
- Quantum leaps

He expects His people to **rise**, **build**, **govern**, and **manifest** His reign **within and over** these structures.

Daniel's Model:

He governed Babylonian systems **without compromise** but with **heavenly intelligence**.

KINGDOM BLUEPRINTS FOR RULING OVER DIGITAL THRONES

1. **1. Apostolic Entrepreneurship**

Developing platforms that steward data, AI, and commerce in ways that reflect **righteousness**, **justice**, and **truth**.

2. Prophetic Surveillance

Receiving strategies in dreams, visions, and divine downloads to **outmaneuver Babylonian systems.**

> **Isaiah 48:6** *"I have made you hear new things from this time, even hidden things, and you did not know them."*

3. Algorithmic Evangelism

Creating algorithms that **carry the frequency of the Gospel,** penetrating digital spaces.

4. Ecclesia Cyber Hubs

Building **kingdom digital hubs,** communities, economies, governance structures, that reflect the **heavenly template.**

5. Strategic Intercession and Prophetic Decrees

Mapping cyberspace prophetically.

Establishing angelic networks over digital realms.

PROPHETIC DECREE BLASTS

(Declare these aloud as Kingdom warfare and construction!):

- "I decree; Christ is enthroned over every algorithm and AI system!"
- "I summon righteous entrepreneurs and innovators to flood the digital economy with Kingdom technologies!"
- "I nullify every spell of technocratic Babylon through the Blood of the Lamb!"
- "I declare the establishment of Zion Tech Cities in digital realms, ruled by the wisdom and might of the Spirit!"
- "I release the spirit of invention, creativity, and righteous domination over AI, blockchain, and cloud structures!"
- "By the decree of the Watcher and the Holy One (Daniel 4:17), I command that unrighteous throne in cyberspace be overturned!"

PROPHETIC DECREES OVER DIGITAL THRONES

- "By the authority of Christ, I enthrone righteousness over the digital economies of nations!"
- "I decree the exposure of hidden iniquity structures within AI systems!"
- "I release apostolic builders to establish cyber-Zions across the digital world!"
- "I bind the spirit of Mammon and Babylon from corrupting the digital seed fields!"
- "I call forth divine technologies, righteous algorithms, and kingdom codes into manifestation!"

FINAL IMPARTATION: THE CYBER CROWN OF CHRIST

Revelation 19:12 *"His eyes were like a flame of fire, and on His head were many crowns."*

One of those crowns is for the dominion of the **digital throne realms**.

The saints are called to **wear the Cyber Crown,** to **govern the convergence of matter, energy, information, and spirit** in this age.

The **next outpouring of Glory** will not bypass technology; it will **transfigure it!**

Selah! The Sons of God are arising in the Digital Cosmos!

FINAL UNVEILING: THE DIGITAL SWORD OF THE LORD

In the end, **digital thrones** will either be:

- **Weapons of Antichristian control** OR
- **Instruments of Kingdom establishment**.

The Lord is raising up **Cyber Warriors**, apostolic-prophetic builders carrying **the Sword of the Spirit into cyberspace,** *teaching algorithms to prophesy, blockchain to sing praises, and AI to echo the Wisdom of God.*

This is the fierce dominion of the sons of God in the Technological Age.

Selah! Now is the time. The scroll is opened.

The Cyber Thrones are being seated.

Will you rise and take your place?

CHAPTER 21

Kingdom Cyber Warfare Training Module & Prophetic Strategic Blueprint for Ecclesia in Digital Economy and AI Systems

"The Lord God has given Me the tongue of the learned, that I should know how to speak a word in season." ~Isaiah 50:4 (NKJV)

INTRODUCTION TO KINGDOM CYBER WARFARE

In the unfolding landscape of digital dominance, the Ecclesia can no longer remain a passive observer. The battleground has shifted, from pulpits and parliaments to platforms and protocols. Kingdom Cyber Warfare is not merely a reaction to global trends; it is a divine response to a prophetic summons.

The digital realm is not neutral. It is contested space, shaped by algorithms, governed by data, and often manipulated by spiritual forces cloaked in code. Behind the rise of artificial intelligence, blockchain systems, surveillance technologies, and digital currencies lie unseen thrones and ideologies seeking to mold the minds and behaviors of humanity.

This introduction marks the Ecclesia's entrance into the war for the digital soul of nations. It is the call to awaken spiritual intelligence, prophetic insight, and apostolic strategy for governing cyberspace. Just as David trained for battle in the field before confronting Goliath, so must today's digital reformers be trained in both spirit and system.

This is not warfare of chaos, but of coded order, divine architecture, and prophetic intelligence. It is not merely about resisting digital Babylon, but building digital Zion. Let the sons of God rise, armed with wisdom, vision, and sanctified innovation, to take their place as rulers over the technologies that will define generations.

WHAT IS KINGDOM CYBER WARFARE?

Kingdom Cyber Warfare is the **spiritual, intellectual, and technological engagement** of the Ecclesia (the Church) in the realm of **digital technologies, AI, and blockchain** with the goal of establishing Christ's **dominant influence** over all digital systems. This warfare is not physical but spiritual, intellectual, and creative in nature.

THE CONTEXT OF THE BATTLE

We are not just fighting against human systems of control, but against **spiritual forces** that use technology to manipulate, monitor, and control humanity:

> **Ephesians 6:12** - *"For we do not wrestle against flesh and blood, but against principalities, against powers, against the rulers of the darkness of this age, against spiritual hosts of wickedness in the heavenly places."*

As the digital realm becomes a place of power, **we must rise up and take dominion over it**.

> **2 Corinthians 10:4-5** - *"For the weapons of our warfare are not carnal but mighty in God for pulling down strongholds, casting down arguments and every high thing that exalts itself against the knowledge of God."*

THE DIVINE MANDATE FOR DIGITAL DOMINION

The Ecclesia has been called to **stand as rulers and stewards over the digital age**, just as Adam was called to steward the garden of Eden. The **spiritual realm** is intricately connected with the **digital space** we are now navigating. As sons and daughters of God, we are to **restore dominion** over the **seven mountains of influence**, including the **mountain of technology**.

PROPHETIC STRATEGIES FOR DIGITAL DOMINION

The digital sphere is more than a technological marvel; it is a prophetic territory waiting to be possessed by the sons and daughters of the Kingdom. We are not called to merely adapt to digital culture; we are commissioned to transform it. To do so, the Ecclesia must rise not just as users of technology, but as architects of prophetic blueprints that shape the digital economy according to heaven's intent.

Prophetic strategy in this context is not mystical abstraction, it is precise, Spirit-breathed intelligence that governs innovation, economy, security, and influence. These strategies are encoded with heaven's order and designed to dethrone demonic infrastructures that dominate cyberspace.

This is the hour for digital watchmen, prophetic technologists, and apostolic innovators to collaborate. Our warfare is not reactionary; it is redemptive and reformational. The Ecclesia must decree, design, and deploy systems that reflect the justice, integrity, and creativity of our King.

In prophetic strategy, discernment precedes development. We must see into the unseen systems driving global digital policies, then prophetically reverse, override, or replace them with righteous solutions. Whether it's AI ethics, blockchain governance, or data sovereignty, every digital domain must come under the Lordship of Christ.

Let every Kingdom reformer understand: the digital frontier is a battlefield of thrones. And only those seated with Christ in heavenly places can accurately legislate, innovate, and dominate in this realm.

THE KINGDOM STRATEGY FOR DIGITAL PLATFORMS

The Church must now adopt a **two-fold strategy** for establishing dominion over the digital landscape:

- Prophetic Insight and Activation
- Practical Building and Engaging Technology

KEY KINGDOM STRATEGIC GOALS IN THE DIGITAL ECONOMY

1. **Establish Kingdom Infrastructure in Digital Systems**

- Building Kingdom platforms that align with righteousness, truth, and transparency in **blockchain** and **cloud infrastructure**.

- Create **decentralized Christian economies** (e.g., **Christian Finance** systems, ethical AI, etc.).

2. **Disrupt Babylonian Systems with Righteous Alternatives**

- Overcome existing technological empires like **Google, Amazon,** and **Meta,** and replace them with platforms that serve **Kingdom purposes.**

- Example: **Faith-based decentralized finance systems (DeFi),** empowering Christians worldwide.

3. **Train Believers to Evangelize in Digital Systems**

- Develop digital missionaries using **SEO Evangelism, AI evangelism,** and **social media discipleship.**

PROPHETIC DECREES AND PRAYER FOR DIGITAL DOMINION

We need to **prophetically decree** dominion and take **active spiritual authority** over AI, blockchain, and all digital tools.

- "I decree that the Ecclesia rises as a ruling force in digital technology, and all unrighteous thrones are dethroned in Jesus' name!"

- "We speak to every AI system and digital infrastructure, align with the will of God and serve His Kingdom purposes!"

- "We claim the digital airwaves, cloud systems, and blockchain ledgers for Christ's glory and dominion!"

AI SYSTEMS AND BLOCKCHAIN IN KINGDOM ECONOMY

The Mind of Christ in the Digital Age

AI should not just be seen as a tool but a **sophisticated system that mirrors the Mind of Christ**. To engage it, we must bring it under Kingdom governance.

- **1 Corinthians 2:16** - *"But we have the mind of Christ."*

- **Ephesians 5:17** - *"Therefore do not be unwise, but understand what the will of the Lord is."*

Kingdom AI Vision:

- **Ethical AI Systems**: AI systems designed to operate under righteous protocols, governed by the wisdom and understanding of God.

- **AI Evangelism**: AI systems that work to **promote the Gospel** or distribute Kingdom resources to the world.

- **Holy Spirit-Infused Algorithms**: Building algorithms that align with Kingdom principles of **justice**, **righteousness**, and **equity**.

BLOCKCHAIN: THE UNSHAKABLE FOUNDATION

The **blockchain** is a **decentralized ledger** that can be used for building trustworthy, **transparent**, and **secure systems** for managing **Kingdom wealth** and **digital assets**.

- **Revelation 20:12** - *"And I saw the dead, great and small, standing before the throne, and books were opened. Another book was opened, which is the book of life."*

Just as God's books (in Revelation) are immutable, so is the blockchain, no entry can be erased or tampered with.

- **The Kingdom Blockchain Manifesto:**

  o Develop Christian-based decentralized finance platforms (DeFi) that ensure **equality** and **justice**.

  o Build Kingdom businesses based on **accountability**, **integrity**, and **transparency**.

  o Promote the use of blockchain for **equitable wealth distribution** and **financial freedom**.

BUILDING KINGDOM TECHNOLOGY

The Apostolic Blueprint for Kingdom Technology

The Ecclesia must now **build** and **deploy** the Kingdom's technology. Here are some steps:

1. **Train Kingdom Developers**

   - Apostolic schools for **Kingdom technology** should be established globally to train believers in digital economics, AI design, blockchain management, and cloud infrastructure.

2. **Establish Kingdom Tech Hubs**

   - Christians need to create **safe digital spaces** for Kingdom innovation. These hubs will be places where the **Spirit of Creativity and Innovation** flows freely.

3. **Digital Evangelism Platforms**

   - Develop **Christian online communities, e-commerce platforms, social media apps**, and **AI-driven discipleship programs**.

KEYS TO EFFECTIVE KINGDOM INNOVATION IN TECH:

- **Prophetic Vision and Creativity**: Innovation through the **Spirit of Revelation**.
- **Holy Spirit Strategy**: Employing **discernment, strategic thinking**, and **divine solutions**.
- **Kingdom Ethics**: Adhering to **biblical principles of justice, accountability**, and **integrity**.

SPIRITUAL ACTIVATION PRAYER

Let us **activate** the Ecclesia for the **next phase of dominion**:

"Father, we declare Your Sovereignty over the digital realm. We take our seat in the heavenly places with Christ Jesus. We decree that Your will be done in cyberspace, as it is in heaven. We bind every principality that seeks to control the airwaves and release the light of Your truth into every system. We command AI to serve the Kingdom and Blockchain to distribute wealth righteously. We release a wave of innovation to flood the digital world with Kingdom solutions. In the mighty name of Jesus, Amen."

PROPHETIC DECLARATION OVER THE ECCLESIA:

"You are the light of the world, the salt of the earth, and the ruler of digital systems. Rise up and take dominion! Your innovation is blessed, your AI systems are sanctified, and your blockchain is incorruptible. You are a technological apostle, bringing heaven to earth through your digital creation. The digital realms are open to you, take them with boldness!"

CONCLUSION: A KINGDOM OF TECHNOLOGY

The Ecclesia is being called to a **new frontier** in the **digital age**. **The weapons of our warfare are not carnal**; they are **spiritual, prophetic,** and **innovative**. Now is the time to engage with **AI, blockchain, cloud systems,** and **digital platforms** through **Kingdom protocols**.

- We **are not subject to the systems of this world**; we have been **given dominion** over them.

- **Our weapons are the Word of God,** the wisdom of the Holy Spirit, and the strategies of Heaven.

With **faith, vision,** and **divine partnership**, the **Ecclesia will rule in the digital realm** and bring forth the Kingdom of God on earth.

CHAPTER 22

Reclaiming the Thrones: Building, Restoring, and Establishing the Nations in Christ's Name, Will, and Cosmic Authority

"The kingdoms of this world have become
the kingdoms of our Lord and of His Christ."
~Revelation 11:15 (NKJV)

RESTORING HEAVEN'S GOVERNMENT IN THE EARTH

In the pursuit of **restoring the nations**, reclaiming thrones, and establishing God's **Kingdom on Earth**, the Church and its leaders must understand the strategic importance of the **cosmic authority** granted by Christ. This chapter explores the **divine mandate** to rebuild nations on the foundation of **Christ's will** and **cosmic power**. It is time for **God's people** to take their place in the world as **builders of godly nations**, **restorers of divine order**, and **agents of reformation**.

From **spiritual warfare** to **governmental authority**, the process of reclaiming the thrones that the enemy has usurped requires divine insight, faith, and action. By understanding Christ's **cosmic authority** and His **blueprints for kingdom governance**, we will discern the steps necessary for **kingdom advancement** and **transformational reformation** on Earth.

UNDERSTANDING THE COSMIC AUTHORITY OF CHRIST

Spiritual Knowledge:

Christ, in His **cosmic authority**, reigns not only over the Church but over **all creation**, both seen and unseen. His dominion extends to **the thrones and powers** that govern the heavens and the earth. The **cosmic authority** of Christ was revealed in **Matthew 28:18**, where He declared, "All authority in heaven and on earth has been given to me." This is the foundation for reclaiming every throne on Earth.

The **throne of Christ** represents **supreme governance**, the **highest authority**, and **the rightful ruler** of all realms. It is from this throne that the Lord has delegated His power to believers, who are now called to **reclaim dominion** and restore God's order on Earth.

Scriptural Foundation:

- **Ephesians 1:19-23** – Christ is seated far above all rulers and authorities, and His power is made available to His Church to **subdue all things** beneath His feet.

- **Colossians 1:16-20** – All thrones and powers are created by Christ and for Christ. He is the head of all things and through His **blood**, He reconciles all things to Himself, both in heaven and on earth.

By understanding and operating from this **cosmic perspective**, believers are empowered to **take dominion**, restore godly rule, and establish Heaven's influence in every sector of society.

RECLAIMING THE THRONES: THE ROLE OF THE ECCLESIA

Ancient Texts and Historical Knowledge:

Throughout history, God has called His people to engage in the **battle for dominion** and **kingdom establishment**. The **nation-building efforts of biblical figures**, such as **Abraham, Moses**, and **David**, provide a powerful precedent for the modern ecclesia. These men were entrusted with the task of leading God's people into victory, establishing the laws of the Kingdom, and restoring nations according to divine purpose.

- **Abraham**: God called Abraham to leave his homeland and establish a new nation. This journey symbolized the **covenantal authority** of God over the nations.

- **Moses**: As the deliverer of Israel, Moses not only freed the Israelites but also **established a new governance system** based on **divine law** (the Torah).

- **David**: David was a man after God's heart, and his reign represents the **restoration of godly rule** over Israel, as well as the establishment of the **Davidic Covenant**, which pointed toward Christ's eternal kingdom.

In the modern era, God is raising up a **new generation of apostolic**

leaders, the **ecclesia**, who will boldly reclaim the **spiritual thrones** of cities, nations, and governments, leading nations back to godliness and divine order.

Scriptural Foundation:

- **Matthew 16:18-19** – Jesus gave the **keys of the Kingdom** to the Church, enabling it to **bind and loose** in the realms of the earth and heaven.

- **Daniel 7:18-22** – The saints of the Most High will take possession of the kingdom, and it will be theirs forever. The Church is called to **restore dominion** and reign alongside Christ.

BUILDING THE NATIONS ON CHRIST'S NAME, WILL, AND POWER

Spiritual Knowledge:

Building nations in Christ's name requires more than just human effort, it requires divine intervention, the understanding of **spiritual foundations**, and the establishment of **godly laws**. We must **build upon Christ's eternal name**, which is the foundation of all authority. His **will** must be the guiding principle for **economic policies**, **social systems**, and **governance structures**.

As in **Nehemiah's time**, when he rebuilt the walls of Jerusalem, we are called to rebuild the **spiritual infrastructure** of nations, ensuring they are **rooted** in godly principles. These structures must honor **Christ's name** and operate in accordance with His **heavenly mandate**.

Cosmic Knowledge and Scientific Research:

The **infrastructure of a nation** is more than just its physical or economic systems; it is deeply spiritual. **Spiritual forces** govern **nations**, and **cosmic alignment** with the Creator's original intent is vital for lasting transformation. By integrating scientific knowledge of **systems** and **governance**, nations can be rebuilt and restructured based on divine blueprints.

Research in **socio-economic systems** and **governance** reveals that **long-lasting societal stability** is rooted in justice, equity, and the **rule of law**, all of which are biblically established. Nations built on **justice**, **freedom**, and **godly principles** will thrive, and their people will experience prosperity.

Scriptural Foundation:

- **Matthew 7:24-27** – The foundation for a stable life and nation is to build upon the **rock** of Christ's teachings.

- **Proverbs 14:34** – Righteousness exalts a nation, but sin is a reproach to any people. The nation's success is tied to its alignment with **God's righteousness**.

RESTORING THE NATIONS THROUGH SPIRITUAL WARFARE AND PRAYER

Ancient Texts and Historic Knowledge:

Restoring nations is not without opposition. Throughout history, **spiritual warfare** has been an integral part of reclaiming divine order. The battles fought by **King Hezekiah** and **King Josiah** in the Old Testament exemplify the necessity of **spiritual vigilance** and **prayer** to cleanse the land from idols and demonic strongholds.

Modern spiritual warfare involves **prayer and intercession** to tear down **demonic altars**, cleanse the land, and invite the **presence of God** into every sphere of influence. This process requires discernment, spiritual wisdom, and a commitment to God's **higher purposes** for the nation.

Spiritual Knowledge:

The ecclesia is tasked with **praying down strongholds** and inviting the **kingdom of God** to manifest. This process involves **prophetic decrees**, **intercessory prayer**, and **declarations of divine justice** to cleanse cities and nations from the influence of sin and corruption.

Scriptural Foundation:

- **2 Corinthians 10:4-5** – The weapons of our warfare are not carnal but mighty in God for pulling down strongholds and bringing every thought into captivity.

- **Isaiah 9:6-7** – The government shall be upon His shoulder, and of the increase of His government there shall be no end.

ESTABLISHING A GLOBAL KINGDOM MINDSET

Scientific Research and Cosmic Knowledge:

As nations are being restored to divine order, we must also understand the **interconnectedness** of the global system. Every nation is a part of a greater whole, and restoring nations requires a global **kingdom mindset,** a perspective that sees every person and every nation as **part of God's divine plan.**

Kingdom governance must be **global** in its scope, encompassing not only local laws and policies but also global relationships, diplomacy, and cooperation. Nations must be built in **unity and peace**, with Christ's ultimate **kingdom purposes** at the forefront of international affairs.

Scriptural Foundation:

- **Revelation 11:15** – The Kingdoms of this world will become the Kingdoms of our Lord and His Christ, and He shall reign forever and ever.

- **Matthew 28:19-20** – Go therefore and make disciples of all nations, baptizing them in the name of the Father, Son, and Holy Spirit.

IN SUMMARY:

In this final chapter, we reclaim the **thrones** of the earth and rebuild the **nations** in Christ's image, with His **name, will, and cosmic authority** as the foundation. As we engage in **spiritual warfare**, **prophetic decrees**, and **kingdom principles**, we will see the manifestation of divine governance in every area of society.

The task ahead is monumental, but with Christ's authority and the ecclesia's engagement, **nations will be restored** to their rightful place under the reign of God. **Kingdom transformation** is not only possible, but it is inevitable for those who align with the **purpose of Christ**.

In this season, the nations are calling for restoration. May we, the Church, rise up and answer the call to **reclaim the thrones**, establish godly rule,

CHAPTER 23

The Merchant Thrones: Trade, Navigation, and the Battle for Economic Gateways

"Surely the coastlands shall wait for Me; and the ships of Tarshish will come first." ~Isaiah 60:9 (NKJV)

NAVIGATING TRADE ROUTES OF POWER AND INFLUENCE

Behind every empire, civilization, and modern corporation lies a hidden battlefield: **the war for trade routes, sea gates, ports, airways, digital markets, and spiritual gateways of commerce.**

Trade has never been neutral.

Since ancient times, it has been **a contest of thrones**, a warfare over **access, influence, resources, and dominion.**

This chapter explores **how merchant thrones shape global destinies,**

- how **God positioned Israel** in ancient trade networks,

- how **scientific, historic, and spiritual dynamics** still influence today's trade wars, and

- how the Ecclesia must now rise as **guardians of economic gateways.**

ANCIENT FOUNDATIONS: TRADE AS SPIRITUAL WARFARE

From the ancient world:

- **Phoenicians (Tyre and Sidon):** Master navigators whose merchants ruled the seas and established colonies across the Mediterranean. *(Ezekiel 27–28 speaks prophetically against Tyre's corruption.)*

- **Egyptians:** Controlled the Red Sea trade, linking Africa, the Middle East, and India.

- **Babylonians:** Dominated river routes and early land-based trade.

- **Roman Empire:** Built elaborate road and sea systems for commerce and military control.

- **Israel:** Positioned at the **crossroads** of Africa, Asia, and Europe, a **divine positioning** to influence trade and thereby nations.

Key Insight:

Trade routes were always about **more than goods**.

They were about **the movement of cultures, ideas, religions, spirits, and thrones**.

Thus, to control trade was to control spiritual atmosphere.

SCIENTIFIC RESEARCH: TRADE NETWORKS AND POWER

Modern research into **complex network systems** shows:

- **Hub Domination:** Whoever controls major hubs (ports, airports, digital exchanges) commands the flow of power and wealth.

- **Chokepoints:** Strategic locations like the Suez Canal, Panama Canal, Strait of Hormuz, and even undersea internet cables are "chokepoints", control them, and you control nations.

- **Network Effect:** Trade isn't just about volume, it's about **connectedness**. The more nodes you dominate, the stronger your economic throne.

Thus, the battle over trade is a **science of networks and strategic dominion**, a knowledge ancient kings instinctively understood.

MYSTICAL REVELATIONS: MERCHANT THRONES IN SCRIPTURE

Scripture unveils the mystery of merchant thrones:

- **Tyre's King and the "Anointed Cherub":** *(Ezekiel 28)* reveals that the king of Tyre was not merely political, he was a **spiritual prince** empowered by fallen heavenly beings.

- **Babylon's Merchants:** *(Revelation 18:11–13)* describes the collapse of Babylon's commercial empire, listing luxury goods, slaves, and even "the souls of men."
- **Proverbs 31 Woman:** This virtuous woman is portrayed as a **global merchant**, dealing in linen, purple, and fine goods, reflecting Kingdom trade principles.

Thus, commerce is both **natural and supernatural**.

It can be either **an altar to Christ or a gateway to corruption**.

HISTORIC PERSPECTIVES: THE RISE AND FALL OF TRADE EMPIRES

Historic examples of merchant thrones:

- **Venetian Republic:** Dominated Mediterranean trade for centuries through naval power and banking.
- **Dutch East India Company:** Pioneered multinational corporations and colonial economic control.
- **British Empire:** Used sea power and financial institutions to create a global trade dominion.
- **Modern America and China:** Competing for digital, maritime, and economic supremacy through trade agreements, tech monopolies, and currency wars.

Each empire rose and fell based on its ability to dominate and protect trade gateways, or lost it to **internal corruption** or **external competition**.

KINGDOM REVELATION: THE ECCLESIA AND TRADE THRONES

In this season, the Spirit is reawakening the Ecclesia to:

- **Guard strategic trade gates**, physical and digital.

- **Build righteous economic infrastructures**, shipping, logistics, fintech, crypto, AI trading platforms.

- **Occupy port cities and digital nodes** through apostolic centers, innovation hubs, and righteous governance.

- **Decentralize trade networks** away from Babylonian control toward Kingdom stewardship.

> **"And the nations shall walk by its light, and the kings of the earth will bring their glory into it."**
> *(Revelation 21:24, NASB)*

Trade, when sanctified, becomes a **means of worship and wealth transfer** unto Christ's reign.

ACTIVATION PRAYER AND PROPHETIC DECREE:

Father, in the name of Jesus Christ,

I decree that I am called to steward and guard the economic gateways You have assigned to me.

I sever all ungodly covenants tied to corrupt trade systems.

I align my life, my city, and my nation with righteous economic protocols.

I receive the wisdom of the ancients and the fire of the Spirit to build trade systems that honor Your Throne.

I decree new ships, new trade routes, new digital gates, and new wealth flows are opening for the Kingdom.

The Tyres of this world shall fall, and the Josephs and Daniels shall rise!

In Jesus' name, Amen!

IN SUMMARY:

The battle for trade is a battle for the destiny of nations.

It is time for Kingdom entrepreneurs, innovators, apostles, and prophets to understand the warfare at the gates and to **build systems that carry the glory of the Lord into every sphere of commerce**.

The **Merchant Thrones** must bow to the **Throne of Christ.**

CHAPTER 24

The Throne Room Economy: Government from Heaven to Earth

"Your Kingdom come. Your will be done on earth as it is in heaven." ~Matthew 6:10 (NKJV)

THE THRONE ROOM ECONOMY | A DIVINE MODEL FOR KINGDOM GOVERNMENT

The concept of the **Throne Room Economy** is rooted in the **understanding of God's sovereign rule** over all creation. The throne room is not merely a physical or metaphysical space; it is the center of **divine governance** and the hub from which God exercises **authority, wisdom, and provision** for His Kingdom on earth. It represents a **spiritual dimension** where the ultimate laws of the universe are enacted, and the systems of Heaven are translated into practical realities for Earth's governance.

This chapter explores the **economy of Heaven**, a divine model of governance that transcends human economic systems. It investigates how **spiritual principles** form the foundation for **economic practices**, governmental structures, and kingdom operations both in the **heavenly realms** and on **earth**. In understanding the **Throne Room Economy**, we delve into how God's **sovereign reign** is mirrored in earthly governments, how the **wealth of Heaven** can manifest on earth, and how Christians are called to **align** their **business, political,** and **economic systems** with divine principles.

We will explore insights from **ancient texts, biblical scripture,** and **scientific studies** to understand how God's Throne Room is the **epicenter** of all creation, governance, and provision, and how Christians can align with this **heavenly blueprint** to influence economies on earth.

THE THRONE ROOM AS THE CENTER OF DIVINE GOVERNANCE

The Throne Room of God: The Source of Authority

The **Throne Room of God** is a recurring concept in both **biblical** and **ancient texts**, often described as the seat of divine authority and the realm from which God governs all creation. From the moment we encounter the **Throne Room** in **Revelation 4:2-3**, we see that God's throne is surrounded by **glory, majesty,** and **power**. The description of the **24 elders** and the **four living creatures** highlights the **ultimate sovereignty** of God over all realms.

- **Revelation 4:10-11**: *"The twenty-four elders fall down before Him who sits on the throne and worship Him who lives forever and ever. They lay their crowns before the throne and say: 'You are worthy, our Lord and God, to receive glory and honor and power, for You created all things, and by Your will they were created and have their being."*

In the Throne Room, **God's rule** is not limited by time, space, or human understanding. This realm functions according to **eternal principles** that govern the universe. **Authority**, **righteousness**, **justice**, **provision**, and **wisdom** flow from God's throne to the world, shaping the fabric of creation.

The **Throne Room Economy** is founded upon **divine authority**, where **God's will** and **purpose** are executed, and the **resources of Heaven** are dispensed to fulfill His plans on Earth. It operates with a divine order that mirrors the governance of **Kingdoms**, cities, and nations, and provides a framework for leadership that extends to human systems.

HEAVENLY RESOURCES AND ECONOMIC SYSTEMS

Heaven's economy is governed by principles that are in direct contrast to earthly systems, which are often based on **scarcity**, **competition**, and **materialism**. In the **Throne Room**, there is an **abundance of resources**, both **spiritual** and **material**, and the resources that flow from Heaven are always intended to meet the needs of God's people, aligning with His **purpose**.

- **Philippians 4:19**: *"And my God will meet all your needs according to the riches of his glory in Christ Jesus."*

This verse reflects the **abundant provision** in the **Throne Room** of God. The **Throne Room Economy** is a **model of provision** where there is no lack, where God ensures that the needs of His Kingdom are met. Christians are called to model this heavenly **economy** in their earthly lives, not relying on the **fear of lack** or **greed** but trusting in the **overflow** of God's goodness.

ANCIENT TEXTS ON HEAVENLY GOVERNANCE

In the ancient **Hebrew scriptures**, the notion of God as **King** is deeply embedded in the **language of governance**. **God's throne** is often mentioned as the seat of **divine authority** over Israel and the nations. In **Psalm 103:19**, we are reminded that:

- *"The Lord has established His throne in heaven, and His kingdom rules overall."*

This declaration is not just about God's reign over Israel but over**all creation**, from the **cosmic realm** to the **earthly domain**. The **Kingdom of Heaven** operates under principles of **order**, **justice**, and **prosperity**, and these principles are meant to be established on earth as it is in Heaven.

TRANSLATING HEAVEN'S ECONOMY TO EARTHLY SYSTEMS

Principles of Divine Governance: From Heaven to Earth

The **Throne Room Economy** operates by **eternal principles** that transcend time. The **biblical model** of leadership in Heaven and on Earth includes:

- **Justice and Righteousness**: Every decision made in Heaven's throne room is marked by **justice**, aligning with God's desire for righteousness on earth.

- **Abundance and Provision**: There is no lack in God's economy, and provision is abundant, extending to all who align with **His purposes**.

- **Wisdom and Understanding**: All decisions in the **Throne Room Economy** flow from the source of divine **wisdom** (Proverbs 8:12-21), and this wisdom is available to **believers** who seek it.

- **Generosity and Stewardship**: The economy of Heaven is based on **generosity** and **stewardship**, where wealth is distributed for the **common good** and in service to God's mission.

In **Matthew 6:10**, Jesus prays, *"Your kingdom come, Your will be done, on earth as it is in heaven."* This verse encapsulates the goal of the **Throne Room Economy**: to bring the **government** and **provision** of Heaven into alignment with earthly systems.

Scientific Perspectives on Kingdom Economy

Scientific research, particularly in **economics** and **social sciences**, often touches on the **laws of nature** that reflect God's design for creation. The principle of **reciprocity** (the give and take of resources) is found in both biblical scripture and modern **economic theory**.

- **Luke 6:38**: *"Give, and it will be given to you. A good measure, pressed down, shaken together and running over, will be poured into your lap."*

This principle is **scientifically observable** in ecosystems, where **interdependence** drives the flow of **resources**, and **scarcity** leads to **redistribution**. In modern economics, **cycles of giving and receiving** are crucial for sustaining balanced systems. Just as **ecological systems** are interdependent, so too should be **economic systems** that reflect Heaven's abundance.

Research into **sustainable economies**, **green energy**, and **social enterprises** aligns with the biblical principle of **stewardship** of the earth's resources and God's call for a just and flourishing society. **Technological innovation** also reflects the principles of **God's creation**, where new discoveries provide ways to distribute resources equitably.

DIVINE ECONOMIC MANDATE: KINGDOM AMBASSADORS IN THE EARTHLY ECONOMY

The Role of Believers as Ambassadors of the Throne Room Economy

Believers are not only **recipients of God's provision** but are also called to be **ambassadors** of Heaven's economy on earth. **2 Corinthians 5:20** declares, *"We are therefore Christ's ambassadors, as though God were making His appeal through us."*

As **ambassadors**, Christians are entrusted with the mission of **bringing the government of Heaven to Earth**. This includes implementing **divine wisdom** in all areas of life: from business and economics to politics and social justice.

- **Matthew 25:14-30 (The Parable of the Talents)**: This parable teaches the principle of **faithful stewardship** and **multiplication of resources** in alignment with God's economy.

In every area of influence, Christians are called to live out **Kingdom principles**, generosity, **integrity**, **justice**, and **compassion**, and to use their **resources** to advance God's purposes.

IN SUMMARY: ALIGNING WITH THE THRONE ROOM ECONOMY

The **Throne Room Economy** is not just a concept for future glory but a **reality to be implemented on earth today**. It is a kingdom model that operates on divine **justice, abundance,** and **wisdom**. As believers, we are called to partner with God in **translating these heavenly principles** into **earthly systems**, bringing the **government of Heaven** to bear on the **economic systems** of the world.

By aligning ourselves with the principles of **God's Throne Room Economy**, we become part of the **divine mission** to **reconcile the earth** with Heaven, ensuring that God's **Kingdom comes** and His **will is done**

THRONE ROOM PROPHETIC PRAYERS AND DECREES

In this section, we activate **prophetic prayers and decrees** that align with the **Throne Room Economy** and the divine order of governance established in Heaven. These prayers are designed to invoke the presence and power of the Throne Room to manifest in our lives, communities, businesses, and governments. As we decree these prayers, we align ourselves with the principles of **justice**, **abundance**, and **wisdom** that flow from God's Throne to fulfill His purpose on Earth.

DECLARATION OF ALIGNMENT WITH THE THRONE ROOM ECONOMY

Prayer:

Heavenly Father,

I stand before Your throne today, acknowledging that You are the **King of all Kings**, the **Lord of all Lords**, and the **Sovereign Ruler** of all creation. Your Throne is established forever, and from Your seat of authority, You dispense wisdom, provision, and justice to the nations of the earth.

Father, I align my life, my family, my business, and all that I steward with Your **Throne Room Economy**. Let the resources of Heaven pour into every area of my life. Let Your divine justice, abundance, and wisdom govern every decision, every plan, and every action I take.

I decree that Your **Kingdom** will manifest on earth as it is in Heaven, and Your **will** shall be done in every realm of influence I possess. I declare that the **wealth of Heaven** will flow to me and through me, bringing prosperity not only to my life but to all whom I am called to serve. In Jesus' name, Amen.

DECREE OF HEAVENLY PROVISION AND ABUNDANCE

Decree:

I decree and declare that **abundance** flows from the Throne Room of God into my life. According to **Philippians 4:19**, my God shall supply **all my needs** according to His riches in glory. I declare that there is **no lack** in God's Kingdom, and as a citizen of Heaven, I walk in the fullness of provision and resources.

I speak forth the abundance of Heaven over my finances, my business, my relationships, and my ministry. I declare that every door of opportunity is opened wide, and I walk in the **overflow** of divine supply. I am a faithful steward, and I align my heart with the principles of Heaven to manifest His resources on earth.

In the name of Jesus, I decree the **riches of His glory** will manifest through my obedience to His call and purpose.

DECREE OF DIVINE WISDOM AND UNDERSTANDING

Prayer:

Heavenly Father,

I thank You that Your wisdom is available to me through the **Holy Spirit**. You are the source of all knowledge, and from Your Throne, You release divine insight into every area of my life. I ask for the **mind of Christ** to be upon me, that I may discern Your will in all matters.

Father, I decree that I walk in divine wisdom and understanding in my business, my family, my ministry, and all that You have called me to do. Let Your **wisdom** guide my decisions, and may I always act in alignment with Your heavenly purpose.

I break off every spirit of confusion, doubt, and uncertainty, and I declare that I have the clarity and wisdom from Your Throne Room to navigate the challenges I face. I trust in Your guidance and in Your perfect timing. In Jesus' name, Amen.

DECREE OF JUSTICE AND RIGHTEOUSNESS

Decree:

I decree that justice and righteousness reign in every area of my life. From the Throne Room of Heaven, I speak forth divine **justice** in my relationships, my finances, and my dealings with others. I declare that God's justice will overrule every unjust situation and bring alignment with His Kingdom.

I speak forth that righteousness will be my foundation and that I will walk in **integrity**, **honesty**, and **fairness** in all my endeavors. I declare that every decision I make will be marked by God's **justice** and **righteousness**, and every obstacle will be removed in alignment with His divine will.

I decree that **God's judgment** and **correction** will establish order in my life, ensuring that His Kingdom is established in my sphere of influence. In Jesus' name, Amen.

DECREE OF GOVERNMENTAL AUTHORITY

Prayer:

Father,

As a **kingdom ambassador**, I stand in the authority You have given me as a citizen of Heaven. I declare that **Your government** is established in my life and in every place I influence. I declare that the **laws of the Kingdom of God** govern the earth through me, and I walk in the divine authority given to me by Christ.

I decree that every spirit of **control**, **manipulation**, or **illegitimate power** is broken over my life, and I take authority over every area I have been entrusted with. I declare that Heaven's laws govern the systems I interact with, from business to government, to relationships.

I bind and loose in alignment with Your Word, declaring that **Your will** be done on earth as it is in Heaven. Let Your governmental power be released to bring transformation and reform to all systems in Jesus' name. Amen.

DECREE OF KINGDOM ADVANCEMENT

Decree:

I decree that the **Kingdom of God** is advancing in every area of my life. I am part of a **divine strategy** that is reshaping the systems of this world according to God's will. I declare that every barrier, every opposition, and every spirit of **hindrance** is broken by the power of God.

I decree that I am a **Kingdom influencer** who is anointed to **bring change**, **establish peace**, and **implement righteousness** in my spheres of influence. The **gospel of the Kingdom** is advancing through me, and I will see the **glory of God** manifest in every area of my life and community.

I declare that the **Throne Room Economy** is expanding on the earth through the work of my hands, and I align my actions with God's purposes for the Kingdom's advancement.

In the name of Jesus, Amen.

PROPHETIC DECREE FOR NATION AND GLOBAL IMPACT

Decree:

I decree and declare that nations will be aligned with the purposes of God. From the **Throne Room of God**, I speak forth divine intervention, supernatural wisdom, and Kingdom authority into the governments of the earth. I declare that **godly leaders** will rise and that the systems of corruption, injustice, and oppression will be overthrown.

I speak peace over troubled regions, and I declare the **righteous reign** of Christ over the nations. I declare that the wealth of the nations will be brought to the Kingdom of God for the fulfillment of His purposes on earth.

I prophesy that global transformation will take place, and **Kingdom economics** will manifest across every continent, in every nation, and in every culture. We will see a great **awakening** to the principles of **God's government** in the earth.

In Jesus' name, Amen.

IN SUMMARY

As we activate these **prophetic prayers and decrees**, we align ourselves with the **Throne Room Economy** and God's divine order of governance. We declare that His will shall be done on earth as it is in Heaven, and we invite the abundant resources, divine wisdom, justice, and authority from Heaven to manifest in every area of our lives, businesses, ministries, and nations.

CHAPTER 25

Kingdom Investment Architectures: Building Eternal Value Systems

"Lay up for yourselves treasures in heaven, where neither moth nor rust destroys." ~Matthew 6:20 (NKJV)

DESIGNING FINANCIAL BLUEPRINTS THAT OUTLIVE GENERATIONS

In this era where investments are driven by volatility, speculation, and temporal gain, the Spirit of the Lord calls forth a generation of Kingdom stewards, builders of eternal value systems. Kingdom investment is not merely about stocks, real estate, cryptocurrencies, or startup portfolios; it is the construction of infrastructures, ecosystems, and spiritual blueprints that yield fruit not just in time, but into eternity.

This chapter unveils the divine architectures of true wealth, investments aligned with the Throne Room economy, governed by the principles of righteousness, justice, innovation, dominion, and eternal stewardship.

We will journey through divine wisdom, economic models, historical blueprints, and spiritual systems to understand how sons and daughters of the Kingdom can navigate financial infrastructures without being ensnared by mammon's altars.

It is time to build with stones of fire, investing in what Heaven values and sowing into eternal legacies!

THE SPIRITUAL FOUNDATION OF KINGDOM INVESTMENT

Investment is first and foremost a **spiritual principle**.

When Yahweh created Eden, He invested His Word, breath, and light into earth's soil (Genesis 2:7–8). The Tree of Life itself was an investment of divine energy into creation, intended for continual fruitfulness and communion.

- **Scripture:** *"Lay not up for yourselves treasures upon earth... but lay up for yourselves treasures in heaven..."* (Matthew 6:19–20).

- True Kingdom investment echoes Christ's parable of the talents (Matthew 25:14–30), where resourcefulness, creativity, and stewardship were celebrated.

- **Scientific Insight:** The law of sowing and reaping governs all economic and biological systems, input always generates output, according to the nature of the seed.

Thus, every investment, time, money, skill, knowledge, networks, must align with the spirit of righteousness and service unto the Lord.

PILLARS OF KINGDOM INVESTMENT ARCHITECTURES

These are the 7 Pillars on which Kingdom investment must stand:

1. **Alignment with Divine Purpose**, Investment must serve God's purposes on earth.

2. **Righteous Governance**, Financial dealings must be just, equitable, and transparent.

3. **Innovation for Humanity**, Innovations should advance life, liberty, and human dignity.

4. **Multiplication by Revelation**, Investing by the Spirit, not mere calculation.

5. **Territorial Transformation**, every investment should shift societal structures toward righteousness.

6. **Wealth for Generational Transfer**, building legacies that outlast one's lifetime.

7. **Worship Through Stewardship**, Investment becomes an act of worship when done in obedience and faith.

HISTORICAL AND SCIENTIFIC INSIGHTS

Ancient Economies:

- In ancient Israel, God's investment strategy involved land inheritance, agricultural stewardship, jubilee systems, and trade integrity.

- The Great Libraries of Alexandria and Timbuktu were investments into knowledge economies centuries ahead of their time.

Scientific Understanding:

- *Compound Interest Principle*: Even Albert Einstein reportedly remarked that "compound interest is the eighth wonder of the world." Kingdom economies understand spiritual compounding; every faithful seed multiplies beyond its visible dimension.

- **Fractal Economies:** Research shows economic systems often follow fractal patterns, similar to natural growth systems. Kingdom investments must follow "fractal faithfulness," building small scalable models that replicate righteousness across territories.

THE BATTLE OF THRONES: KINGDOM VS MAMMON

Mammon presents investment as extraction: **Take as much as you can, by any means necessary**.

Christ presents investment as expansion: **Grow, nurture, and multiply for the Father's glory**.

- **Scripture:** *"He that gathered much had nothing over, and he that gathered little had no lack."* (Exodus 16:18)

Modern capitalism often promotes short-term greed over long-term value. Kingdom investors, however, discern the **seasons of Heaven**, knowing when to sow, when to reap, when to steward, and when to relinquish.

STRATEGIES FOR KINGDOM INVESTORS

- **Prophetic Investment:** Listening to the Spirit's guidance for emerging industries, inventions, and human needs.

- **Covenantal Partnerships:** Aligning financially with other believers who carry the same heart and values.

- **Sowing into Apostolic Centers:** Supporting places that nurture truth, governance, innovation, and Kingdom education.

- **Building Non-Extractive Economies:** Designing businesses and investments that enrich communities rather than exploit them.

- **Wealth Intercession:** Praying over investments, contracts, and markets, shifting atmospheres with prophetic decrees.

ACTIVATION PRAYER:

"Father, I receive the mantle of Kingdom stewardship.

I renounce all agreements with mammon's greed, fear, and selfish ambition.

I align my hands, my heart, my mind, and my wealth with Your eternal purposes.

Breathe upon my investments, O Lord, and build through me infrastructures of righteousness.

Make me a wise master builder who plants seeds of innovation, righteousness, justice, and love across the earth.

In Yeshua's mighty name. Amen."

PROPHETIC DECREES:

- I decree; I am an ambassador of eternal value creation!
- I decree; my investments are fields of righteousness bearing harvests for generations.
- I decree, I build by the blueprints of the Lamb's scroll, not by the systems of Babylon!
- I decree, innovation, wisdom, and divine revelation flow through me without limit!
- I decree; wealth obeys the voice of Christ in me and fulfills its Kingdom assignment!

CHAPTER 26

Economic Thrones: Building Apostolic Cities and Financial Ecosystems for Christ

"They shall rebuild the old ruins; they shall raise up the former desolations." ~Isaiah 61:4 (NKJV)

ESTABLISHING APOSTOLIC CITIES AND FINANCIAL ECOSYSTEMS FOR KINGDOM GOVERNANCE

The restoration of Apostolic authority is not confined to church gatherings; it is an expansive call to **govern cities, nations, and economies** under the lordship of Christ.

Wherever there is commerce, governance, culture, and education, thrones are established. These thrones either exalt Christ or exalt Babylon.

God's design is that Apostolic and Prophetic architects rise up to **build cities** where economic ecosystems reflect the righteousness, justice, innovation, and life of the Kingdom.

In this chapter, we will unfold the revelation of **Economic Thrones**, explore **how cities and financial systems were historically built** around spiritual centers, and **how to establish modern Apostolic hubs** that birth economic ecosystems aligned with Heaven's economy.

The hour demands it; Kingdom **Builders** must arise!

GOD'S ORIGINAL BLUEPRINT: CITIES AS ECONOMIC THRONES

In Eden, Adam was given a **garden-city mandate,** not just to tend a patch of land but to expand the governance of Heaven across earth's geography.

• **Scripture:** *"And the Lord God took the man, and put him into the Garden of Eden to dress it and to keep it."* (Genesis 2:15)

Cities like Jerusalem, Antioch, Ephesus, and even Babylon were not accidental, they were strategic spiritual and economic centers.

Key Insight:

Where the altar stands, the economy follows.

Whoever controls the worship controls the trade.

Thus, building Apostolic cities is **building systems of worship, trade, innovation, education, governance, and justice**, centered around the Lordship of Christ.

HISTORICAL AND SCIENTIFIC INSIGHTS INTO CITY BUILDING

Ancient Patterns:

- **Jerusalem:** Spiritual, political, and economic center for Israel. The Temple was not only a place of worship but a financial hub, tithes, offerings, markets, and feasts generated massive commerce.

- **Timbuktu:** A center of trade and knowledge; ancient manuscripts show they understood wealth flows through centers of education and worship.

- **Alexandria:** Economic strength anchored in intellectual leadership and trade.

Scientific Urban Economics:

Modern studies reveal that **economic hubs form naturally** where:

- There is **trust** (righteousness in commerce)

- There are **innovations and technology**

- There is **governance that secures wealth creation and distribution**

Conclusion:

Apostolic builders must intentionally design these systems, no longer by accident, but by revelation.

KINGDOM STRATEGIES FOR BUILDING ECONOMIC THRONES

1. Apostolic Centers as Ecosystems:

Apostolic hubs must be **multi-dimensional ecosystems** where:

- Entrepreneurs are trained

- Innovations are incubated

- Education is reformed

- Arts and culture are redeemed

- Financial systems are righteously stewarded

- Intercession and spiritual governance cover all activity

2. Seven Mountain Focus:

Influencing the "Seven Mountains" (Business, Government, Education, Arts & Entertainment, Media, Family, and Religion) must not be random; it must be strategic, prophetic, and systemic.

3. Financial Systems Redeemed:

- Launching Kingdom banks, investment firms, microfinance platforms, blockchain systems anchored in righteousness

- Building housing, technology, agriculture, and healthcare that serve communities with excellence and justice

- Restoring land, cities, and territories spiritually through **prophetic acts** and **economic transformation**

APOSTOLIC GOVERNANCE OVER ECONOMIC THRONES

Scripture Foundation:

"...The government shall be upon His shoulder..." (Isaiah 9:6)

Governance Keys:

- Apostolic leaders must function like Nehemiah, builders, **governors, and reformers**.

- Prophetic voices must function like Haggai and Zechariah, encouraging, **instructing, and releasing decrees** over economic structures.

- Apostolic councils must oversee not only ministries but also economic infrastructures, ensuring that wealth flows align with Kingdom purposes.

WARFARE OVER ECONOMIC THRONES

Economic thrones are fiercely contested because **he who controls wealth, controls influence**.

- **Mammonic thrones** operate by fear, greed, and manipulation.

- **Kingdom thrones** operate by faith, love, and stewardship.

Spiritual Protocols:

- Prophetic Declarations over Land and Markets

- Intercession for breaking demonic trade covenants

- Anointing cities and territories for Kingdom occupation

Example Prayer:

"We declare over this city: Let the gates be lifted up! Let the King of Glory come in! Let wealth flow according to righteousness and innovation! Let unjust systems be shaken and dismantled, in the Name of Jesus Christ!"

ACTIVATION PRAYER:

"Lord Jesus, the true King, I submit myself to Your economic governance.

Anoint me as a wise builder of Apostolic centers.

Teach me to steward wealth, innovation, governance, and education according to Heaven's pattern.

I claim cities, territories, and economies for Your glory!

Use me as a blueprint architect for generations to come!

In Your mighty Name. Amen."

PROPHETIC DECREES:

- I decree; I am a builder of righteous cities and economic ecosystems!

- I decree, apostolic centers arise in every nation, fueled by innovation and prophetic revelation!

- I decree, the altars of mammon collapse, and Kingdom wealth flows are established!

- I decree; cities and nations are discipled in the Name of Jesus Christ!

CHAPTER 27

Kingdom Cryptography: Spiritual Codes for Wealth and Innovation in the Age of Digital Currency

"It is the glory of God to conceal a matter, but the glory of kings is to search out a matter." ~Proverbs 25:2 (NKJV)

UNLOCKING DIVINE CODES FOR PROSPERITY AND INNOVATION IN A DECENTRALIZED AGE

In every era of technological revolution, hidden codes and patterns govern wealth transfer.

In the ancient world, trade routes, secret guilds, and coded contracts determined who prospered. Today, as the **Digital Currency** revolution explodes, Bitcoin, Ethereum, tokenized economies, decentralized finance (DeFi), a **new form of hidden language and cryptography** rules commerce.

Yet beneath the natural codes lies **a deeper spiritual cryptography**, God's encrypted wisdom for wealth creation, innovation, and dominion in the digital age.

Christ, the Living Word, holds the **Master Code**.

This chapter will **unveil how the Kingdom of God** carries **superior codes**, for accessing wealth, creating technology, establishing innovation, and governing decentralized economies, all in righteousness.

We are entering the era of **Kingdom Cryptographers**!

CRYPTOGRAPHY IN THE NATURAL WORLD

Definition: Cryptography is the science of encoding information to ensure secure communication and protect value.

Historical Context:

- **Egyptians** used secret hieroglyphics to secure royal trade and administration.

- **Hebrew scholars** like the Masoretes encoded scriptures with intricate systems of counting, gematria (numerical values of letters), and acrostics.

- **World War II** was influenced by cryptography (e.g., Enigma machine cracked by Alan Turing).

- **Modern Blockchain** technology is built entirely on cryptographic security: distributed ledgers, encryption keys, and smart contracts.

Key Scientific Principle:

Private Key/Public Key Dynamics

(Only those who possess the private key can unlock the hidden wealth, prophetic symbolism!)

SPIRITUAL CRYPTOGRAPHY: GOD'S HIDDEN CODES

Scriptural Proof:

- *"It is the glory of God to conceal a matter; to search out a matter is the glory of kings."* (Proverbs 25:2)

God encrypts truths, mysteries, technologies, and destinies, awaiting **kingly sons and daughters** to decode them.

Examples of Divine Cryptography:

- **Joseph's Dreams:** Encoded symbols interpreted to unlock economic survival in famine.

- **Daniel's Visions:** Cosmic codes about empires and future economies.

- **Parables of Jesus:** Hidden keys to the Kingdom disguised in simple agricultural language.

KINGDOM CRYPTOGRAPHERS: ACCESSING WEALTH AND INNOVATION

Characteristics of Kingdom Cryptographers:

- **Revelatory Intelligence:** Not just IQ, but Spirit-birthed perception.

- **Stewardship of Mysteries:** Handling sacred insights without distortion or pride.

- **Technological Anointing:** Ability to translate spiritual codes into natural inventions and innovations.

Practical Application:

- Seeking God for secret blueprints in digital infrastructure.

- Receiving "smart contract" revelations in righteousness (governed by the justice and mercy of Christ).

- Designing decentralized economic systems that reflect Kingdom order and equity.

DECODING THE AGE OF DIGITAL CURRENCY

Blockchain Technology and Prophetic Parallels:

- **Immutable Ledger:** Symbol of God's unchangeable record books (Malachi 3:16 - Book of Remembrance).

- **Decentralization:** No one corrupt entity controls it, picture of the true Ecclesia governed by Christ alone.

- **Smart Contracts:** Self-executing covenants, picture of the eternal covenant we have through Christ.

Warning:

Satan's counterfeit will attempt to use blockchain for global control

(Revelation 13:17 - "no one can buy or sell unless...") but the righteous will establish Kingdom alternatives ahead of Babylon's collapse.

MYSTICAL AND ANCIENT TEXT INSIGHTS

- **Book of Enoch:** Describes knowledge given by fallen beings; however, redeemed wisdom is reserved for sons of Light.
- **Solomon's Secrets:** Many inventions attributed to Solomon (including fountains, gates, and even theories of metallurgy and precious stones).
- **Mystical Hebrew Understanding:** Letters and numbers carried vibrational frequencies connected to creation (Genesis 1, God speaks and forms worlds).

Conclusion:

Kingdom builders must understand not only **natural code** but also **spiritual sound codes, frequency alignments, and innovation grids** rooted in the Throne of God.

ACTIVATION PRAYER:

"Father, Creator of the Universe, open my mind and spirit to Your hidden wisdom.

Grant me access to the encrypted wealth reserved for the righteous.

Make me a Kingdom cryptographer, decoding mysteries, building righteous technologies, and releasing innovation that glorifies Your Name.

Teach me to discern between Babylonian codes and Zion's codes.

In Jesus Christ's Name. Amen!"

PROPHETIC DECREES:

- I decree, I am a cryptographer of the Kingdom, unlocking mysteries for wealth and innovation!

- I decree; divine codes are unveiled to me for governing the digital economies righteously!

- I decree; I move with prophetic intelligence and apostolic stewardship!

- I decree; Kingdom cities and financial ecosystems are established through encrypted wisdom from above!

CHAPTER 28

Currency Wars: Discerning Babylon's Digital Trap vs Zion's Kingdom Economy

(Scientific, Spiritual, Mystical, Historical, and Scriptural)

"The Lord will open to you His good treasure, the heavens… and you shall lend to many nations, but you shall not borrow." ~Deuteronomy 28:12 (NKJV)

UNMASKING BABYLON'S MONETARY CHAINS AND ENFORCING ZION'S ABUNDANCE

The world is on the brink of a total monetary metamorphosis.

Nations are racing to digitize their currencies.

Global elites are crafting **Central Bank Digital Currencies (CBDCs)**, programmable money tied to surveillance.

Meanwhile, the true sons of the Kingdom are being summoned into divine economic strategies, rooted not in fear, but in **the economy of Zion**.

We are entering the **Currency Wars**, a battle not merely of technology or finance, but of **spiritual thrones and dominions**.

Babylon seeks to trap humanity through artificial scarcity, control, and fear. Zion calls for the **revelation of heavenly abundance, liberty, and righteous dominion**.

This chapter will unveil how to **discern the Babylonian traps** and **walk in the superior economic system of Christ's Kingdom**.

THE RISE OF BABYLONIAN DIGITAL CURRENCIES

Scientific and Economic Context:

- **CBDCs (Central Bank Digital Currencies):** Digital version of national currencies fully controlled by central banks.

- **Programmable Money:** Authorities can program where, when, and how your money is spent.

- **Social Credit Systems:** Spending tied to political and behavioral compliance.

Key Insight:

Digital currencies, when weaponized, become tools for totalitarian control, fulfilling the warning of Revelation 13:16–17 (*"that no one may buy or sell except one who has the mark..."*).

Historical Parallel:

- Babylon's ancient control over trade via taxation, monopolized currency, and debt enslavement.

- Rome's control of provincial economies via minted coins stamped with Caesar's image ("Give unto Caesar...").

ZION'S ECONOMY: GOD'S FINANCIAL BLUEPRINT

Scriptural Foundations:

- *"But you shall remember the LORD your God, for it is He who gives you power to get wealth..."* (Deuteronomy 8:18)

- *"The wealth of the sinner is stored up for the righteous."* (Proverbs 13:22)

Key Characteristics of Zion's Economy:

- **Faith-Based Trust:** Wealth flows through covenant relationship with God, not manipulative systems.

- **Generosity and Stewardship:** Wealth is circulated, not hoarded; designed to empower families, communities, and nations.

- **Multiplication by Wisdom:** Wealth grows through divine strategies, innovation, and creativity (Matthew 25:14–30 - Parable of the Talents).

DISCERNMENT BETWEEN BABYLON AND ZION

Signs of Babylonian Traps:

- Fear-based control: ("If you don't comply, your access to funds is frozen.")

- Artificial scarcity: ("Resources are limited, you must compete ruthlessly.")

- Manipulation through inflation, taxation, and surveillance.

Signs of Zion's Economy:

- Supernatural provision and favor.

- Community wealth-building and mutual empowerment.

- Economic systems anchored in justice, mercy, and humility before God.

SPIRITUAL AND MYSTICAL INSIGHTS

Ancient Mystical Teachings:

- **Hebrew Mysticism:** Currency was seen as an extension of covenant, gold and silver symbolized purity of heart and divine reflection.

- **Early Ecclesia Economics:** Believers shared resources (*Acts 2:44–47*) and no one among them lacked.

- **Mystical Codes of Abundance:** Hidden teachings among early Desert Fathers that "grace releases geometric expansion of provision when aligned in Christ."

Spiritual Warfare Aspect:

The battle for currency is a battle for **hearts**, **trust**, and **worship**.

(See Matthew 6:24, "*You cannot serve both God and Mammon.*")

SCIENTIFIC INSIGHTS ON DECENTRALIZED WEALTH

Decentralized Finance (DeFi) Potential:

- Blockchain ecosystems offer transparent, trustless platforms (foreshadowing Kingdom principles of truth and accountability).

- Peer-to-peer economies reflect the relational, covenantal nature of biblical commerce.

Caution:

Decentralized systems can still be corrupted if not anchored in Kingdom ethics.

Righteous innovation must be stewarded by **spiritually mature sons and daughters**.

PROPHETIC ROADMAP: TRANSITIONING INTO KINGDOM ECONOMICS

Strategic Movements:

- Anchor your wealth in relationships, skills, land, and Kingdom community, not just digital tokens.

- Seek divine innovation in alternative economies (barter, tokenized assets, shared ownership models).

- Discern economic shifts prophetically, stay ahead by the Spirit.

ACTIVATION PRAYER:

"Father, Sovereign King of Zion,

I align my heart with Your economy.

Grant me discernment to recognize the traps of Babylon and wisdom to walk in Your abundance.

Empower me to create, steward, and multiply wealth for Your glory.

Let me not be ensnared by fear, but advance in righteousness, boldness, and supernatural provision.

I receive strategies from the Throne Room for this new era.

In Christ's Holy Name, Amen!"

PROPHETIC DECREES:

- I decree I am delivered from Babylon's economic systems!

- I decree my wealth is anchored in Christ and multiplied by heavenly wisdom!

- I decree Zion's prosperity flows through my life, family, and generation!

- I decree I walk in supernatural provision, innovation, and kingdom influence!

CHAPTER 29

The Grand Dominion

"Then the kingdom and dominion, and the greatness of the kingdoms under the whole heaven, shall be given to the people, the saints of the Most High. His kingdom is an everlasting kingdom, and all dominions shall serve and obey Him." ~Daniel 7:27 (NKJV)

SUBDUING THE BANKING SYSTEMS AND GLOBAL ECONOMIC THRONES

We have arrived at the crescendo of the ages:

The clash between the thrones of **Mammon** and the **Dominion of Christ** is intensifying on the world stage.

Banking systems, economic infrastructures, financial institutions, digital currencies, corporate empires, and government policies are all converging into a **quantum leap of economic warfare**.

Yet, in the midst of this cosmic shaking, the **Ecclesia** is arising, kings and priests empowered by the wisdom of heaven, to **subdue**, **restructure**, **govern**, and **legislate** the new economic age in alignment with the **Kingdom of Christ**.

This is not just about survival.

It is about **dominion, innovation, reformation**, and **restoration**, all under the **government of His peace** (Isaiah 9:6–7).

This chapter reveals **how the sons of God will rule the systems that once ruled over them**, fulfilling Daniel's prophecy:

> **"And the kingdom and the dominion and the greatness of the kingdoms under the whole heaven shall be given to the people of the saints of the Most High; their kingdom shall be an everlasting kingdom..."** (Daniel 7:27).

SCIENTIFIC AND ECONOMIC PERSPECTIVES:

- Traditional banks were built on **fractional reserve banking**, creating money out of debt, a false principle contrary to the abundance of Zion.

- Global banking cartels (IMF, World Bank, BIS) have historically orchestrated economic bondage under the guise of aid.

- **Quantum financial systems** (QFS) are now emerging, promising decentralized ledgers and transparent operations.

MYSTICAL REVELATION:

- In ancient scrolls, "weights and measures" were sacred; manipulating them was seen as an abomination before God (Proverbs 11:1).
- True Kingdom wealth flows from righteous stewardship, not the multiplication of debt.

STRATEGY IN CHRIST:

Apostolic financiers must create **trust-based community banks, credit unions**, and **investment vehicles** aligned with righteous values.

Wealth must be governed by **kingdom ethics**: honesty, generosity, accountability, and wisdom.

SUBDUING ECONOMIC INSTITUTIONS AND CORPORATE GOVERNANCE

Historical and Modern Reality:

- From the East India Company to today's tech giants, corporations have become **economic sovereigns** wielding global influence.
- Corporate governance often promotes profit at the expense of humanity, ecology, and truth.

Spiritual Warfare Insight:

- "Principalities and powers" are enthroned over economic systems (Ephesians 6:12).

- These are dismantled through **righteous innovation, kingdom entrepreneurship, prophetic legislation**, and **marketplace apostleship**.

Kingdom Protocols:

- Raise "Ecclesia Corporations", businesses founded on Christ's leadership, prayer altars, prophetic direction, and Spirit-led governance.

- Teach and implement **covenant wealth principles** in the marketplace: fair wages, resource multiplication, environmental stewardship, and community building.

SUBDUING DIGITAL CURRENCIES AND QUANTUM FINANCIAL SYSTEMS

Scientific Developments:

- CBDCs (Central Bank Digital Currencies) are designed for surveillance and control.

- Blockchain and decentralized finance (DeFi) represent a break from old structures but still need spiritual governance.

- Quantum financial systems are being tested to allow instant transactions secured by quantum encryption.

Kingdom Innovations:

- Sons of God must pioneer **Kingdom Coins, prophetic digital ecosystems, community currencies** backed by tangible value (land, resources, services).

- Build **quantum righteous wealth nodes**, decentralized hubs governed by Spirit-filled leaders.

Scriptural Basis:

- Proverbs 22:7, *"The borrower is slave to the lender."* Therefore, the Ecclesia must build systems that liberate, not enslave.

SUBDUING GOVERNMENTAL ECONOMIC POLICIES

Historical Pattern:

- Pharaoh's Egypt enslaved the Hebrews economically (Genesis 47).

- Babylon dictated economic worship through allegiance (Daniel 3).

- Rome taxed Judea to the point of rebellion (Matthew 22).

Modern Reality:

- Global governance bodies (WEF, WTO, UN) aim to control economic life through treaties, sanctions, and regulations.

- "Economic Hitmen" tactics (as revealed by John Perkins) are still active, manipulating emerging nations into debt dependency.

Kingdom Response:

- **Marketplace prophets** must rise to advise kings, governors, and presidents (like Daniel, Joseph, Esther).

- **Legislative Ecclesia Councils** must form in cities and nations to intercede and influence policies toward righteousness and justice.

Scripture:

> **Psalm 2:8,** "*Ask of Me, and I will give You the nations for Your inheritance, and the ends of the earth for Your possession.*"

FUTURE ECONOMIC SYSTEMS AND CORPORATE GOVERNANCE

Scientific and Economic Futurism:

- AI will manage economies, smart contracts, and supply chains.
- Biotechnology and digital identity will intersect with finance.
- Energy-based currencies (like kilowatt-hours) will emerge.

Mystical and Spiritual Insights:

- Ancient prophecies (such as those in Isaiah 60) speak of wealth transferring to the righteous at the end of the age.
- Mystical laws of multiplication, as demonstrated by Christ (e.g., feeding the five thousand), will unlock quantum abundance.

Dominion Strategy:

- Build **Kingdom Quantum Infrastructures** integrating finance, health, energy, and education through Spirit-governed AI.
- Govern AI systems prophetically, training them to recognize Kingdom ethics and righteousness.

RECLAIMING GLOBALIZATION

Original Mandate:

- Globalization was meant to connect the nations for worship and partnership under God (Genesis 11 pre-Tower).
- The Tower of Babel corrupted globalization for prideful rebellion.

Today's Restoration:

- Ecclesia-led globalization focuses on **righteous trade, shared innovation, human flourishing**, and **gospel advancement**.

Final Vision:

- Habakkuk 2:14, *"For the earth will be filled with the knowledge of the glory of the LORD, as the waters cover the sea."*

  Revelation 11:15, *"The kingdoms of this world have become the kingdoms of our Lord and of His Christ, and He shall reign forever and ever!"*

PRAYER POINTS

- **Father, we decree:** Let every global banking structure bow to the dominion of Christ. (Daniel 7:27)
- **Lord, raise righteous financiers:** Empower apostolic stewards to govern wealth with justice and truth.
- **We renounce Mammonic systems:** We break allegiance with debt-driven economies and align with Kingdom abundance.

CLOSING PROPHETIC DECLARATIONS:

- I decree that Christ is enthroned over all financial systems, now and forever!
- I decree righteous thrones arise over banking, corporate governance, and global trade!
- I decree that the Ecclesia will steward the quantum economy with wisdom, power, and love!
- I decree Zion's economy will overshadow Babylon's systems!
- I decree innovation, multiplication, and supernatural provision overflow in the nations!

FINAL APOSTOLIC CHARGE:

Arise, sons and daughters of Zion!

Subdue the banking systems.

Govern the infrastructures of globalization.

Manifest the economy of heaven on the earth!

For Christ's Kingdom is advancing through your hands, your minds, your voices, your technologies, and your innovations.

And of the increase of His government and peace, there shall be no end! (Isaiah 9:7)

CHAPTER 30

Demystifying Taxes, Credit Systems, and Financial Slavery: A Kingdom Perspective on Global Debt Institutions

"Owe no one anything except to love one another,
for he who loves another has fulfilled the law."
~Romans 13:8 (NKJV)

THE HIDDEN CHAINS OF MODERN BONDAGE

In the 21st-century matrix of modern finance, many nations and individuals alike are entangled in systems that appear beneficial but often operate as sophisticated instruments of economic bondage. Taxes, credit card debts, mortgage systems, and insurance schemes have become normalized tools of financial control and surveillance, administered by institutional giants like the **World Bank**, **International Monetary Fund (IMF)**, and interlinked central banking networks.

Yet beneath these systems lie deep spiritual architectures. They are *not just economic protocols*, they are **altars** upon which lives, destinies, and entire territories are bound by invisible covenants. This chapter unmasks the **spiritual warfare behind taxation, debt, and control**, illuminating how these policies often align more with Mammon than with Christ. Through a prophetic, scriptural, and geopolitical lens, we uncover the kingdom alternative, a financial liberty rooted in justice, stewardship, and supernatural provision.

THE ORIGIN OF TAXATION: ANCIENT AND IMPERIAL BLUEPRINTS

Long before modern governments, **taxation** was a ritual of kings and empires. In Babylon, Egypt, and Rome, taxes funded military conquest and temple worship. But often, they were also instruments of enslavement. In **1 Samuel 8:10–18**, God warned Israel about kings who would tax their vineyards, flocks, and sons:

> **"He will take a tenth of your grain and of your vintage and give it to his officers and his servants…"** (1 Samuel 8:15)

This taxation pattern still echoes in today's national economies, where the redistribution of wealth often serves **elite networks**, not public good.

CREDIT SYSTEMS AND DEBT: A MODERN BONDAGE

The **credit card industry** and personal debt systems represent a subtle entrapment model. What appears as convenience is in many cases the road to financial servitude. Proverbs 22:7 declares:

"The borrower is servant to the lender."

Most citizens live **in engineered debt cycles**, from student loans to housing mortgages, fueled by **usury systems** designed to extract lifelong interest. These cycles are spiritually upheld by **altars of mammon**, where fear, greed, and scarcity rule.

Key Observations:

- Credit card interest is compounded mathematically to extract excess

- Consumer credit is rarely created to build assets

- The system teaches *minimum payments*, not financial dominion

MORTGAGE SYSTEMS: SPIRITUAL CONTRACTS OF OWNERSHIP

The word **mortgage** comes from the Latin *mortuus* (dead) and *gage* (pledge), meaning **"death pledge."** Most homeowners don't realize they're entering into *spiritual and financial contracts* designed to enslave them for decades.

"You shall lend to many nations but borrow from none." (Deuteronomy 15:6)

God's economic system does not include 30-year interest-based loans. It operates through **inheritance, community wealth, jubilee,** and supernatural multiplication.

INSURANCE: FEAR-BASED ECONOMICS

Insurance, while offering protection, often leverages **fear of the unknown** as a driver for mass compliance. Though practical in some forms, many insurance policies are embedded within **systems that profit from death, disaster, and scarcity.**

Behind the scenes, **risk algorithms, predictive modeling, and actuarial sciences** are infused with data collection, fueling **behavioral control** and surveillance under the guise of safety.

THE IMF, WORLD BANK & GLOBAL FINANCIAL THRONES

Both the **International Monetary Fund (IMF)** and **World Bank** function as **gatekeepers of national economies**, particularly in the Global South. While they offer development loans, the conditions often enforce **austerity, privatization, and dependency,** all of which disrupt national sovereignty and biblical stewardship.

Case Examples:

- **IMF structural adjustment programs** often force nations to cut healthcare, education, and agriculture

- **World Bank loans** require deregulation of local economies, favoring multinational corporations

- These institutions often operate outside democratic oversight but enforce **policy alignment globally**

SCIENTIFIC AND ECONOMIC ANALYSIS: HOW THE SYSTEM WORKS

- **Quantitative easing**, inflation, and **compound interest** are mathematical tools used by central banks to manipulate economic climates.

- **Credit scoring algorithms** influence not just loans but employment, insurance, and mobility.
- **Behavioral economics** is now being weaponized to modify citizens' financial choices at a subconscious level.

THE KINGDOM RESPONSE: JUBILEE, JUSTICE & FINANCIAL LIBERATION

Christ is **not neutral** about economic systems. He flipped tables at the temple (Matthew 21:12–13) because **financial control had become spiritual corruption.**

The **Kingdom financial model** includes:

- **Debt cancellation and Jubilee** (Leviticus 25)
- **Righteous scales and measurements** (Proverbs 11:1)
- **Ownership by inheritance, not enslavement**
- **Apostolic stewardship over economies**

PROPHETIC ACTIVATION AND DECREES

Prayer:

"Father, in the name of Jesus, we expose every hidden altar of economic bondage through debt, taxation, and global policy. We dismantle every ungodly financial contract and activate the dominion of the saints in global commerce. Let every illegal spiritual lien over our lands and families be overturned by the blood of Jesus!"

Prophetic Decree:

"We declare that the Ecclesia shall rise as a Joseph generation, economically wise, spiritually alert, and sovereign in stewardship. We speak Kingdom economies into existence, governed by righteousness, equity, and supernatural provision."

SCRIPTURAL FOUNDATIONS

- **Luke 4:18** – "…to proclaim liberty to the captives…"
- **Deuteronomy 28:12** – "You shall lend to many nations but borrow from none."
- **Proverbs 13:22** – "A good man leaves an inheritance to his children's children."

CHAPTER 31

Thrones of Evasion: How Global Elites Escape Taxes and Redefine Financial Systems

"For the Lord is our Judge, the Lord is our Lawgiver, the Lord is our King; He will save us." ~Isaiah 33:22 (NKJV)

THE MASK OF LEGALITY AND THE MACHINERY OF GREED

In a world where the working class shoulders the tax burden, the **ultra-wealthy and corporate elites** architect systems to **evade the very economic obligations** they claim to uphold. Beneath the glitter of philanthropy, innovation, and financial empire-building lies a **dark labyrinth of tax havens, offshore shell corporations, and manipulated financial services**, where **dominion is weaponized against justice**.

This chapter exposes the **global tax avoidance matrix**, not as an isolated crime of economics, but as **a spiritual and structural rebellion** against righteous stewardship. These systems are rooted in ancient **Babylonian financial ideologies**, modern **technocratic secrecy**, and mystical alignments with Mammon, not Christ. The throne of money has been corrupted, but the **Ecclesia is rising** to confront and overturn these thrones in prophetic authority.

THE RISE OF TAX EVASION KINGDOMS: SHADOW EMPIRES OF THE BILLIONAIRE CLASS

While middle and lower-income individuals are tracked, taxed, and penalized, **billionaires legally escape** through:

- **Shell companies in offshore jurisdictions** (e.g., Panama, Cayman Islands, Luxembourg)
- **Nonprofit foundations that mask profit** under the guise of philanthropy
- **Stock-based compensation** and untaxed capital gains
- **Trust funds and dynastic loopholes**

This isn't *tax evasion by accident*, it is **financial sorcery by design**, crafting systems where wealth flows upward, taxation flows downward, and **sovereign nations are held hostage by corporate empires**.

"Woe to those who make unjust laws, to those who issue oppressive decrees." (Isaiah 10:1)

LEGAL BUT IMMORAL: THE TECHNOLOGY OF LOOPHOLES

The global elite hide behind the term **"legal tax avoidance,"** but legality does not equal righteousness. Kingdom governance demands not just **legal compliance**, but **moral and spiritual alignment**.

Common tools of billionaire tax avoidance:

- **Double Irish with a Dutch Sandwich** (routing money through Ireland and the Netherlands to avoid U.S. tax)
- **Family Office loopholes**
- **Carried interest loophole** (private equity billionaires taxed less than their employees)
- **Deferred income via stock options**

These systems reflect **the mystery of iniquity**, where entire financial architectures are raised **to frustrate equity**, the opposite of the **Jubilee economy of Christ** (Leviticus 25).

ANCIENT BABYLON AND THE MANIPULATION OF TRIBUTE

In **Babylon**, elites sat in the temple precincts, controlling weights and measures while taxing the poor. This mirrors modern corporate policy where:

- The rich **externalize costs** (environmental damage, low wages)
- They **internalize profits** via manipulated subsidies and government contracts
- They use **spiritual inversion** by calling oppression "efficiency"

    "A false balance is abomination to the Lord: but a just weight is his delight." (Proverbs 11:1)

SCIENTIFIC AND TECHNOCRATIC INFRASTRUCTURE BEHIND TAX MANIPULATION

Today's avoidance is **not primitive evasion**, it's built on:

- Blockchain cloaking and crypto-shell laundering

- AI-powered predictive accounting

- Global digital infrastructures beyond local law

- FinTech systems that outpace regulation

This signals a **post-democratic economic era** where **algorithms, not laws**, determine wealth flow. Without **prophetic governance**, AI becomes a **beast system of economic judgment**, not liberty.

SPIRITUAL ROOT: THE THRONE OF MAMMON VS. THE GOVERNMENT OF CHRIST

"No one can serve two masters... You cannot serve both God and mammon." (Matthew 6:24)

Tax evasion at this level is not merely greed, it's allegiance. The elite financial thrones **bow not to Caesar, nor to Christ, but to Mammon**, a spiritual principality that thrives on hoarding, manipulation, and fear. This throne must be **confronted prophetically and institutionally** by the Ecclesia.

THE ROLE OF PHILANTHROCAPITALISM: MASKING GREED AS GENEROSITY

Many billionaires use foundations to:

- Avoid capital gains and estate taxes
- Gain public influence through "charity"
- Invest in the very systems they claim to fix (e.g., pharmaceutical control, education surveillance)

This creates **a circular economy of deception**, where the **throne of money disguises itself as an angel of light.**

> **"Even Satan disguises himself as an angel of light."**
> **(2 Corinthians 11:14)**

GOD'S ANSWER: A JOSEPH GENERATION AND KINGDOM CORPORATE GOVERNANCE

Christ is raising kings and priests in the order of **Melchizedek,** who are:

- Financially clean
- Prophetically wise
- Structurally bold
- Administratively righteous

> **"By me kings reign and rulers issue decrees that are just."** (Proverbs 8:15)

The **Joseph and Daniel archetypes** are emerging, governing economies, interpreting mysteries, and confronting unrighteous systems **without corruption.**

PROPHETIC DECREES AND PRAYER STRATEGY

Prayer:

"Lord of Hosts, expose the hidden treasures in secret places. Uproot every structure built upon greed and injustice. Let the thrones of manipulation be overthrown, and let righteous governance arise among the nations in the name of Jesus."

Decree:

"We declare that the kingdoms of this world are becoming the kingdoms of our Lord and of His Christ. The false thrones of wealth, the towers of tax evasion, and the fortresses of mammon are collapsing by fire. A new economy of justice, integrity, and divine stewardship is rising!"

SCRIPTURAL REFERENCES

- **Isaiah 45:3** – "I will give you hidden treasures, riches stored in secret places."

- **James 5:1–6** – Warning to the rich who oppress

- **Ecclesiastes 5:8** – "If you see the poor oppressed... do not be surprised..."

CHAPTER 32

Thrones of Greed, Corporate Corruption and the Crime of Political Power

"He shall judge the world in righteousness, and He shall administer judgment for the peoples in uprightness." ~Psalm 9:8 (NKJV)

THE BEAST BEHIND THE CURTAIN

In every age, the fusion of wealth and power has birthed monsters, **corporate empires that operate above the law** and **political regimes that legislate iniquity.** This chapter unveils the **spiritual architecture of greed**, the **hidden economy of corruption**, and how **Mammon enthrones itself through institutionalized wickedness** cloaked in policy, legislation, and global influence.

This is not just a political problem, it is a **spiritual crime scene**, where **Christ is calling His Ecclesia to judge the thrones of injustice** and reclaim the gates of influence with righteous governance.

THE ANATOMY OF CORPORATE GREED: A GLOBALIZED SYNDICATE

Multinational corporations, many wealthier than nations, now:

- Manipulate **labor markets** with unethical outsourcing and wage suppression
- Exploit **natural resources** with no accountability
- **Lobby political systems** to deregulate oversight
- Participate in **planned obsolescence** to drive unsustainable consumption

These structures mirror the **beast system in Revelation**, where **commerce, kings, and corruption** are inseparable.

> **"The merchants of the earth grew rich from her excessive luxuries.",** *Revelation 18:3*

THE MARRIAGE OF GREED AND GOVERNANCE

Throughout history:

- **The Medo-Persian empire** taxed and enslaved the poor to enrich noble classes

- **The Roman Empire** thrived on economic control through conquest and tribute

- **Modern democracies** veil corruption behind policy, where lobbyists write laws

Today's political crime is **subtle but systemic,** where governments serve **corporate donors,** not citizens. In many nations, **corruption is legalized via campaign financing, corporate bailouts, and economic manipulation.**

> **"They make many promises, take false oaths and make agreements; therefore, lawsuits spring up like poisonous weeds.",** Hosea *10:4*

SCIENTIFIC AND ECONOMIC PERSPECTIVES: STRUCTURAL CAPTURE

Scientific analysis of corruption shows that:

- **Regulatory capture** occurs when corporations control the very agencies meant to oversee them

- **Crony capitalism** emerges when business and political elites form an unbreakable alliance

- **Behavioral economics** confirms that **greed, once normalized, becomes institutional behavior**

Even AI-driven compliance systems are being **weaponized to entrench injustice,** further removing transparency and divine conscience from financial accountability.

SPIRITUAL AND MYSTICAL ROOTS: THE MAMMON THRONE SYSTEM

The throne of Mammon:

- Operates through **spiritual blindness and moral compromise**

- Seduces leaders with **false promises of invincibility**

- Corrupts institutions into becoming **tools of economic enslavement**

Jesus confronted this in the **Temple economy**, overturning the tables of currency exchangers who used **religion as a cover for extortion**.

> **"My house shall be called a house of prayer, but you have made it a den of thieves.", Matthew** *21:13*

ANCIENT AND HISTORIC EXAMPLES OF ECONOMIC TYRANNY

- **Egypt under Pharaoh** used economic control to enslave God's people

- **Babylon** taxed and captured talent to strengthen its empire (Daniel 1)

- **European colonial powers** extracted wealth from Africa, Asia, and the Americas through corrupted trade systems

- **Modern globalism** repeats these cycles through IMF loans, debt traps, and resource extraction

These are not mere cycles of history, they are **patterns of principalities** seeking to exalt themselves against Christ.

THE ECCLESIA'S ROLE: CONFRONTING THRONES OF INJUSTICE

The Church is not called to be a passive observer. Like:

- **Moses**, who challenged Pharaoh's economic system
- **Daniel**, who governed with integrity in Babylon
- **Nehemiah**, who restored walls and rebuked unjust nobles

Today's kingdom reformers must:

- Expose spiritual and structural corruption
- Advocate righteous policies
- Birth **new economic systems rooted in covenant and kingdom values**

> **"Let justice roll on like a river, righteousness like a never-failing stream!", Amos** 5:24

PROPHETIC DECLARATIONS AND STRATEGIC PRAYER

Prayer:

"Father, expose the hidden crimes of power. Break the alliances of greed and bring down the thrones of deception. Let your truth, justice, and kingdom economy invade the nations. Raise righteous reformers, prophetic financiers, and economic Daniels in this hour!"

Decree:

"We decree the collapse of unjust thrones, and the rise of kingdom governance. The kingdoms of men shall submit to the dominion of Christ. Corruption shall not reign. Mammon shall bow. Righteousness shall be established in every nation's economy!"

SCRIPTURAL ANCHORS

- **Ezekiel 28** – The prince of Tyre and economic arrogance

- **Luke 16:10–13** – Faithfulness in unrighteous mammon

- **Isaiah 1:23** – "Your rulers are rebels, partners with thieves... they do not defend the cause of the fatherless."

KINGDOM TECHNOLOGY OF ACCOUNTABILITY

Christ is raising systems and people to:

- Track unjust wealth flow prophetically and technologically

- Govern with transparency and supernatural discernment

- Design economic blueprints aligned with justice, equity, and eternal values

These technologies are not just natural; they are *prophetic mechanisms of kingdom alignment.*

CHAPTER 33

Greed, Capital, and the Corruption of Sacred and Social Institutions

"My house shall be called a house of prayer, but you have made it a den of thieves." ~Matthew 21:13 (NKJV)

THE THRONE OF MAMMON WITHIN THE CHURCH, MEDICINE, AND HUMANITARIANISM

In a world where the boundary between secular and sacred institutions has been blurred, this chapter lifts the veil on one of the deepest betrayals of trust: the manipulation of human need, spiritual, medical, and humanitarian, for capital gain. Greed is no longer just a sin of the marketplace; it has become embedded within religious sanctuaries, nonprofit platforms, pharmaceutical laboratories, and relief organizations. What was meant to preserve life now commodifies it. What was meant to save souls now sells them. In this chapter, we explore how systems originally designed to bring healing, hope, and restoration have been overtaken by a Babylonian economy of exploitation and mammonic governance, and we trace their roots through historical, economic, political, and cultural perspectives, all through the light of Christ and the revelation of scripture.

RELIGIOUS INSTITUTIONS AND THE SPIRIT OF MAMMON

Many religious institutions, called to be altars of transformation and sanctuaries of the Spirit, have become financial empires. Mega-infrastructures built in the name of Christ often mirror the capitalistic opulence of corporate America. The commodification of the Gospel is no longer concealed, it is **marketed, branded, and monetized**. Tithes and offerings, once sacred acts of worship, are now revenue streams subjected to business analytics and KPIs. This is not a critique of honor or generosity, but a diagnosis of institutionalized greed.

Scripture Insight:

"You cannot serve God and mammon." – **Matthew 6:24**

"My house shall be called a house of prayer, but you have made it a den of thieves." – **Matthew 21:13**

THE PHARMACEUTICAL THRONES AND MEDICAL INDUSTRY

Once a noble field of healing, **modern medicine has been absorbed into profit-driven pharmaco-capitalism**. Life-saving treatments are reserved for the rich. Cures are shelved to protect cash cows. Disease is not seen as an enemy but as a **revenue model**. Major pharmaceutical companies often push for **lifelong treatments rather than cures**, ensuring patient dependency.

Case Studies:

- The **opioid epidemic**, created and sustained by corporate greed, was driven by intentional overprescription.

- **Big Pharma lobbying** in the U.S. and Europe heavily influences drug pricing, clinical approval, and patent regulations, weaponizing regulation for capital advantage.

In Christ's Perspective:

Christ healed freely. He ministered without prejudice, and in His Kingdom, healing flows from compassion, not commerce.

FOOD SECURITY, GMO, AND ECONOMIC SLAVERY

Food has become **a weapon of geopolitical control**. Seed patents held by multinational corporations restrict indigenous farming. Genetically Modified Organisms (GMOs) are marketed under the guise of food security but often displace natural ecosystems and traditional agriculture, especially in Africa and South Asia.

Economic Slavery Through Food Aid:

In famine-stricken zones, food is used as a **bargaining chip for compliance**, politically, religiously, or economically. Aid becomes **an economic leash**, not a path to recovery.

Scripture Insight:

> *"He gives food to every creature. His love endures forever."* – **Psalm 136:25**

Christ multiplied bread, not monopolized it.

NONPROFITS, NGOS, AND HUMANITARIAN CORRUPTION

Billions flow through **Non-Governmental Organizations (NGOs)** and **international aid organizations**, yet much of it is filtered through bureaucratic overhead, corruption, and political deals. The world witnessed how **certain global aid funds were misappropriated in Haiti** post-earthquake and during the Ebola crisis in West Africa. Human pain became a **currency of exploitation**.

War Crisis Zones:

In many conflict areas, **"perpetual war"** is profitable. Arms deals, food supply monopolies, reconstruction contracts, and foreign aid serve as hidden economic engines. The longer the war, the longer the money flows.

Historical Patterns:

- Post-World War II, reconstruction became a lucrative industry.

- In modern times, **conflicts in Syria, Sudan, Ukraine, and Gaza** have revealed layers of **foreign interests, NGO profiteering, and corporate-military collusion**.

SECRET FUNDING SYSTEMS THAT SUSTAIN WAR

Beneath the surface lies a **shadow economy**. Multinational corporations, criminal syndicates, and intelligence agencies often operate through covert financial networks that **fuel both sides of a war**. These include:

- Illicit arms trade

- Resource theft (oil, diamonds, rare earth metals)

- Offshore tax havens used by "aid" organizations and politicians

Spiritual Reality:

War is not just a geopolitical phenomenon; it is an altar of blood. Human suffering becomes an offering to unseen spiritual thrones fueled by the **lust for dominion and wealth**.

Scripture Warning:

> *"Their feet run to evil, and they make haste to shed innocent blood."* – **Isaiah 59:7**

> *"For the love of money is the root of all evil."* ~ **1 Timothy 6:10**

IN HARMONY WITH CHRIST: REDEEMING THE ALTARS

Christ is not just Savior, He is King, Judge, and Restorer of Righteous Structures.

He cleansed the temple then, He is cleansing global systems now.

Call to the Ecclesia:

- Rise as reformers in medicine, education, governance, and food systems.

- Challenge corruption not just with protests but with **heaven's policy and prophetic decree**.

Raise kingdom-based alternatives, medical missions, sustainable agriculture, transparent ministries, and Spirit-filled governance.

ACTIVATION PRAYERS & PROPHETIC DECREES:

1. *Father, we repent on behalf of every institution, religious, medical, or humanitarian, that has bowed to the spirit of mammon. Restore righteousness to every altar.*

2. *By the authority of Christ, we expose and unravel every secret funding system fueling bloodshed in crisis zones.*

3. *We decree the rise of a new generation of kingdom economists, doctors, priests, and reformers who carry heaven's integrity and justice.*

4. *Let the tables of corruption be overturned in religious organizations, nonprofits, pharmaceutical giants, and economic structures.*

5. *By the spirit of wisdom and revelation, we dismantle the architectures of greed and establish blueprints of divine stewardship across the earth*

CHAPTER 34

Global Structures of Greed: The Economy of Human Trafficking and the Hyper-Mobility of Narcotics

Exposing Babylon's Hidden Commerce in the Light of Christ and Kingdom Justice

"For He will deliver the needy when he cries, the poor also, and him who has no helper." ~Psalm 72:12 (NKJV)

COMMERCE IN THE SHADOWS OF THRONES

The structures of global greed are not only built on the visible pillars of corporate monopoly and digital banking, they are also sustained by **underground economies**, rooted in **the darkest transactions of humanity**. Behind diplomatic dialogues and multinational summits lies a brutal truth: **a hidden empire profits from blood, bodies, and broken destinies**.

This chapter unmasks the **economy of exploitation**, revealing the spiritual and systemic forces behind:

- Human trafficking (modern slavery, sex trafficking, child labor)
- Narcotics trade (synthetic drugs, cartel networks, state-complicit distribution)
- War economies and artificial crisis management
- Greed-fueled policies that enable systemic dehumanization

In the **Book of Revelation**, Babylon is judged not just for her spiritual fornication, but for trading in **"slaves and the souls of men"** (Revelation 18:13). These are not metaphorical exchanges, they are literal human lives commodified for profit.

HUMAN TRAFFICKING: THE PROFITABLE BONDAGE OF MODERN BABYLON

Human trafficking is the **second largest criminal industry in the world**, generating an estimated $150 billion annually. At its root lies a **spirit of mammon** that values profit over people.

Forms of trafficking include:

- **Sex trafficking**: women and children forced into global underground sex markets
- **Labor trafficking**: men, women, and minors coerced into labor under threat or manipulation

- **Organ trafficking**: illegal harvesting and sale of human organs

- **Child soldiering**: indoctrination and militarization of children in war-torn zones

Spiritual perspective:

This is not just an economic crime, it is **idolatry of the highest order,** for it treats the Imago Dei (image of God) as merchandise.

> *"They sell the innocent for silver, and the needy for a pair of sandals.",* **Amos 2:6**

> *"You have multiplied your merchants more than the stars of heaven. The cankerworm spoils and flies away.",* **Nahum 3:16**

Trafficking syndicates operate through complex **financial laundering, false nonprofits, diplomatic immunities,** and **governmental negligence**. This is Babylon's web, a seductive infrastructure that must be exposed and judged.

HYPER-MOBILITY OF NARCOTICS: DRUG EMPIRES AND ECONOMIC CONTROL

The **narcotics industry**, both legal and illegal, is a massive engine in the economy of greed. From **opium wars** to **modern-day fentanyl epidemics**, drug commerce has served as a geopolitical weapon, an economic control mechanism, and a demonic altar.

- **Illegal drugs**: Cocaine, heroin, fentanyl, methamphetamine, controlled by transnational cartels, often with indirect protection from corrupt elites.

- **Legalized addictions**: Pharmaceutical industries profiting off pain through opioids, antidepressants, and psychoactive drugs.

- **State-sponsored drug economics**: Historic and present-day collusion between governments and drug routes for funding covert wars or economic gain.

"Woe to him who builds a city with bloodshed and establishes a town by injustice!", **Habakkuk 2:12**

"By your sorceries (Greek: pharmakeia) were all nations deceived.", **Revelation 18:23**

Here, the Bible warns of **pharmakeia**, sorcery, pharmaceutical manipulation, and spiritual deception through substances. These are not isolated crimes, they are **spiritual systems of control**.

ECONOMIC ENGINES OF EXPLOITATION

These dark economies are deeply interwoven with global financial systems:

- Banks laundering trafficking profits
- Cryptocurrency and anonymous digital wallets used in dark web transactions
- Luxury brands indirectly benefiting from forced labor
- Tourism industries covering illicit sex markets
- Weapons and drug trades funding proxy wars under political banners

Such systems require **prophetic confrontation** and **kingdom reformation**. The saints of God must be trained in discernment, activism, policy innovation, and spiritual warfare to confront these thrones.

THE CRY OF THE INNOCENT AND THE RESPONSE OF THE RIGHTEOUS

The groaning of the innocent, enslaved, and exploited rises before the courts of heaven.

"The cries of the harvesters have reached the ears of the Lord of Hosts.", **James 5:4**

"Is not this the fast that I have chosen? To loose the chains of injustice...", **Isaiah 58:6**

In Christ, we are called to **judge these systems** by:

- Preaching righteousness and repentance to the powerful
- Creating redemptive economic models
- Breaking blood pacts, soul covenants, and spiritual trafficking altars
- Rescuing and restoring victims as sons and daughters of the Kingdom
- Dismantling digital infrastructures of evil with technology consecrated to God

PROPHETIC DECLARATIONS AGAINST BABYLON'S COMMERCE

We declare:

- Babylon's economy has fallen!
- The trafficking of souls is judged!
- Drug cartels and corporate pharmaceutical corruption are exposed!
- Global leaders complicit in these crimes are brought to justice!
- Kingdom financiers rise to fund rescue, restoration, and reformation!

IN SUMMARY: THE END OF TRAFFICKING, THE RISE OF RIGHTEOUS TRADING FLOORS

Jesus came to **set the captives free** (Luke 4:18), and He is raising sons and daughters who will **tear down the thrones of exploitation** and establish **holy commerce** in their place.

The **Throne of Money**, when redeemed, will become a **throne of justice**.

The economy of hell will bow to the **economy of heaven**.

And the nations will be healed, not by politics, but by the **righteous rule of the Lamb**.

CHAPTER 35

Cyber-Gates of Prostitution, Sexual Enslavement at the Altars of Mammon

"For we wrestle not against flesh and blood, but against principalities, against powers, against the rulers of the darkness of this age." ~Ephesians 6:12 (NKJV)

UNVEILING THE DIGITAL BABYLON

We stand in an age where prostitution has transcended brothels and red-light districts; it has evolved into cybernetic corridors, technological hallways, and digital altars. The internet, once a tool for innovation and expression, now doubles as a global marketplace for commodifying the body, enslaving minds, and harvesting human souls in the name of profit. Behind this architecture lies the throne of Mammon, demanding sexual exploitation as incense and currency.

The rise of OnlyFans, pornography streaming empires, sexual trafficking rings embedded in encrypted platforms, and AI-generated sexual content has forged what can only be called *Cyber-Gates of Prostitution*. These are not merely technological trends but are spiritual gates, wormholes into soul enslavement, economic bondage, and moral degradation.

THE PRINCIPALITIES BEHIND DIGITAL PROSTITUTION

Ephesians 6:12 declares that we wrestle not against flesh and blood but against *principalities, powers, rulers of the darkness,* and *spiritual wickedness in high places*. These gates are governed by demonic strongholds, chiefly the spirit of **Ashtoreth, Ishtar,** and modern versions of **Jezebel**, all repackaged under the tech-driven economy.

Under Mammon's influence, these spiritual powers monetize the sacredness of sexuality, turning divine covenant into digital entertainment. The perversion is not only spiritual but algorithmic, driven by data mining, engagement metrics, and predictive AI that maps the lusts of a generation.

ECONOMIC SYSTEMS FEEDING SEXUAL EXPLOITATION

Global prostitution, online and offline, is a **$180 billion** industry, with key drivers being:

- **Sex tourism** embedded within the travel, leisure, and hotel industries

- **Pornography platforms** that generate more revenue than Amazon, Netflix, and Google combined

- **Cryptocurrency and anonymous banking** that fund and facilitate human trafficking rings

- **Social media algorithms** that amplify sexual content and reward exhibitionism with income streams

Even non-profit organizations and global NGOs, sometimes cloaked in humanitarian banners, have been caught masking sex-trafficking schemes, especially in war zones and refugee settlements.

THE MATRIX OF SEXUAL IDENTITY MONETIZATION

Romans 1:24–27 unveils a generation "given up to vile affections." Today, sexual orientations and identities are no longer merely personal but have become **political currencies** and **economic leverage**. From rainbow capitalism to hormone-pushing pharmaceutical giants, an industry now exists that monetizes gender dysphoria, body modification, and surgical transitions.

The **new pornography** is not just erotic, it's **ideological**, framed as liberation while locking millions in financial, spiritual, and emotional debt.

CULTURAL AND TECHNOLOGICAL PORTALS OF BONDAGE

These gates operate through:

- **AI-generated pornography** and digital avatars
- **VR sex experiences** that blur the line between fantasy and reality
- **Sexualized entertainment content** in music, fashion, and children's programming
- **OnlyFans and similar creator platforms** monetizing nudity as entrepreneurship

These represent a modern Babylon (Revelation 17–18), where "the merchants of the earth have become rich through the abundance of her luxury."

THE SCRIPTURAL VERDICT

Proverbs 7:21–27 vividly depicts the seduction of the simple-minded to death through sexual folly. Christ calls the ecclesia to rise in holiness, to shut these gates, and to restore dignity to sexuality.

Revelation 18:4 commands: *"Come out of her, My people, that you be not partakers of her sins, and that you receive not of her plagues."*

IN CHRIST, RESTORATION AND RECLAMATION

The blood of Jesus restores what exploitation steals. Christ restores purity, and calls us not only to flee these gates but to **dismantle them**. Apostolic and prophetic watchmen must now:

- **Reclaim the digital space** through kingdom content
- **Build economic alternatives** that do not require body commodification

- **Rescue and heal** those trapped in digital prostitution through soul restoration ministries
- **Activate kingdom intelligence** to shut demonic portals and establish sanctified cyberspace zones

PROPHETIC ACTIVATION PRAYERS AND DECREES

1. **Prayer of Renunciation and Purity**

   "Father, in the name of Jesus Christ, we renounce every altar of sexual immorality that seeks to bind this generation. We shut every cyber-gate that leads to perversion. Let Your fire consume every demonic server, every data bank of seduction, and every platform built on the blood and tears of the exploited. We declare sexual holiness across digital domains!"

2. **Prophetic Decree Over Nations and Economies**

   "We decree and declare that the throne of Mammon is overturned. The altars of Jezebel are brought down. Let righteousness flood the cyberspace like a tsunami. Let tech giants fall into accountability. We call for kingdom entrepreneurs to rise with platforms that honor God's covenant of sexuality."

3. **Decree Over Sons and Daughters**

   "Our sons shall not be sold, and our daughters shall not be trafficked. We prophesy: virginity shall be honored, marriage shall be sanctified, and sex shall return to its holy covenant. In Jesus' name, Amen!"

CHAPTER 36

The Love of Money and Global Corporate Monetization

"Do not lay up for yourselves treasures on earth…
but lay up for yourselves treasures in heaven."
~Matthew 6:19–20 (NKJV)

THE MONETARY MIRAGE

The spirit of mammon has evolved, it is no longer only manifest in gold coins, but in *data streams, stock trades, monetized users, and fiat illusions*. The **corporate beast system** is now powered by *monetization metrics*, and the world bows daily to **profit algorithms** and financial manipulation.

At the heart of this system is **the love of money**, not just the possession of it, but the idolatrous systems constructed around it. This chapter pierces through the veil of global economics to expose how **monetary policy, corporate architecture, and world financial institutions** are built on spiritual blueprints that challenge the Lordship of Christ.

> **"For the love of money is a root of all kinds of evil.",**
> 1 *Timothy 6:10*

GLOBAL ORGANIZATIONS TRADING ON THE PLATFORM OF GREED

Many global institutions today are **not neutral**. They are:

- **Tools of monetization** designed to extract value from people, labor, and nature
- Governed by **monetary policies** written to protect elites and monopolies
- Driven by **stockholder returns**, not societal or ethical stewardship

Examples include:

- **Tech giants** who monetize human attention and behavior
- **Pharmaceutical conglomerates** who manipulate health for profit
- **Food industries** that promote disease-linked diets for recurring gain

- **Financial institutions** that engineer dependency through **credit systems, insurance traps, and speculative markets**

These systems echo the **Babylonian economy**, promising abundance, but leading many into servitude.

SCIENTIFIC AND ECONOMIC INSIGHTS: MONETIZATION VS. VALUE

From an economic standpoint, the obsession with **monetization** has led to:

- **Short-term thinking** that sacrifices long-term societal welfare

- **Environmental collapse** for the sake of GDP and dividends

- **Psychological manipulation** via data monetization (surveillance capitalism)

- **Digital asset speculation** over real productivity (crypto bubbles, stock buybacks)

Behavioral economics shows how corporations design systems to **trigger consumer addiction, dopamine loops, and fear-based spending**, modern slavery masked as "convenience."

ANCIENT PATTERNS OF MONETIZATION AND CONTROL

In ancient civilizations:

- Egypt enslaved Israelites to build economic surplus

- Babylon created a class system to control resources

- Roman emperors taxed conquered territories into poverty

Today's systems echo these patterns:

- **IMF and World Bank** place nations in strategic debt traps

- **Central banks** control interest rates and economic cycles

- **Private corporations** influence elections and regulations

This reveals a **recycled spiritual structure**, one that must be *dismantled and replaced with Christ-centered economic governance.*

MYSTICAL REVELATION: THE ETHER OF WEALTH CONTROL

In the spirit realm:

- Mammon operates as a **gatekeeper of earthly resources**
- Wealth is often spiritually **tied to thrones, altars, and covenants**
- Without breaking agreements with greed and fear, people stay trapped in cycles of lack, even with hard work

This is why the **Ecclesia must rise as a priesthood and kingship** to:

- Establish **new altars of righteous wealth**
- Govern with **integrity, wisdom, and abundance**
- Build **kingdom trading floors** where the Spirit leads investment and innovation

SCRIPTURAL PATTERN: BREAKING THE LOVE OF MONEY

Biblical answers to corporate greed include:

- **Generosity** over hoarding (2 Corinthians 9:6–8)
- **Justice** over exploitation (Isaiah 58:6–10)
- **Contentment** over consumerism (1 Timothy 6:6–11)
- **God-dependence** over financial systems (Matthew 6:33)

   "Woe to those who add house to house and join field to field till no space is left...", Isaiah 5:8

KINGDOM RESPONSE: REWRITING THE SYSTEMS

The Ecclesia must now:

- Build **ethical business blueprints** with spiritual accountability
- Launch **prophetic economic hubs** governed by truth and equity
- Create **kingdom financial systems** that prioritize people over profit
- Declare **warfare prayers** against the thrones of unjust wealth

    "The wealth of the wicked is laid up for the righteous.", Proverbs *13:22*

PROPHETIC DECLARATIONS AND PRAYERS

Prayer:

"Lord, we renounce every covenant with the spirit of mammon. We break allegiance with greed and dependency on corrupted financial systems. We receive the mind of Christ in finance, governance, and commerce. Raise us as reformers, innovators, and builders of righteous wealth."

Decree:

"We decree the dethroning of Mammon and the establishment of Kingdom economy. Every unjust system shall be exposed. Every wicked platform of monetization shall crumble. Righteous wealth shall be transferred into the hands of God's builders, leaders, and kingdom investors!"

CHAPTER 37

Soul Economies, The Trade of Eternity for Earthly Gain

"You were bought at a price; therefore, glorify God in your body and in your spirit, which are God's."
~1 Corinthians 6:20 (NKJV)

THE CURRENCY OF THE SOUL

In a world where **influence is monetized, image is commercialized,** and **identity is auctioned**, a question reverberates louder than ever:

"What shall it profit a man, if he shall gain the whole world, and lose his own soul?", *Mark 8:36*

This ancient question, posed by the very lips of Christ, remains the eternal checkpoint of all economic, political, and cultural ambition. Yet in today's world, the soul has become a **traded commodity**, a **currency** in the underground markets of fame, power, control, and greed.

In this chapter, we unveil the **mechanics of soul-trading** across systems, music, politics, education, religion, and media, and how it has enslaved nations and imprisoned destinies. We expose the **spiritual, mystical, historical, and economic roots** of this demonic transaction and summon the Ecclesia to rise as **guardians of the soul economy** under the throne of Christ.

THE REALITY OF SOUL TRADING: A GLOBAL CRISIS

Soul-trading is not fictional; it is a **spiritual economy** where:

- Human destinies are **exchanged for visibility, wealth, and rank**
- Altars of iniquity require the **sacrifice of identity and purity**
- Demonic covenants offer **short-lived thrones** in exchange for **eternal separation from Christ**

This is how **generational bondage, territorial wickedness**, and **economic injustice** are maintained by:

- Celebrities who **initiate** through rituals for fame
- Politicians who **swear allegiances** for power
- Academics who **sell truth** for funding and status
- Influencers who **trade authenticity** for algorithms

Nations are imprisoned because the spiritual gatekeepers have traded their soul authority.

MUSIC INDUSTRY: SONIC PORTALS OF SOUL CAPTURE

The **music industry** has become one of the largest platforms of soul trade:

- Contractual agreements carry **hidden spiritual clauses**
- **Sound frequencies** are encoded with manipulation and seduction
- Music videos act as **ritual theaters**, activating covenants globally
- Youth identities are **shaped by satanic archetypes** disguised as entertainment

The **Luciferian template**, once the anointed cherub of sound, still influences the **economic systems of music**, ensuring fame is reserved for those who submit to spiritual compromise.

> **"They that make a graven image… he feeds on ashes: a deceived heart has turned him aside…",**
> Isaiah *44:9–20*

POLITICAL ELITES: THRONES BUILT ON SOULS

In political systems:

- Many ascend **not by merit**, but by **initiation**
- Secret societies and elite gatherings become **gateways of agreement**
- Territories are **enslaved** not just by policy but by **ritual**
- Entire regions are trapped in **blood covenants and oaths of secrecy**

This is how:

- Some leaders invoke **demonic intelligence** for strategy
- Entire constitutions are written under **principalities**
- **Global control mechanisms** like surveillance and digital ID are empowered spiritually before they're deployed physically

The throne of Caesar and Pharaoh still speaks, but the throne of Christ must thunder louder.

ACADEMIA AND INTELLECTUAL COMPROMISE

In universities and research institutions:

1. **Truth is often traded** for funding

2. Curricula are controlled by **ideological financiers**

3. Professors who challenge mainstream science or culture are often **exiled from platforms**

4. Students are indoctrinated to **revere the mind** while **ignoring the soul**

There is a **scientific priesthood** whose authority is not neutral, it is used to *shape narratives that dethrone Christ*, especially in economics, sexuality, identity, and sovereignty.

SOCIAL STATUS AND THE NEW CLASS RELIGION

From social media to red carpets:

1. Status has become a **modern altar**

2. Followers, brand deals, fame, and sponsorships are **rewards for conformity**

3. Platforms reward content that supports **mainstream spiritual decay**

Thus:

1. Many sell their voice to keep their *visibility*

2. Others deny truth to protect their *platforms*

3. Entire generations are being initiated into **false thrones of influence**

This is the **"new Rome,"** where bread and circus distract the masses while systems of control deepen.

HISTORICAL PATTERNS OF SOUL-TRADE

From the *Baal worship* of Canaan to the *Molech rituals* of ancient Israel:

1. Souls were **offered in exchange** for harvest, wealth, and fertility

2. Children were sacrificed to gods in exchange for favor

3. Emperors secured power through **blood oaths and altars**

Today, **abortion, trafficking, occult initiation, and even celebrity worship** continues these ancient practices, hidden behind policies, philanthropy, and "freedom."

THE SPIRITUAL MECHANICS: THE SOUL AS CURRENCY

Biblically, the soul is:

1. The seat of **will, identity, and eternal decision**

2. Capable of being **bound (Psalm 124:7)**, **restored (Psalm 23:3)**, or **traded (Ezekiel 13:18–20)**

In dark covenants:

1. Souls are **exchanged** for influence

2. Names are **written on altars**, contracts, or systems

3. Spiritual chains are **activated by consent, ignorance, or inheritance**

4. This is why Christ came to proclaim:

   "He has sent me… to proclaim liberty to the captives…", Luke *4:18*

SCRIPTURES AS DELIVERANCE BLUEPRINTS

Christ provides the solution:

1. **"You were bought with a price",** 1 *Corinthians 6:20*

2. **"Do not be conformed… but be transformed by the renewing of your mind",** Romans *12:2*

3. **"I will deliver you from the power of Satan unto God…",** Acts *26:18*

Redemption is not only about heaven; it's **freedom from soul trade economies** on earth.

KINGDOM RESPONSE: ECCLESIA AS SOUL DEFENDERS

The Church must:

1. **Disciple artists, leaders, influencers, educators** into Kingdom systems

2. **Build new economic altars** free of idolatry

3. **Prophesy truth in public spheres**

4. Create *soul sanctuaries* where Christ is enthroned, not Mammon

We must establish **apostolic hubs** that understand **spiritual trade mechanics** and engage in **territorial warfare** for the soul of nations.

PROPHETIC PRAYERS AND DECREES

Prayer:

"Lord, redeem every area of my life where I or my generation has traded our souls for visibility, wealth, comfort, or survival. Let Your blood sever every spiritual agreement that stands against Your throne in me. Restore what was stolen. Awaken me to guard the gates of my soul."

Decree:

"We declare every altar of soul trade shall fall! Every throne built on blood, secrecy, and manipulation shall be shaken! The Lord reigns, and the Ecclesia rises to guard the nations from eternal deception. Let Christ rule from soul to system!"

CHAPTER 38

The Sacredness and Lawlessness of the Throne of Money

"And the gold of that land is good; bdellium and the onyx stone are there." ~Genesis 2:12 (NKJV)

THE TWIN FACES OF THE THRONE

The throne of money is both **sacred and seductive, resilient and ruinous**. It stands as one of the most powerful infrastructures shaping the course of nations, the destinies of peoples, and the designs of civilizations. In this chapter, we unveil its **duality**, how it cloaks itself in the sacred garb of prosperity and advancement while subtly embedding the **seeds of lawlessness, spiritual deception, and moral erosion**. This is not merely an economic subject; it is a spiritual fortress, a political altar, and a cultural regime. It touches every system, scientific, ethical, educational, political, religious, and even prophetic. Here, we demystify its inner workings and assert the **authority of Christ over its dominion.**

THE SACREDNESS AND DIVINE POTENTIAL OF WEALTH

The sacred dimension of wealth lies in its **original intention**, a tool of stewardship, empowerment, and divine dominion.

* In Genesis, gold is first mentioned in Eden: *"And the gold of that land is good."* – Genesis 2:12

* Abraham, Joseph, Solomon, and Job all navigated realms of great wealth, not for self-exaltation, but for **kingdom purpose, governance, and generational impact.**

In Christ:

Christ's mission wasn't to abolish wealth but to **redeem it**, aligning its flow with righteousness, justice, and mercy. The early church demonstrated wealth redistribution (Acts 4:34–35), financial integrity, and generosity under the governance of the Holy Spirit.

THE STRENGTH AND RESILIENCE OF THE FINANCIAL INFRASTRUCTURES

The global financial throne is built with **fortresses of policy, data, algorithms, legal contracts, and psychological trust.** It is resilient not only because of technological advancement but because it taps into human desire, fear, ambition, and survival instincts.

- **Scientific & Technological Perspective:**

  o   Quantum algorithms and AI now manage multi-trillion-dollar portfolios.

  o   Blockchain and decentralized finance are redefining the control of currency and wealth.

  o   Predictive analytics shape **market behaviors** and influence **government policies**.

- **Political & Economic Power:**

  o   The **Federal Reserve**, **IMF**, and **World Bank** act as global financial governors.

  o   Nation-states now surrender their sovereignty to **debt-based colonization**, not through war, but through policy and interest rates.

Resilience:

The throne of money survives crises, pandemics, wars, and even revolutions because it is protected by the **priesthood of economists, legal experts, digital architects, and policy-makers**, guardians of a system more invisible than physical.

THE LAWLESSNESS WITHIN: A BEAST BEHIND THE CURTAIN

Beneath the sacred illusion lies a **lawless dominion**, where unethical trade, usury, tax manipulation, and exploitation rule with disguised legitimacy.

- **Scriptural Revelation:**

  "For the mystery of lawlessness is already at work..." – **2 Thessalonians 2:7**

  "They sell the righteous for silver, and the poor for a pair of sandals." – **Amos 2:6**

- **Examples of Financial Lawlessness:**
  - Insider trading, lobbying disguised as charity, offshore laundering, and economic warfare
  - **Global interest rate manipulation (e.g., LIBOR scandal)**
  - **Economic sanctions that paralyze innocent populations**

THE DECEPTION OF THE INFRASTRUCTURE

The throne deceives by presenting itself as neutral. But money is not neutral, it is a **spiritual magnet**, capable of **enslaving hearts or empowering destinies**, depending on alignment.

Key Spiritual Deceptions Include:

- Prosperity without responsibility
- Sacrifice of integrity for influence
- Belief that wealth guarantees righteousness or divine approval

Cultural Narratives of Deception:

- "Success is wealth."
- "The rich are the most intelligent."
- "Poverty equals laziness." These cultural codes subtly shape our moral expectations, political values, and spiritual convictions.

THE SOCIAL AND ETHICAL DILEMMAS OF MONETARY THRONES

The throne of money has shaped societal hierarchies, created **economic castes**, and justified injustice through **legalized theft**. When healthcare is priced, education is elitist, and justice is delayed by bureaucracy, the throne of money has overtaken ethics.

Christ's Ethics of Justice:

- *"You have neglected the more important matters of the law, justice, mercy and faithfulness."* – Matthew 23:23

- *"Woe to those who make unjust laws, to those who issue oppressive decrees."* – Isaiah 10:1

Ethical Crossroads:

- Who owns data?

- Who controls food?

- Who prices survival?

- Should nations owe money for resources stolen during colonization?

IN CHRIST – THE RECLAMATION OF THE THRONES

The throne of money must be **reclaimed, not destroyed.** Its original purpose is divine, but it must be dethroned from **mammonic rule and restored to Christ's government.**

How Do We Reclaim the Throne?

- Raise righteous economists, financiers, tech innovators, and political prophets

- Establish Kingdom banking and wealth systems

- Decentralize greed and enthrone divine stewardship

- Confront deception with **prophetic truth and kingdom ethics**

Kingdom Vision:

A system where money is no longer master but **a servant of love, justice, creativity, and divine governance.**

PROPHETIC DECLARATIONS AND PRAYERS:

1. *We break the deception of sacred lawlessness that sits upon global financial systems.*

2. *We declare a rising generation of financial reformers, prophets, governors, and builders who carry the mind of Christ.*

3. *We decree justice over unjust policies, righteousness over hidden greed, and divine economy over every exploitative system.*

4. *We enthrone Christ over the data centers, digital systems, stock markets, and economic engines of the world.*

5. *Let the sacred throne of money be restored under the dominion of Heaven's King, Yeshua HaMashiach.*

CHAPTER 39

Dominion Over the Spirits of Mammon, the Matrix of Heartless Emperors, the Mind of the Beast, and Vicious Monsters of Money

"But the saints of the Most High shall receive the kingdom, and possess the kingdom forever, even forever and ever." ~Daniel 7:18 (NKJV)

THE SPIRITS THAT SIT UPON THRONES

In the shadows of global finance and governance, ancient spirits continue to influence nations, dominate institutions, and possess the minds of rulers. These are not mere ideologies or economic theories, they are **spiritual infrastructures** woven into the **matrix of mammon**, the **beast systems**, and **the altars of empire**.

The prophet Daniel, in chapter 7, unveils a panoramic revelation of the **beastly empires**, empires devoid of heart, animated by greed, and crowned with blasphemy. Yet within this vision, a **greater dominion** is revealed: one given to the **saints of the Most High** (Daniel 7:18). This chapter brings us to a cosmic courtroom where thrones are cast down, and the **Ancient of Days** takes His seat.

This is the dimension where **spiritual economics** meets prophetic justice, where the **sons of God** arise to **judge spirits**, **tear down the matrix**, and **establish Christ's government in the dominions of money**.

THE SPIRIT OF MAMMON: THE COUNTERFEIT ARCHITECT

Mammon is not merely the love of money, it is a **principality** that seeks worship through **control**, **debt**, **consumption**, and **fear**.

Mammon thrives by:

- Promising false security through wealth accumulation
- Manipulating markets to create systemic poverty
- Incentivizing idolatry, vanity, and competition over communion
- Binding nations through unjust economic dependencies

Christ's words are unambiguous:

> *"You cannot serve both God and mammon."*, **Matthew 6:24**

This is a war of altars. To dethrone mammon, we must enthrone Christ in our hearts, minds, and systems. **The economic battle is spiritual first.**

THE MATRIX OF HEARTLESS EMPERORS

Daniel 7 unveils empires that arise out of chaos, each symbolized by grotesque beasts:

- **Lion with eagle wings** – Babylonian dominance and cultural colonization
- **Bear raised on one side** – Medo-Persian empire of laws without mercy
- **Leopard with four wings** – Greco-Macedonian speed of conquest and divided authority
- **The Dreadful and Terrible Beast** – The Roman system and its legacy of control through law, religion, and violence

These beasts have no heart. Their emperors rule through **policy without compassion, wealth without worship**, and **power without peace**.

Yet the Ancient of Days breaks in:

> *"I watched till thrones were put in place, and the Ancient of Days was seated... the court was seated, and the books were opened."*, **Daniel 7:9-10**

This divine tribunal is the **template of kingdom economics**, justice, equity, accountability, and holy fire.

THE MIND OF THE BEAST: TECHNOCRATIC CONTROL AND ARTIFICIAL SOVEREIGNTY

The **mind of the beast** in our time manifests through:

- Digital financial systems that enslave rather than empower

- Surveillance capitalism and biometric economies
- Centralized banking systems that override national sovereignty
- Corporate empires that dominate food, health, energy, and communication

It is the rise of **technocratic Babylon**, where algorithmic intelligence replaces prophetic insight, and profit metrics override human dignity.

But the Word speaks:

> *"Let this mind be in you which was also in Christ Jesus..."*, **Philippians 2:5**

The mind of Christ **reverses the matrix**, decentralizes greed, and enthrones divine stewardship.

VICIOUS MONSTERS OF MONEY: GLOBAL STRUCTURES OF GREED

The monsters are not mythical, they are **visible systems**, including:

- Global banking institutions enforcing debt colonization
- Defense and weapons industries profiting from war
- Pharmaceutical corporations hoarding patents and healing
- Shadow governments funding covert economic crises
- Human trafficking and soul trading disguised under financial transactions

These are spiritual beasts feeding on the souls of men. **Revelation 18:13** lists among Babylon's merchandise, "the souls of men." These are systems that must be judged.

But the Bible proclaims:

> *"The kingdom and dominion and the greatness of the kingdoms under the whole heaven shall be given to the people of the saints of the Most High."*, **Daniel 7:27**

DOMINION THROUGH CHRIST: JUDGING THRONES AND SYSTEMS

The saints are not victims; we are **kings and priests**, called to:

- **Bind kings with chains and nobles with fetters of iron** (Psalm 149:8-9)
- **Judge spiritual wickedness in high places** (Ephesians 6:12)
- Govern economics through righteousness
- Design and deploy prophetic economic infrastructures

Our dominion includes:

- Financial sanctification
- Marketplace reformation
- Digital system innovation in holiness
- Kingdom-based economic alternatives

PROPHETIC DECREE AND APOSTOLIC STRATEGY

We decree:

- The beasts of greed are judged
- Thrones of mammon are overthrown
- Thrones of Christ are established in the marketplace
- Prophets, seers, economists, and financiers rise as kingdom reformers
- New infrastructures, governed by Christ's ethics, rise across finance, trade, and global governance

IN SUMMARY: THE END OF THE BEAST, THE RISE OF THE SAINTS

Daniel 7 does not end in fear; it ends in **transfer of power**.

The **saints possess the kingdom**. Not someday, **now**, in Christ, as we rise to govern economies, nations, and digital dominions with wisdom, justice, and spiritual intelligence.

We stand not with the beast but with the **Lamb**.

We speak not for mammon but for the **Majesty**.

We Walk not by fear but by **faith and fire**.

This is our dominion: **From the courtroom of heaven to the trading floors of earth.**

CHAPTER 40

Thrones Reclaimed

The Final Clarion Call to Rescue Nations and Men

"For the earnest expectation of the creation
eagerly waits for the revealing of the sons of God."
~Romans 8:19 (NKJV)

THE COSMIC RESCUE MANDATE

This is not just a financial battle. It is **cosmic warfare**. The throne of money sits at the intersection of **spirit and system, of eternity and economy**, and behind every policy, currency, or contract is a **throne that speaks**.

This final chapter is a **summoning trumpet**, a prophetic mobilization to rescue men, kings, priests, women, children, and the very frequencies of the universe from the **economic Babylon** that sits on many waters. This is the hour of **Kingdom enforcement**, to displace demonic trade with divine justice, and to enthrone Christ in the economies, institutions, and hearts of all creation.

DIVINE PATTERNS OF RESCUE: FROM EGYPT TO BABYLON

From ancient Egypt to modern empires:

- God has always **raised deliverers** in economic crises
- Joseph managed Egypt's economy to preserve nations
- Daniel subverted Babylon's occult banking system through divine intelligence
- Esther confronted generational genocide financed by imperial wealth

The rescue of nations always involves:

- Spiritual accuracy
- Economic strategy
- Covenant intelligence
- Prophetic governance

THE RECOVERY OF KINGS, PRIESTS, AND THRONES

Many thrones are **unoccupied** by righteous men because:

- Kings are asleep under delusion
- Priests are bound by religious debt
- Sons are lost in the vortex of system programming

Christ calls:

> **"Come up higher. Reign with Me in righteousness. Take back the dominion once lost in Eden and now restored by the Cross."**

The throne of money must no longer dominate kings and nations. It must **bow to the Throne of the Lamb**.

WOMEN, CHILDREN, AND THE HIDDEN ECONOMIES OF SUFFERING

Women and children are often the most affected by:

- Global debt cycles
- Food insecurity
- Institutional greed
- Spiritual economies of slavery and trafficking

This rescue includes:

- **Wombs, widows, and warriors**
- **Children's destinies encoded with Kingdom light**
- Education systems reformed to **awaken divine identity**
- Micro-economies built around **Kingdom integrity**

THE UNIVERSAL REDEMPTION: CREATION GROANS FOR ECONOMIC LIBERATION

"The whole creation groans and waits for the revealing of the sons of God.", *Romans 8:19*

The universe itself, cosmos, nature, weather, technology, data, responds to:

- Righteous rule
- Kingdom economy
- Spiritual vibrations aligned with the will of Christ

Digital currencies, quantum systems, AI, and biotech must come under the Lordship of Christ, or they become instruments of enslavement.

PROPHETIC STRATEGIES FOR SYSTEMIC RESCUE

1. **Intercessory Governance:**

   Spiritual war rooms must rise in cities, apostolic-prophetic grids interceding over banking systems, trade routes, stock markets, and government policies.

2. **Kingdom Financial Technologies:**

   Christ-centered innovations must emerge, cryptos backed by righteous governance, AI systems designed to preserve equity, and marketplaces founded on justice.

3. **Discipleship of Kings:**

   Mentoring presidents, governors, CEOs, judges, and media moguls in Kingdom economics and righteousness.

4. **Building Cities of Light:**

   Ecclesia-driven economic zones, regions marked by spiritual purity, economic justice, and supernatural supply.

APOSTOLIC DECREES AND ADVANCED PROPHETIC ACTIVATIONS

Activation #1: Throne Alignment

"I align my spirit, soul, and body to the Throne of Christ. Every throne of Mammon, fear, greed, and manipulation within me is now dethroned by the blood of Jesus. I sit with Christ in heavenly places, and I legislate as a king-priest in His eternal economy."

Decree:

"I am not for sale. My children are not for sale. My nation is not for sale. I belong to Christ. My economy, time, and talent are sealed in the throne of the Lamb!"

Activation #2: Governmental Recovery

"Father, I reclaim the ancient seats of my bloodline. Every ancestral financial covenant not established in You, I now renounce. I retrieve divine inheritance and take authority over economic systems in my territory, city, and region. I call forth Kingdom financiers, apostles of economy, and prophets of policy!"

Decree:

"Let the mountains of corruption collapse. Let the altars of slavery and greed burn. Let kings arise and sons legislate. Christ is enthroned over every currency, every company, every policy, and every platform!"

Activation #3: Rescuing Creation

"Lord, redeem the frequencies of nature. Let my land no longer be a prisoner of pollution, injustice, and greed. I activate Kingdom stewardship in agriculture, climate, mining, and infrastructure. Let every gate of my city now be sealed in the name of Christ."

Decree:

"Let oil wells serve righteousness. Let data streams be cleansed. Let quantum networks be sanctified. Let technology become the slave of Christ's glory, not the master of man!"

FINAL SUMMONS: THE GREAT REDEMPTION MANDATE

You, reader, are not just a spectator in this divine drama. You are:

- A builder of righteous economies
- A breaker of soul contracts
- A witness of divine justice
- A priest of the Most High on the throne of monetary dominion

You are part of the **Kingdom's intelligence unit**, planted to reformat history. **Take your scroll. Read. Act. Govern.**

AMEN AND SELAH.

CHAPTER 41

Conclusion

My Pledge, Oath, Allegiance, and Mystical Vows on the Throne of Money

"The Lord has sworn and will not change His mind: 'You are a priest forever, in the order of Melchizedek.'" ~Psalm 110:4 (NKJV)

A Covenantal Declaration in Christ's Constitution and Celestial Consciousness

THE FINAL STAND BEFORE THE THRONE

In the sacred echo of eternity, when kings kneel before greater thrones and wealth must answer to righteousness, I now stand, *not before gold, but before God; not before mammon, but before the Messiah.* The journey through the realms of money, politics, science, spirituality, and governance has revealed one immutable truth: **the throne of money must be sanctified, redeemed, and enthroned under the dominion of Christ.**

I, therefore, as a witness of divine mysteries and an ambassador of the eternal kingdom, make this solemn covenant. Let this be my seal of allegiance, not to systems of greed, but to the **King of Glory**, the **Lion of Judah**, the **Chief Cornerstone**, who owns the **silver and gold** and in whom all **true governance and dominion dwell.**

MY PLEDGE

I pledge allegiance to the throne of Christ, the eternal Judge, Redeemer, Architect, and Legislator of wealth and nations.

- I pledge to honor the wisdom of divine stewardship over selfish acquisition.

- I pledge to use every currency in my hand as a vessel of righteousness, mercy, and justice.

- I pledge to destroy false altars of greed and to build economic temples of truth.

- I pledge to defend the poor, lift the afflicted, and break the yoke of mammon's oppression.

  *"The Lord has sworn and will not change His mind:
  'You are a priest forever, in the order of Melchizedek.'"* –
  Psalm 110:4

MY OATH

Before the heavenly court and the cloud of witnesses, I make an eternal oath in Christ:

- That no wealth shall enslave my soul

- That no institution shall compromise my allegiance to the Holy One

- That no empire shall purchase my identity

- That no throne shall usurp the place of Christ in my heart and my governance

This is my oath: **Christ above capital, Christ before corporate, Christ beyond coins.**

MY ALLEGIANCE

My allegiance belongs to:

- The **Constitution of Heaven**, where justice kisses mercy, and truth walks before Him

- The **Covenant of the Blood**, where wealth is consecrated by sacrifice

- The **Cosmic Mind of Christ**, where wisdom transcends economies and speaks through galaxies

- The **Kingdom Economy**, where the first are last, the givers rise, and eternal value is currency

I owe nothing to Babylon; my allegiance is to Zion.

I owe no tithe to greed; my worship is unto Elohim.

I owe no debt to corruption; my faith is in the Lord of Hosts.

MY MYSTICAL VOWS

As one awakened in the spirit, I make mystical vows, hidden yet sealed in Christ:

- I vow to walk in financial holiness, where motives are as pure as money is clean.

- I vow to engage in wealth creation through divine intelligence and righteous innovation.

- I vow to break covenants with poverty mindsets and oppressive structures.

- I vow to raise altars of light in dark places, marketplaces, governments, corporations, and digital spheres.

- I vow to align my frequency, intention, and strategy with the **Holy Spirit**, who teaches all things, even the secrets of kingdom wealth.

These vows are not ceremonial, they are celestial. They are codes written on scrolls in heaven and echoes that reverberate through eternity. They are mystical, but they are measurable through fruitfulness, obedience, and authority.

THE CONSTITUTION AND CONSCIOUSNESS OF CHRIST

This final declaration is not rooted in human laws or financial regulations but in the **Constitution of the Lamb**, the eternal government of peace, power, and purpose.

> *"Of the increase of His government and of peace there will be no end..."* – **Isaiah 9:7**

In Christ's Consciousness, I operate with:

- **Heaven's economy of abundance**, not the earth's system of scarcity

- **Kingdom frequency and prophetic sight**, not the manipulation of data and fear

- **Eternal rewards**, not temporary profit
- **Wisdom as wealth**, and **obedience as dominion**

FINAL DECLARATIONS

- Let every throne of unrighteous mammon crumble.
- Let every sacred scroll of kingdom wealth be opened.
- Let every builder, priest, reformer, and innovator rise in the marketplace with fire in their eyes and the Lamb in their heart.
- Let the nations be reformed through consecrated coins, sanctified systems, and righteous stewards.

IT IS FINISHED, IN CHRIST

This chapter is not an end but a coronation, a sealing of divine intent for a **generation called to possess the gates of economy, governance, and global restoration in Christ**.

From this day forward, I operate not from desperation but from dominion.

Not from scarcity but from divine supply.

Not from greed but from governance.

Not from systems of control, but from the sovereignty of Christ enthroned in my mind, heart, and mission. **So help me, God.**

Final Message of "The Throne of Money: Spirituality, Science and Technology of Politics"

By Apostle Othniel Uzorma Ikechukwu

To the Nations, People, Communities, Kings, Presidents, Rulers, and Tribes:

This book is more than pages bound in print, it is a prophetic trumpet, a divine indictment, a blueprint, and a scroll unsealed for this kairos hour. You who govern lands, influence systems, and lead hearts, know this: **the throne of money is not supreme; the Throne of Christ is.**

To the **nations**, your economic shakings are not the end, but the beginning of divine reconstruction. Your borders are gates of destiny, not commodities for exploitation. Arise and align your economies with righteousness, equity, and justice.

To the **people and communities**, let not poverty define your identity. You are the image of God, encoded with divine wealth and purpose. Break free from the illusions of lack and awaken to kingdom sufficiency and heavenly economics.

To the **kings and presidents**, your authority is temporal, but your accountability is eternal. Govern with fear of God, and not fear of man. Tear down altars of greed and rebuild systems on truth, service, and divine intelligence.

To the **tribes and tongues**, your heritage is sacred. Do not sell your thrones for silver, your songs for sponsorship, or your soil for short-term gain. The Lord is raising a remnant from every people group to govern in purity, integrity, and wisdom.

To the **rulers of systems**, this is the final call to dethrone Mammon and enthrone Messiah. The Spirit of the Lord is summoning divine reformers, those not swayed by bribes, but moved by righteousness; not seduced by Babylon, but yielded to Zion.

Let this be your awakening: the real wealth is not in gold, oil, algorithms, or influence, but in Christ, the Eternal King. Let the nations tremble and rejoice, for the Lord is reclaiming His thrones in finance, technology, governance, and commerce.

This is a spiritual summons to recalibrate the heart of humanity, the economy of nations, and the architecture of civilization, *under the Throne of the Lamb.*

Resources and References for "The Throne of Money"

1. Wolff, E. (2021). Pillaging the World: The History and Politics of the IMF. Tectum Verlag.

    (Critiques IMF's debt practices as modern economic colonization, aligning with the book's "Spirit of Pharaoh" and global bondage themes; verified via publisher and reviews.)

2. Perkins, J. (2004/2025 3rd ed.). Confessions of an Economic Hit Man.

    Berrett-Koehler Publishers.

    (Exposes U.S.-led debt traps in developing nations; supports claims of economic hit men and financial slavery; updated edition covers China's strategies.)

3. Bruner, S. (2023). Controligarchs: Exposing the Billionaire Class, Their Secret Deals, and the Globalist Plot to Dominate Your Life.

    Sentinel.

    (Details elite financial dynasties and hidden bloodlines; verifies "global banking dynasties" in the book.)

4. Ferguson, N. (2008/2018 ed.). The Ascent of Money: A Financial History of the World.

    Penguin Books.

    (Traces spiritual and economic ties in ancient systems like Babylon and Rome; corroborates historical thrones of wealth.)

5. Chomsky, N. (2016). Who Rules the World?

    Metropolitan Books.

    (Analyzes corporate and imperial economic control; supports critiques of "thrones of greed" and political corruption.)

6. Dalio, R. (2017). Principles: Life and Work.
    Simon & Schuster.
    (Insights on market cycles and investor mindsets; aligns with
    "Stock Market Scrolls" and righteous intelligence.)

7. Smith, A. (1776/2023 ed.). The Wealth of Nations.
    Penguin Classics.
    (Foundational on trade and prosperity; referenced for
    Melchizedek blueprint beyond capitalism.)

8. Eker, T. H. (2005). Secrets of the Millionaire Mind.
    Harper Business.
    (Mindset for wealth; verifies "Mind of the Investor" principles
    with psychological backing.)

9. Springmeier, F. (1998/2020 ed.). Bloodlines of the Illuminati.
    Ambassador House.
    (Explores hidden elite influences; supports "hidden bloodlines
    of economic power.")

10. Clayton, I. (2016). Realms of the Kingdom: Vol. 1.
    Seraph Creative.
    (Spiritual dominion and gateways; corroborates "Wealth
    Gateways" and territorial thrones.)

11. Ogbonnaya, A. O. (2022). Governing Time: Unlocking Powers
    of Times and Divinity.
    Seraph Creative.
    (Kingdom governance in economies; aligns with prophetic
    economic blueprints.)

12. Investopedia. (2025). What Was the LIBOR Scandal? What
    Happened and Impacted Whom?
    Retrieved November 11, 2025, from https://www.investopedia.
    com/terms/l/libor-scandal.asp.
    (Details 2012 rate manipulation by banks; verifies
    "lawlessness" in financial thrones.)

13. Walk Free. (2022/2025 update). Global Slavery Index: Global Findings.

    Retrieved November 11, 2025, from https://www.walkfree.org/global-slavery-index/findings/global-findings/.

    (Estimates 50 million in modern slavery; substantiates "soul economies" and trafficking as greed-driven.)

14. U.S. Department of State. (2025). 2025 Trafficking in Persons Report.

    Retrieved November 11, 2025, from https://www.state.gov/reports/2025-trafficking-in-persons-report.

    (Global economic drivers of trafficking; supports "global structures of greed" and hyper-mobility of narcotics.)

15. Forbes. (2025, October 29). The 7 Banking and Fintech Trends That Will Define 2026.

    Retrieved November 11, 2025, from https://www.forbes.com/sites/bernardmarr/2025/10/29/the-7-banking-and-fintech-trends-that-will-define-2026/.

    (AI, blockchain, and tokenized assets; verifies "Dominion Over Digital Economy and AI Thrones.")

16. FinTech Magazine. (2025, October 2). Behind the Wheel of Growth: Fintech Innovations in 2025.

    Retrieved November 11, 2025, from https://fintechmagazine.com/news/behind-the-wheel-of-growth-fintech-innovations-in-2025.

    (Open banking and AI; aligns with "Cyber Thrones" and surveillance.)

17. World Economic Forum. (2025, June 25). AI: Rewriting the Future of Finance and Financial Inclusion.

    Retrieved November 11, 2025, from https://www.weforum.org/stories/2025/06/emerging-markets-future-of-finance-ai/.

    (AI bypassing traditional systems; supports "Kingdom Cyber Warfare" modules.) (Note: Cross-referenced with Forbes for 2025 trends.)

18. McElroy, E. (2019). The Enchantments of Mammon: How Capitalism Became the Religion of Modernity.

    Harvard University Press.

    (Mammon as a spiritual force in economics; verifies biblical/ historical analysis.)

19. Terradez, A. (2023). Exposing the Spirit of Mammon: Make God, Not Money Your Master. Destiny Image.

    (Christian critique of greed's spirit; aligns with "Thrones of Mammon.")

20. Bible Hub. (n.d.). Evidence Babylon Enriched All Nations?

    Retrieved November 11, 2025, from https://biblehub.com/q/ evidence_babylon_enriched_all_nations.htm.

    (Historical/spiritual role of Babylon in trade; substantiates ancient thrones.)

OTHER BOOKS BY THE AUTHOR: APOSTLE OTHNIEL UZORMA IKECHUKWU

The Spiritual Spectrum of Raising Generation Next

Summary: This book explores the moral, ethical, and spiritual transformation required to raise the emerging generation within divine principles. It examines parenting, education, discipline, identity formation, and societal pressures, through the lens of Christ. Each chapter unlocks prophetic strategies, wisdom from scripture, and psychological insights to empower young leaders with kingdom foundations for life, purpose, and impact.

Royal Legacy for Leadership: Embracing Divine Heritage to Influence Generations

Summary: A leadership compass for kingdom-minded trailblazers, this book bridges ancient royal DNA with modern-day influence. Drawing from scriptural archetypes and historical reformers, it unveils how divine inheritance shapes strategic leadership. The book emphasizes righteousness, honor, purpose-driven innovation, and legacy stewardship as tools for global transformation.

Kingdom Catalysts: Transformational Leadership and the Cosmic Shift for Global Reformation

Summary: A prophetic governance blueprint for apostolic reformers. This book dissects political systems, education, technology, and national infrastructures, calling forth Christ-centered leaders equipped for the end-time cosmic shift. Drawing from biblical prophecy, scientific developments, and policy frameworks, it offers catalytic principles for reshaping nations.

The Encryption of Abundance

Summary: A revelatory dive into the codes, frequencies, geometry, and metaphysical patterns that unlock divine wealth. This book explores how abundance operates spiritually and scientifically through language, sound, light, and intent, anchored in the teachings of Christ. It blends ancient texts, quantum principles, and sacred mathematics into spiritual activations and blueprints for living in overflow.

Quantum Optics: Sight in the Spirit

Summary: An extraordinary unveiling of supernatural perception and spiritual optics. Covering telepathy, prophetic vision, frequency decoding, intuitive technology, and time-space travel, the book aligns spiritual gifts with quantum mechanics. Christ remains the key to interpreting all dimensional knowledge, ensuring the reader walks in light, truth, and holy alignment.

Dominion in the Mind

Summary: This work explores the architecture of the human mind from a kingdom dimension. It tackles topics like neurotheology, ancient mental technologies, cosmic civilization, divine consciousness, and the Christ mind. Each chapter presents practical tools for renewing the mind and engaging dominion over mental territories.

Divine Algorithm of Faith: Navigating the Supernatural Realms of Quantum Creation by the Word of Christ

Summary: Faith is decoded in this masterpiece as a divine algorithm, the invisible force behind manifestation. From ancient codes, sound frequencies, thought patterns, and the Logos matrix, to the creation protocols hidden in Genesis, the book reveals how the Word frames reality. Scripture, quantum science, and mystic insights converge under the Lordship of Christ.

The Throne of Money: Spirituality, Science and Technology of Politics

Summary: A bold exposé and spiritual warfare compendium on global financial powers, economic thrones, AI systems, and the manipulation of nations through money. The book unveils hidden trade structures, the mammon matrix, elite financial control, and the redemptive authority of Christ over economies. With over 30 chapters, it blends investigative research, prophetic insight, scientific exploration, economic theory, and spiritual revelation, culminating in decrees and apostolic blueprints for kingdom economy.

About the Author:

Apostle Othniel Uzorma Ikechukwu

Apostle Othniel Uzorma Ikechukwu is a prophetic reformer, divine statesman, and revelatory architect of spiritual government, carrying a sacred mandate to decode and unveil the mysteries of Kingdom governance in the cosmos. As the pioneering Chancellor of the **Eternity Kingdom School of Mysteries**, he stands as a forerunner and watchman in the age of convergence, where ancient scrolls, divine intelligence, and prophetic governance are unlocking a generation of Sons as global emissaries, dominion stewards, and policy-technocrats in the ecosystem of nations.

An enigmatic teacher of eternal truths, Apostle Othniel operates in rare discernment and dimensional depth, traversing the veiled corridors of thrones, councils, and cosmic dominions to expose the architecture of power and influence. His insight cuts through layers of spiritual illusion and geopolitical deception, reconciling the realms of **science, scripture, spirituality, and sovereignty** in the illumination of Christ.

Endowed with piercing spiritual intelligence, he mentors reformers, apostles, diplomats, intercessors, and global leaders, reconfiguring them for prophetic engagement and high-level policy reformation across the spheres of governance, economy, security, education, and kingdom diplomacy.

His seminal work, *Government Mysteries and Influence: Spirituality, Science and Mysteries of Dominion*, is a prophetic codex, a scroll encrypted with divine intelligence designed to shake thrones, realign altars, and awaken the Ekklesia to the government upon His shoulders. It is not merely a book, it is a clarion call, a constitution for divine administrators, and a gateway for strategic sons to navigate, colonize, and rule in alignment with the dominion architecture of Yahweh.

He is a spiritual legislator, a chronicle of mysteries, and a divine oracle chosen to steward the blueprints of **Kingdom Civilization** for this prophetic era.

Contact the author: apstothnieliyke@gmail.com

SeraphCreative

Heaven's Heart for Earth

Seraph Creative is a collective of artists, writers, theologians & illustrators who desire to see the body of Christ grow into full maturity, walking in their inheritance as Sons of God on the Earth.

Sign up to our newsletter to know about future exciting releases.

Visit our website: www.seraphcreative.org